Don
HARRON

A Parent
Contradiction

Don
HARRON

A Parent
Contradiction

A
BIOGRAPHY
BY
Martha
Harron

COLLINS TORONTO

First published 1988
by Collins Publishers
100 Lesmill Road, Don Mills, Ontario

© 1988 by Martha Harron

CANADIAN CATALOGUING IN PUBLICATION DATA

Harron, Martha
   Harron : a parent contradiction

ISBN 0-00-215440-4

1. Harron, Don, 1924-   .   2. Actors – Canada –
Biography. 3. Humorists, Canadian – Biography.
4. Authors, Canadian (English) – 20th century –
Biography.* I. Title.

PN2308.H37H37 1988   792'.028'0924   C88-094973-2

Second Printing

Typeset by Jay Tee Graphics Ltd.
Printed and bound in Canada

to F.B.
Love, Goneril

CONTENTS

Don
HARRON

A Parent
Contradiction

PREFACE

I wrote Don Harron a hate letter on my twenty-first birthday. I tell you this not because I am proud of it but because of what it reveals about my father, who is the subject of this book.

I was just finishing my third year of university in Nice, on exchange from Victoria College in Toronto, and had gone to the bank to cash my very last (official) handout. Like many other men with three kids and marriages to match, my father had a lot of support payments to make over the years. Unlike many other men, he actually paid them. Now I was supposed to stand on my own two feet. Halfway through endorsing the cheque, I fainted and collapsed on the floor of the bank. It was a great start.

When I had revived and pocketed the cash, I went straight back to my one-room apartment. With a pen in one hand and Kleenex in the other, I poured every bit of filial frustration I could think of onto soggy sheets of paper and hurled them at my father. "I hate you for leaving my mother." (Read "me.") "I hate you for letting your wives walk all over me." And so forth. It was terribly childish, but after all this was my last fling. I was going to support myself, but not until I'd unloaded a lot of emotional baggage.

My boyfriend tried to talk me out of mailing the letter. I said, "It's all right, he'll understand. He's cut the cord and I have to cut it too." I was full of confidence as I marched to the post office, but over the ten days that followed I felt progressively queasier. Thank God that was sixteen years ago: these days return airmail between Nice and Toronto can take months.

11

I needn't have worried. Father's reply began: "Dear Martha, Thank you for the wonderful letter" and went on to talk of other things. I should have known. You can put him down as much as you like, but you can't pin him down no matter what you do.

About eight years ago, a journalist named David Cobb came to see me. He was writing a profile of my father for *Maclean's* magazine, and he looked awful, even for a writer. There was a desperate look in his eyes. I said, "I know, you're trying to paint an intimate portrait of Don Harron, and you're not having any luck, are you?"

He suddenly looked hopeful. "You're absolutely right, and I've been following him around for days! What should I do?"

I said, "Forget it. *Anyone* who claims to know my father intimately is a liar."

The next time I saw that look, it was on my father's face. He told me he was trying to write his autobiography. I was tempted to ask "Whose?" It turns out this was precisely the problem. *Harronside* is the only book he's ever had trouble writing, probably because he couldn't get close enough to his subject.

Mind you, it was partly my fault. His eldest daughter, researcher and sometime co-author had been less than encouraging about the manuscript. "This book should be called *It's Only Me*," I told him. "It's so humble, it's sickening. Stop being so bloody *Canadian*." This hurt his feelings, but only because he's so patriotic.

I told one of Canada's bestselling authors that I could do a better job of writing his life story than he could and, being Canadian, he believed me.

The only thing that bothers me about writing my father's biography is that it makes my mother so happy. She lives for literature and her family, and is only satisfied when the latter is churning out the former. For years she's been saying "Why don't you write?" I know a lot of mothers say that, but mine means books, not letters. It's hard for me to do something she approves of, but I comfort myself with the knowledge that following in the footsteps of literary giants like Christina Crawford and Nancy Sinatra is not exactly what Mother had in mind.

1

A PUN HIS FATHER'S KNEE

DONALD Hugh Harron made his first entrance at two in the morning on September 19, 1924. He says he was born at home in bed with a naked woman, and hopes to exit the same way. I hope that won't happen for a long time.

Looking back, it is easy to see the influences which propelled him toward a career in showbusiness. At the same time, it is difficult to imagine what other career (apart from college professor) he could have pursued. I've never met anyone else so totally at odds with the physical world. This star of stage and screen has to wait for another member of the family to come home and turn on the VCR for him. He has written books, plays and musicals in the time it takes some of us to read one, but he can't change the ribbon on his old manual typewriter without having to take a bath afterwards.

No one knows where this curious trait came from. His father was a draughtsman and graduate engineer. His mother was a supremely efficient homemaker, which makes her a genius in my book. Yet their son once climbed into the back seat of his own car and shouted, "Jesus Christ, someone's stolen my steering wheel!"

Both of his parents loved to perform, on stage and in the living room. Wordplay came as naturally to them as breathing. Grandpa's specialty was cartooning, and he continued to perform "chalk talks" until the year he died. These are humorous lectures illustrated by cartoons and caricatures drawn on the spot. At university, he had been staff cartoonist on the college paper.

13

It was my grandmother, however, who had the most irrepressible sense of fun. Her son was particularly impressed with the perfor- mance she gave one Hallowe'en as the rear end of a heavy draft horse. Inside her half of the costume Grandma was holding an ample supply of brown paper bags, which she crumpled into balls and shoved through an opening at the back.

In 1916, shortly after they became engaged, Lionel Harron joined the Royal Canadian Engineers and went overseas, into the mud- diest, most gruesome battlegrounds of the muddiest war in history. Delsia Hunter stayed in Toronto, working as a stenographer at her brother Tom's insurance company, and spent her holidays at Camp Billie Bear near Huntsville, Ontario, with other young ladies whose men had gone to war. Delsia and her friends seem to have spent their days dressing up and posing for snapshots. I suspect Grand- ma's influence had a lot to do with the choice of costumes.

After Armistice was declared, Lionel did a chalk talk for his fellow soldiers in Paris before coming home with a military cross. They married, Delsia left the steno pool and they moved into a flat on Rushton Road. Lionel went to work for the thriving family business, Harron's Cleaners and Dyers, although he had hopes of becoming a professional cartoonist. He was joined by his brother Roy, who much preferred being a divinity student. Their widowed mother had been holding down the fort until the war was over.

In 1920 Lionel and Delsia moved into the little house that was to be their home for the rest of their lives, although they couldn't always afford to live in it. Pinewood Avenue, now practically downtown, was a new street outside the city limits, and was filled with young married couples.

All of their social activities were centred around the Methodist church, which in the year of Don's birth merged with the Episcopalians to form a uniquely Canadian compromise known as the United Church. The Harrons' temple of worship, Bathurst Street United, retained that Methodist excuse for mixed socializing known as the Epworth League. The League, not the bowling alley, was the place to go on Thursday nights. Lionel also belonged to the "Hustlers" Bible class, and Delsia was one of the "Joy Girls." It must have been an innocent time indeed.

They had a lot of fun, and spent most of their time putting on shows. Many of them were black-faced minstrel shows, with Grandpa as ''interlocutor,'' the lone paleface in the centre of the front row, resplendent in tux or tails. Grandma was an ''end-woman,'' kind of like a ''sideman'' in a rock and roll band, and went by the name of Odessa. Don refers to these as ''racist entertainments'' which of course they were, but the Hustlers and the Joy Girls would have been surprised by the accusation.

Lionel and Delsia were the most playful couple I ever met. Family gatherings always included games, especially charades, the perfect vehicle for Grandma, and something called ''the drawing game'' which was Grandpa's specialty. We never bothered to keep score for charades, but the drawing game was intensely competitive. Like a secret agent, Lionel would flash a card at two opponents, standing with pencils at the ready. They would race to their battle stations and draw whatever was named on the card, with a point going to the team which guessed it first.

When they weren't playing games, they were singing and playing musical instruments. This is a talent Don claims he failed utterly to inherit. He loves music, but don't ask him to sing it or play it. When his parents weren't actually performing, they continued to ham it up around the house by teasing each other, while giving the rest of us knowing winks. This kind of creative bickering seems to be a textbook recipe for a happy marriage.

I heard my grandparents call each other a bewildering variety of pet names, and with names like Lionel and Delsia you can hardly blame them. He called her ''Dutzie'' most of the time and she called him ''Fat,'' which he wasn't, or ''Big Bum,'' which he wasn't either. Fat called his Dutzie from work every lunchtime, and when little Donny came along he got to talk on the phone too.

The first event in his life that my father remembers took place when he was barely a year old. His father carried him down the front steps of their house and took him for a ride in his brand new Maxwell. Donald swears that his perfect recall of the occasion is in no way aided by the photograph which recorded the event.

His first public performance, about six months later, was unscheduled and a total disaster. He had been taken to church to hear his father, who was the Sunday school superintendent, give a special sermon. The only problem was that a pillar obscured the speaker from his son's view. Wriggle as he might on his mother's knee, little Donald could hear his father but couldn't see him. Just as Lionel paused for dramatic emphasis, his son's voice rang out with amazing clarity, calling his father's name not once but several times, "Big Bum! Big Bum!" Dutzie and child beat a rapid retreat out the church door.

Don's next vivid memory is of the first time he was upstaged. He never got over this traumatic experience, although it happened over sixty years ago. He was taken to Grace Hospital to meet Mary, his new baby sister. Come to think of it, *she* never got over it either — having Don Harron for a big brother, I mean. The first thing he did when he entered his mother's room was to stomp all over the bed, shouting, "Where is she? Where is she?" She was in her crib, fortunately.

Apart from the horror of sharing his parents' attention with a sibling, life was good. After Mary they got a dog, thereby becoming a statistically average family with one of each. The family business was booming. They couldn't have been more settled, in fact, when Lionel got the chance to fulfil his greatest ambition — an offer from King Features Syndicate in Chicago to become a full-time professional cartoonist.

This was in 1929. My father blames his mother for the decision to turn the job down. Be that as it may, the Harrons decided to play it safe and stick to drycleaning. Instead, Grandpa satisfied his wanderlust by attending spot removal conventions.

Two years later the stock market crashed, the economy collapsed and luxury trades like drycleaning were hit hardest of all. Don noticed the change first when his parents traded in their new car for an older, cheaper model. Then the phone was taken out of the house, and he discovered that even their house did not belong to them, but to the man who held the mortgage, the dreaded Mr. Slade. Even today the name sends shivers down my father's spine.

When business became too bad, the Harrons were forced to rent out the house to people who could afford it, and move into a small apartment. I don't know whether Don was aware of it yet, but the lesson was not lost on him that playing it safe is not necessarily the smart move. One industry that thrives even in hard times is entertainment. People learn to live with stains on their clothes, but they'll still spend their last nickel on a good laugh. Lionel would have done better to follow his dream. There is no substitute for conviction, and despite the Harron brothers' best efforts, Harron's Cleaners and Dyers became a pale shadow of its former self. Only the iron determination of their tiny, fragile-looking mother, Margaret, kept it going.

Holidays were spent mostly at Dunbarton, twenty-five miles from Toronto, where Delsia's parents lived. Don called them Bampa and Nanna. Christopher Hunter was a tall, stately gentleman whose father had been a tavernkeeper before he took to farming near Buttonville. Farming was too strenuous for Christopher, however, so he became storekeeper and postmaster in a little town called Painswick, three miles from his grandson Donald's present country retreat. He lost the post office position when John A. Macdonald went out and Wilfrid Laurier came in, which caused him to vote Conservative ever after.

According to Don, his grandfather's distaste for work became a lifelong aversion rivalled only by his loathing for the Liberals. He retired in 1898, at the age of 49, and was supported for the rest of his life by his son Tom, the successful member of the family. The only physical exertion he indulged in thereafter was a dignified stroll into the street, shovel in hand, to return with a steaming load of road apples. These he gallantly and gracefully would deposit around his wife Florrie's rosebushes. (Funny, all my gardening books say not to do that.)

Florrie Hunter, fifteen years younger than her husband, was Don's favourite grandparent. She spoiled him with plates of taffy and brown sugar sandwiches, when she wasn't waiting on her husband hand and foot. Country living in Dunbarton tasted sweet in spite of the lack of electricity or plumbing. He would sit with his grandfather on the side porch living a man's life, swatting flies by the hundreds while Bampa smoked his pipe and read the Bible.

The fact that both grandparents adored him was the icing on a rich cake. To the little boy from the city, that white clapboard cottage represented peace and contentment, freedom and adventure, all the finer things in life. You could say it was the birthplace of my father's alter ego Charlie Farquharson, the rural philosopher who goes against the grain because it's too far to go back to the house.

At school, Don claims to have been a normal, undistinguished student, apart from his inability to write legibly or with his right hand. Much was expected of him because his parents were so active in the Home and School Association, and starred in all the Association's entertainments. He would have liked to be the class clown, but this career was cut short by a teacher who was discussing the way that a cat's ears are multi-directional. When he caught Don giving an unsolicited demonstration, he gave him a verbal tar-and-feathering for being a show-off that stuck. Not being rebellious by nature, Don quit clowning for good — but only in class.

Fortunately, another teacher at Humewood Public School encouraged those very same qualities. Oliver Thompson cast his protégé as a little slave boy in *Uncle Tom's Cabin*. Harriet Beecher Stowe may be a cut above minstrel shows, but Don is still embarrassed about his burnt cork début. His next appearance was as Peter Cratchett in Dicken's *A Christmas Carol*. This was too much like real life because his little brother Tim got all the attention.

The twice and future actor decided he would rather pursue a career in sports — a laughable prospect to those of us who have watched him wrestle with his socks. He tried out for the soccer team, but when the list of players went up on the notice board, he found his name at the very bottom: HARRON — LEFT OUTSIDE. Not realising this was a position on the team, Don figured he'd been eliminated and went sadly home.

At home, there were his father's books: Dickens, Ernest Thompson Seton, G.A. Henty and R.M. Ballantyne. Not to neglect the visual arts, Lionel Harron taught his son to draw cartoons. But it was the theatre that seems to have left the most indelible impression on the boy's mind. By theatre, I am referring to that bastion of culture known as Shea's Hippodrome, where Shoeless Joe Jackson did his clown bicycle act and Red Skelton was king. It stood right next to the old City Hall, on the corner now occupied by the new City Hall Square.

The most famous act he saw at Shea's turned out to be a big disappointment. The seats they had for a show by Howard Thurston, the great magician, were on the side. Thurston's greatest illusion was being blown to bits by a cannon onstage and reappearing intact, after the smoke cleared. From where he was sitting, Don saw Thurston slip out of his robe just as the assistant lowered the hood in place, and was bitterly disillusioned. Lionel couldn't understand his son's lack of enthusiasm, but Don never explained, not wanting to destroy his father's childlike sense of wonder.

Another fallen hero in Don's young life was the principal of Humewood Public School. A tall, thin man with a Hitlerian moustache, Mr. Watson had seemed to him the most awesome authority figure this side of Jehovah. Don was particularly fascinated by his habit of stroking his Adam's apple in a sensuous way. The disenchantment came from his discovery that the principal was incapable of controlling his own two small sons, who ran wild through the house. One day they coated their mother's new sofa with green paint. On a visit to a farm, they smuggled a live pig into the back seat of their father's car, and Mr. Watson didn't notice it until they got back to the city. (This reminds me of my own father. Blessed are the unobservant, for they shall see very little of what their children are up to.)

While life in the city got tougher and tougher, summers in Dunbarton remained much the same, thank Heaven, with his Bampa reading the Bible or the daily *Toronto Star*, 2 cents. If Don got tired of waiting for the comics section, he'd head for Morrish's General Store next door.

The store was truly General, just like the one in *Anne of Green Gables*. As the song says, "A General Store is just the place / To meet the needs of the human race." The one in Dunbarton had straw hats and pitchforks, cheese, pickles and all kinds of penny candy: hard hats, B-B bats, conversation lozenges and tart powdered sugar sucked up with licorice straws. The store had one other great selling point — a boy his own age, the owner's son Lyle Morrish.

If Lyle wasn't around, Don would head over to the other side of his grandparents' property to visit Joe and Elsie Gormley. Joe was the first real farmer he ever knew. Joe's clothes looked at least as old as he did, which must be where Don got the notion that this is how real farmers dress. Charlie Farquharson wore the same sweater for over thirty-five years, and he's still wearing the same cap. When I complained that he was supposed to look like a farmer, not a derelict, my father smiled sadly and replied, "Tried farming lately?"

In the evenings, Don would watch his grandfather and Joe Gormley pitch horseshoes, the former standing straight and tall and aristocratic after a strenuous session of reading the paper and swatting flies, the latter bent with the work of the day. In spite of his grandfather's devotion, Don began to despise the old man's idleness. In his defense, it should be stated that Christopher Hunter suffered from allergies, and had been referred to since childhood as "the sickly one" in the family. If Don noticed this infirmity, he considered it a poor excuse.

In the summer of 1932 his friend Lyle Morrish died. Don doesn't remember what Lyle died of, but he remembers the shock of the news. It was his first intimation of mortality. He couldn't understand how his grandfather could survive a heart attack to celebrate his eighty-second birthday, while his Dunbarton friend could die before his eighth.

From then on, Lyle's mother would look at Don as if he could bring her son back to her. Watching him grow up must have reminded her of her own boy who never had the chance. Don felt guilty, as if he were personally responsible for Lyle being taken instead of him. He also wondered if he might be next.

He almost was. He had brushes with death both the following summer and the next. While visiting a farm he fell through a hole in the barn floor that led to a thirty-foot-deep pile of loosely packed hay. He was sliding blithely into certain suffocation when his father saw what was happening and managed to catch hold of him just in time. Typically, my father feels guilty for that too — guilty that he made no attempt to save himself.

Don Harron is the most guilt-ridden person I ever met, and I don't know where it came from. But, I can give you *his* explanation. He bought it at great expense from an analyst in 1963. The analyst was curious to know why, on his (first) wedding day in 1949, Donald gave his parents a car, a reversal of the usual ritual. The explanation he offered was that as a young boy Don had (of course) suffered from the Oedipus complex, wanting to kill his father and marry his mother. When the Depression came, and his father was wiped out, Don felt personally responsible. These feelings of guilt were compounded in the summer of 1933 by the knowledge that he was about to be sent into exile, before his ninth birthday. It seemed like a punishment for the fulfilment of his wicked desires. "The car was a guilt-offering to your father to assuage his wished-for murder."

That was the professional opinion. If you want *my* opinion, I think he did it because he's a nice guy, who felt badly that he wouldn't be around to run errands for his parents any more.

Whether or not Don's complex was responsible, by 1933 the drycleaning business had shrunk to the point where the Harrons couldn't even afford their apartment, let alone their house. Dutzie and daughter Mary went to stay with her parents in Dunbarton, Lionel stayed at his mother's place across from the drycleaning plant, and Donald was sent to board with second cousins so he could continue his schooling.

The McKelvies were nice people but they weren't family, at least not the family he was used to. During that year he sought refuge in books, and the person he identified with most was a red-headed orphan named Anne of Green Gables. He felt homeless, helpless and terribly alone but he hoped, like Anne, to triumph over adversity with imagination and determination.

The next time Don almost died was by drowning. In the summer of '34, the family went to Little Lake Tourist Camp near Midland, Ontario in the wheezy old Pontiac. After dark, nine-year-old Don would have to ride on the front fender holding a flashlight, because the headlights had gone. They drove from there to Dunbarton the same way. I don't know what Lionel did for emergency illumination the rest of the summer, commuting up from Toronto on weekends. He was once pulled off the highway and given a ticket for driving too slowly.

At the tourist camp, Don took up with a gang of ten-year-old boys who spent their time trying to outdo one another in everything. They shinnied up and down poles in playgrounds, mooched buns from the baker's wagon and ice from the ice wagon, smoked cedar bark and stole apples, until they were chased by a farmer and almost ended up with a buttful of B-B shot.

Little Lake had boats for two bits (25 cents) an hour, and the

swimming was free. There were rafts all over the lake, and some
had slides on them. One such raft had too many people on it, all
yelling and shoving and screaming with delight. It finally tilted so
steeply that Don was pitched overboard. When he rose to the surface, he found himself trapped underneath the raft. He tried to
surface a few times, but each time ran up against the sharp rusty
points of the nails holding the platform together. After that he
started running out of air and sinking. He remembers very clearly
seeing himself on the murky bottom, and watching the bubbles as
they rose from his body.

He accepted the fact that he was going to die, just like his friend
Lyle. He observed the event as if from above, like the people
Elizabeth Kubler-Ross writes about who have been to the brink of
death and returned to tell the tale. It may have been watching the
re-run of his life that shook him out of his death trance: the film
was too short, and he didn't like the ending. He was feeling no
pain, but suddenly became furious with himself. "You stupid twit!
What are you doing lying down here? Get the bloody hell out !"
(He talks to himself like that all the time.)

On this try he had sense enough to take a few strokes forward
as well as upward, and managed to reach the surface. When he came
up, his face was purple, which attracted a grown-up swimmer's attention. This was fortunate, as Don had not uttered a sound. His rescuer
grabbed him by the hair and dragged him to shore, where his mother
sat brushing little Mary's hair, oblivious to what had just happened.
Don threw himself down on the sand beside them and said nothing,
confused and frightened by the fact that he almost let himself die.

He didn't know it, but his exile was already over. It had ended
with the school year in 1934. It was over because that spring, Don's
"lazy" eighty-four-year-old grandfather had collapsed while digging
up his half-acre vegetable garden. The doctor said he had six weeks
to live, but he hung on until the Harron clan arrived from the tourist
camp.

It was to be their last summer in Dunbarton. Don learned that
for years his grandparents had been living off their son, the
successful member of the family. Tom decided his parents should
give up the place in the country and stay with relatives in town.

Not at his house of course — his wife would not have approved — but with his sister Delsia and her family, the city churchmice.

The churchmice didn't mind. The allowance provided by Uncle Tom meant that they could move back to Pinewood Avenue. The addition of two more family members might have made the little house seem crowded had they been living in it all along, but the Harron family was delighted to be back in their own home again, and didn't mind the togetherness one bit.

Don was happy to give up his bedroom to Nanna and Bampa. He moved into his father's den, which was more like a closet with a window, but had enough room for a ten-year-old boy and his father's collection of cartoon books from World War I. Nanna went on spoiling her husband and grandson, and Bampa went on reading the Bible and transferring fresh manure from road to rosebush. He managed to stretch those six weeks into eleven years.

2

FROM CHALK TO BOTTOM

HAVING survived his first decade, young Donald grew like a wild weed. He read Horatio Alger books with stirring titles like *Work to Win, Strive and Save,* and one more ominously entitled *George Pulls It Off.* His favourite book, *Peck's Bad Boy,* which I remember him reading to me with undiminished enthusiasm some decades later, described the antics of a juvenile delinquent who drove his father crazy. My father must have found this so amusing because he himself was such a model son.

The Harrons spent the rest of the Thirties sans phone, sans car, sans country retreat. Don credits the lack of phone calls for the fact that he got this homework done, but I'm sure he would have done it anyway, considering that he was reading *Work to Win* in his spare time. When the old Pontiac finally wheezed its last, it was even past selling for parts and was towed away to a quiet burial. For rustic contemplation, Don went camping with his Wolf Cub pack and learned the hard way that poison ivy is no substitute for toilet paper.

At home, thanks to Bampa's piety, ministers of the Gospel would frequently come to visit. Reverend Chandler used to shake the rafters with his powerful voice. It was worse when the bearded Reverend Garnham would stop by. Donald would be summoned in from play to join the family in prayer. Reverend Garnham was a marathon speaker, or as my father would say, he had a long-praying record. Don furtively opened one eye during a particularly lengthy prayer and was delighted to discover his grandmother, seated next to the

Reverend, slowly rotating her hand at his side as if winding up a phonograph.

These interminable prayers must have been easier for Nanna as she was hard of hearing. On the occasion of her husband's ninetieth birthday, she asked him if he had received a present from the next-door neighbour. "Kind regards," replied her husband with some irony.

Nanna looked delighted. "Nine cigars?"

Don's attempts to earn money were many and varied and not very successful. Asking his father for an allowance was out of the question, so he earned some pocket money delivering "Harron's Cleaners and Dyers" handbills. One hot day the friend who was supposed to split the work and the pay suggested they dump the bills under a porch and hit the swimming hole instead. Young Harron was outraged and finished the route by himself.

Like lots of other boys, he sold *Liberty* magazines door to door, hoping to win a bicycle. He never made more than thirty-five cents a week that way, but he got plenty of exercise because the few regular customers he managed to acquire lived miles apart and, of course, he had no bike.

His father managed to earn some money on the side too. About once a month he would put on his old interlocutor's tuxedo and go off into the night to perform a chalk talk at a banquet. The first time Don remembers seeing his father's act was when Lionel performed for free at a church "Father and Son" banquet. I wish I could report that it was a witty and polished performance. My grandfather was a wonderful cartoonist, but the humour was sexist and laden with racial stereotypes. At a 1935 church social this was considered "good clean fun."

Donald dates his lifelong love affair with puns from that memorable evening. About halfway through his act Lionel drew a potato, and talked about an Irishman named Richard Murphy who went to Italy to get a job. The potato was transformed into a caricature of Benito Mussolini while Lionel explained that the Irishman had changed his name to "Dick Tater."

Don was deeply impressed. He thought he could do a chalk talk himself, and longed for the bright lights that went with it. Lionel not only encouraged him to follow in his footsteps, he taught him his act word for word. Don mastered the patter without any trouble. The drawings were more of a problem only because he wasn't tall enough for the huge sheets of paper. However, with the help of a chair he was able to reproduce all his father's cartoons quite successfully.

He tried out his act at a Wolf Cub banquet, and was a big hit. This led to his being featured as a solo divertissement in the "Eighth Annual All-Star Thirtieth Troop Boy Scout Revue." It ran for three nights and led to two more offers.

The first person who actually paid Don Harron to show off, after eleven years of doing it for free, was the president of Tippet-Richardson Movers. He was having a banquet for his staff at the Ellen Bradley Grill, and hired Don to do his chalk talk for ten dollars. Lionel went along to carry the drawing board and collect the fee. He never complained at being relegated to the sidelines as coach and manager, and never kept a cent of his son's earnings for himself.

For his professional début, Don again wore his Wolf Cub uniform, probably because they were his best clothes. He must have presented quite an irresistible picture, perched on a stool turning an egg into a portrait of bald-headed President Basil Tippet.

The second offer to come out of the Boy Scout Minstrel Revue was much more than a one-night stand — it was an adventure series for the Canadian Radio Commission. The CRC was Canada's first attempt to nationalize radio, and the first link from sea to sea since the railroad. A scriptwriter named Iola Plaxton had already chosen one of the Boy Scout "end-men" from the Minstrel Revue to play the older of the two boy heroes, and asked Donald to audition for the part of the younger one. She and Len Robinson came over to Pinewood one evening, and the three of them read through an episode of *Lonesome Trail,* as the series was to be called.

The lines on the page came naturally to Don at first reading, and Mrs. Plaxton hired him on the spot. There would be three broadcasts a week, and he would be paid two dollars and fifty cents for each one. Already feeling like a real boy hero adventurer, he saw himself leading his family out of the valley of the shadow of debt single-handed. To hell with Mr. Slade and his mortgage!

This was April 1936, however, and the series didn't start until September. With fame and fortune still months away, he had to content himself with life, *Liberty* and the pursuit of subscribers, still without a bicycle.

At school, due to lack of space and budget, Don's class had to share a classroom and teacher with the grade above them. Luckily the teacher was Oliver Thompson, the one who encouraged Don to show off. He was a magnificent teacher, somehow managing to instruct both classes and maintain order at the same time. Don tried to do his Junior Fourth (Grade Seven) classwork, but he would find himself listening to the Senior Fourth Entrance lessons instead.

June came at last and Don "passed without trying," as did most of the Junior Fourths, which meant his marks were good enough to exempt him from writing examinations. The smartest boy in the class, according to my father, was Jimmy Harrold, a mathematical whiz and actuary-to-be. He decided to try the entrance exams just for fun, and persuaded Don to try them too. Mr. Thompson agreed, so every day when the Junior Fourth class was excused, the two boys would stay behind and write exams. It's amazing what some people will do for kicks.

When it came time to write the history exam, Jimmy decided not to bother. Math and science were his meat and potatoes, but history was not his cup of tea. Why waste an afternoon trying to write about topics only vaguely overheard all year? Don agreed, so they packed a lunch and went off to the wilds of Cedarvale, now a scrupulously manicured municipal park, like a golf course without holes.

They had eaten their sandwiches and were folding up the waxed paper (to be washed and used again, no doubt) when they heard the Humewood School bell ringing in the distance. The Entrance class would be filing in to write the exam. Suddenly Don was seized by a wild impulse, and said, "Jimmy, history is just bullshit! Let's go write that exam!" It was a long way and a hot day. They ran as fast as they could, but by the time they knocked on the door of the examination room, everyone else was scribbling away. Mr. Thompson smiled as he handed the papers over to the panting, sweaty pair.

Perhaps inspired by the *Lonesome Trail* that lay ahead, Donald wrote the history exam as if it were a boy's adventure story, which if you think about it is how many of the protagonists lived it. What he didn't know, he filled in with diversionary tactics, bits of theatrical derring-do and a couple of attempts at humour.

When the results came out, Don and Jimmy were summoned to the principal's office. Mr. Watson sat behind his desk stroking his Adam's apple as usual, but with a curious smile on his face. He informed them that Jimmy had received the highest math mark in the school, and Donald had received a 74 in history, one percentage point below first-class honours. They had a choice: stay for the Senior Fourth year, or go straight on to high school.

That September Don Harron was the only kid in short pants climbing the steps of Vaughan Road Collegiate Institute. He was still eleven years old, although soon to be twelve, and the Fifth Form (Grade Thirteen) students looked like giants. Future Stratford star William Hutt even sported a moustache.

Like every other public school, Vaughan Road Collegiate was over-crowded and underfunded, with the result that classes were staggered. Some students attended from 8:00 to 2:30, others staggered in from 10:00 to 4:30. But Don didn't take much notice of his new school, or his schoolmates. He was too busy being a boy hero adventurer, which turned out to be very hard work. *Lonesome Trail* was broadcast live (like everything else in those days) at 6:30 p.m. every Tuesday, Thursday and Saturday. Monday, Wednesday and Friday they rehearsed, leaving only Sundays free — for homework. He would come straight home from school every day, grab the street car tickets his mother always left for him and rush downtown, either to the studio to do a broadcast, or to the advertising agency where the CRC had rented them a room to rehearse.

How he envied the other kids on the street, who could kick a football around while he slaved. One day he couldn't stand it any more. After a half-hearted attempt to find the streetcar tickets, which were under the mirror of the dining room centerpiece as usual, Don ran out to play touch rugby with his friends. His mother was at a Home and School meeting, and of course they had no phone, so it was some time before the truant was caught. There were stern faces around the dining room table that night, and a special rehearsal had to be held after supper for Don's benefit and everyone else's inconvenience. To my knowledge, he hasn't missed a radio rehearsal since.

Parental disapproval of his playing hooky had nothing to do with needing the money. They never intended to spend it, which is pretty noble when you consider how hard up they were. The notion of rescuing his family was all Don's own. He wanted to save up to buy them a refrigerator, but this young hero business was turning out to be a lot more of a grind than he had anticipated. What he needed was an independent mode of transportation, and what he wanted was a shiny red C.C.M. bicycle.

With his first month's salary of thirty-five dollars and his parents' permission, Don bought the bike as a belated twelfth birthday present to himself. His dream had come true, if he could only learn to ride the damn thing. This was no easy task, not only because he has trouble with any mechanical object but also because he was terrified that the other kids on the street would see his struggles and laugh at him.

Fortunately, by the time Don returned home from work and had his supper, the other kids were inside doing their homework. From eight to nine o'clock nightly, with his father's patient guidance and support, he wobbled furtively down laneways and sidestreets. Finally — and suddenly, as so often happens — he got the hang of it. From then on he was whizzing around corners, no hands, everywhere he went. His father warned him to slow down and be more careful. Quite apart from risk to life and limb, Don had a responsibility toward the sponsor of *Lonesome Trail,* which happened to be the Ontario Department of Highways.

At the end of each show, an Irish cop named Mickey O'Something would deliver a message about traffic safety to all the children listening. The cop was really Don Harron putting on a thick Irish brogue. It seems odd that they would have chosen the youngest member of the cast to impersonate a policeman. I can only assume that his was the best Irish accent, which is no slight on the others because he does all kinds of accents superbly, and at every available opportunity.

Don quickly became bored with rehearsals, but he loved doing the broadcasts, especially in their new studio. When the CRC became the Canadian Broadcasting Corporation, they moved to the top floor of the Eveready Flashlight Building, next to the streetcar barns on Davenport Road. The new building was an exciting place for a starstruck lad. Conversations about exotic places like Hart House Theatre and summer stock in Bala, almost a hundred miles away, wafted by him enticingly in the halls.

He found himself in pretty distinguished company on *Lonesome Trail,* with young Eric Clavering already typecast as a lovable geriatric, and their announcer Charles Jennings looking and sounding very much like his ABC anchorman son Peter does today. When Charles couldn't make it, his replacement was a very funny guy named Bud Walker, who became a very sober-faced CBC mandarin.

Don was particularly impressed with the sound effects man Billy McLintock. All effects were done live. When the boy adventurers walked through the snow, Billy would punch a bag of cornmeal. When it rained, he'd take a box full of dried peas and roll them around. If the boys made a fire, he'd take a cellophane wrapper off a chocolate bar and crackle it close to the microphone. If it was supposed to be windy, he'd spin a corrugated drum against a piece of canvas. The sound of horses' hooves was made by coconut shells, à la Monty Python. For paved roads, Billy would clap the halves together. For dirt roads, he'd unbutton his shirt and pound them on his chest. McLintock's bag of tricks was a constant source of wonder, but the trick that impressed young Donald the most was when, on the air, Don was supposed to be zipping up his radio mother's evening gown, and Billy used his own fly for the sound effect.

One day, hurtling to work down Bathurst Street hill on his shiny red C.C.M., Don turned the corner onto Davenport Road without slowing down and ran straight into the path of an oncoming taxi. The cab driver did his best to avoid him, enough that the cyclist's life was spared, but the bike was demolished.

Considering the fact that the accident was entirely Don's fault, the driver was extremely decent about it. He slung the wreckage into the back seat and offered to take the boy where he wanted to go, which happened to be the radio station just around the corner.

By the time he had dragged his bruised body and crippled steed up the four flights of stairs, Don was half an hour late. The logical thing would have been to leave the bike down below, as it was no longer worth stealing, but this would not have occurred to him. Like King Lear carrying the corpse of Cordelia, he dragged the earthly remains of his broken dream into the studio.

There was just enough time for a quick dress rehearsal before they went on the air. The show went smoothly until it came time for Don to put on his Irish accent and tell all the little children to look both ways before crossing the street. This was too much for the rest of the cast, who had to stuff the velvet curtains into their mouths to muffle their howls of merriment. The twelve-year-old traffic cop failed to see the humour in the situation. As soon as the broadcast was over, he burst into tears.

A month later, the Department of Highways withdrew its sponsorship and the series was cancelled. Don put showbusiness behind him, claiming he didn't mind a bit, and returned to the delights of playing hockey after school. With what was left of his fortune, he bought a second-hand bike, and this time kept his hands on the handlebars.

A month after that, tired of poverty and idleness, he took a job as delivery boy for the Little Pie Shoppe on St. Clair Avenue, about a mile from Vaughan Road Collegiate. He would rush over during lunch hour and after school to deliver home-baked bread, butter tarts and lemon meringue pies. The two ladies who ran the Shoppe were very generous with free samples, so much so that he practically lived on butter tarts that year.

Don found the transportation of delicate goods to be very difficult work. He kept at it, though, until the day came when he had to deliver a lemon meringue pie to a lady he swears lived ten miles from the store. It was pouring with rain, and he couldn't find the address. When he finally made it back to the shop, he returned the water-logged meringue and resigned his commission on the spot.

Unemployed again, Donald tried hard to mis-spend his youth, but without much success. He lost interest in smoking because cedar bark made him cough, and a few puffs on his father's cigar made

him want to die. That summer at his Uncle Tom's cottage he raided

the liquor cabinet, and guzzled enough gin to put him off drinking for life. He laughed helplessly for half an hour, but this did
not make up for the vomiting and hangover which followed. Cigar-
ets and whiskey were out. It looked as if wild, wild women were
his only hope.

Don was aware of girls, but hadn't the faintest idea what to do
with them. Over the next year he spent a lot of time putting Orange.
Blossom Brilliantine or Hollywood Wave Set on his cowlick, hoping to make himself more acceptable to the opposite sex. Like most
twelve-year-old boys, he only pursued girls who ignored him. He
says this is Mother Nature's way of making sure that nothing will
happen.

The following summer, his thirteenth, something finally did happen, although certainly not what he had expected. Hanging around
the old Humewood schoolyard, he shinnied up one of the poles
holding up the swings, and slid down again. To his amazement,
this produced a sensation in his shorts that was better than butter
tarts. So much better, in fact, that he spent the rest of the summer
climbing up and sliding down that pole, but the sensation was never
repeated.

I mention this because I think it's funny, and it is included in
my father's unpublished autobiography which I am contradicting,
but I have to be honest and tell you that discussing my father's libido
makes me uncomfortable. It's indecent of parents to have a sex life,
and I would be tempted to ignore this aspect completely, if there
were any hope of stringing his life story together without it.

He fell madly in love with a girl named Jane Elmore, although
she probably didn't know it. He was never able to stammer more
than a few words in her presence. He managed to ask her to dance
once, but slunk away in embarrassment afterwards, when he saw
that his perspiring right hand had soaked its imprint right through
the back of her dress.

He had unclean thoughts about the policeman's wife up the street.
She had nice legs, and when she mowed the lawn in her shorts Don
would spy on her from his mother's bedroom and writhe in frustration. One hot summer afternoon he took part in a group sex experi-
ment — a bunch of thirteen-year-olds watching a fourteen-year-
old attempt to masturbate. It was a dry run.

Puberty is such a trying time in anyone's life. The usual outlet for thirteen-year-olds' frustrations, at least in those innocent times, was contact sports. Don became a member of the Vaughan Road Junior-B football team. It was this, by a curious twist of fate, that led him back to showbusiness.

In order to prepare a presentation for parents' night, the drama teacher, Miss Waugh, dragooned a group of Junior-B footballers into putting on a scene from *A Midsummer Night's Dream*. The scene she had chosen, for which her cast was most appropriate, was the rehearsal of *Pyramus and Thisbe* by the "rude mechanicals." Don was assigned the role of Bottom the Weaver. Miss Waugh kept telling them it was a comedy, a sure-fire hit, but none of them had much faith in the material.

Parents' night came all too soon. There was no time for a dress rehearsal with the set, which was a cardboard forest nailed to lengths of two-by-four. As the reluctant football players made their entrance, Don accidentally tripped over one of the pieces of wood and fell flat on his face. Under the mistaken impression that they were watching a comedian, not a klutz, the audience roared with laughter. It was music to his ears, a sound never heard on the *Lonesome Trail*. (Except through velvet curtains.)

Getting laughs was sweeter than butter tarts, possibly even sweeter than sliding down that pole, and easier to repeat — much easier than he could have imagined. Forgetting all about the two-by-fours, Bottom tripped again on his way out and fell flat on his namesake. It hurt like heck, but he didn't care — it got the biggest laugh of the night. Don Harron was beginning to think he had found his forté, at last.

3

PASSING THE PHYSICAL

DON'S next brush with the Bard was a shameful episode. His class had been taken to Oakwood Collegiate to see a performance of *Henry IV, Part 1*. Finding himself on the wrong side of the footlights was such torture, he attempted to upstage the cast with a series of what he thought were wildly funny ad libs. When Owen Glendower began to play his Welsh flute, Harron yelled "Swing it, Artie!" At the end, when Hotspur stammered "O! I could prophesy, but that the earthy and cold hand of death lies on my tongue," Harron added "Th-th-th-that's all, folks!" in his best Porky Pig imitation.

The abused Hotspur was future Stratford star William Needles, and the "semi-professional troupe" (i.e., polished but unpaid) was Dora Mavor Moore's Village Players. Their next encounter was to have a profound influence on Donald's life. Thank heavens they didn't recognise the heckler.

Later that year, the editor of the high school magazine persuaded him to go along on an interview with the members of Canada's most popular radio show, *The Happy Gang*. Don was eager to meet Bert Pearl and the rest of the gang, but it wasn't easy to climb the stairs of the Eveready Building again, this time as an outsider.

You may be wondering why he hadn't been back there in two years, not even to audition for a part, if he wanted one so badly. No longer a child, not yet a man, at fourteen Don was burning with desire for fame and females — and too shy to do anything about either. Not much has changed over the last half century. My mother described him perfectly the other day when she said to my sister, "Mary, you're just like your father — all that ambition and no push." Never mind. Somehow or other, they rev up the motor and climb hills without ever putting the car in gear.

Meanwhile, there was still the little matter of high school to get through. There doesn't seem to have been any teacher at Vaughan Road Collegiate with whom he had a special rapport, like Oliver Thomson at Humewood. He wanted to develop one with the German teacher, but so did all the other boys. They were constantly dropping their pencils for a better view of her shapely legs.

Most of the teachers he remembers for their quirks. If Miss Roach, which was really her name, caught him leaning back to whisper with the pupil behind him, she would yell, "Harron! Are you sitting so as to invite intercourse?" Another, who shall remain nameless, had the habit of furtively rubbing her crotch on a corner of the desk while she lectured. The boys rubbed chalk on that corner to emphasize the point — which it did, to their delight.

Don remembers two new boys in the class that year. One was named Donald Herron, with an "e", which caused some confusion. The other was a Jewish refugee from Germany. Klaus Goldschlag paid a lot more attention in English class than his fellow students did in German class, and mastered the language in a very short time. He went on to take top honours in the school.

To Don's parents and their circle of acquaintances, centred around their Protestant church, anti-Semitism was just a harmless habit, or so it seemed before World War II. It would never have occurred to them to be anything but polite and friendly to the Jewish friends Don brought home, but there was always a veiled resentment of foreigners who came to Canada, worked far too hard at school and took good jobs away from the "Canadian" descendants of immigrants who had done exactly the same thing.

Some years earlier, Don remembers a friend of his mother's coming back from Germany and announcing that everything was going to be fine there since a man named Hitler had taken charge. Now all the classes in his school were being taken down to the auditorium to hear the voice of this same take-charge type scream and rant about the Saar, or the Sudetenland, or the Semites.

When the war started in September 1939, Don was just turning fifteen. At first everyone thought it would be a repeat performance of World War I, forgetting how ghastly that had been. Even his father, who had been at Paaschendael, started singing *Oh, Oh, Oh What a Lovely War* and all the other old Dumbbells' songs. One of the members of that famous troupe, Red Newman, lived just down the street. He and Pat Rafferty and the rest found themselves suddenly popular again, and *We're Gonna Hang Out Our Washing on the Siegfried Line* replaced *Oh Johnny* on the radio. Don thought the older boys looked like movie stars in their dashing new uniforms, and it all seemed terribly exciting.

He kept on with school, and spent Saturdays bagging groceries in a Power store. As Norway fell, followed by the Low Countries, things began to look ominous, but the reality didn't sink in until June, 1940, with the fall of France. He remembers the Power store lunchroom was as quiet as the grave on the day of the Dunkirk evacuation. Only one man spoke: "It'll take a miracle, a fuckin' miracle." Nobody replied.

Not yet old enough to serve as a soldier, Don enlisted in a non-paying summer job which required almost as much courage. He became a Councillor-in-Training at a Lions' Club boys' camp for juvenile delinquents. The Big Brothers transported the young lads up to Beausoleil Island in Georgian Bay, and left Don in charge of a group including a sixteen-year-old arsonist/psychopath, a fourteen-year-old seduced by his stepmother and rapidly turning homosexual, and a ten-year-old charged with thirty-two break-and-enters. Don survived by making them laugh all day, and scaring the willies out of them at bedtime with Edgar Allan Poe.

He says that summer job convinced him it was people, not machines, he wanted to work with. Anyone else could have figured that out from watching him with his first set of building blocks. Even so, his ambition right through high school was to please his father by following in his footsteps to the University of Toronto's School of Practical Science. Ironically, Lionel had already followed in his son's footsteps by going to work as a draughtsman for Don's old sponsor, the Ontario Department of Highways, giving up the ghost of the drycleaning business to his brother Roy.

In order to enter S.P.S. at the U of T, Don had to pass high school physics, and to do that he had to get past the physics teacher, the formidable J.C. Harston. J.C. was also the physical education teacher, and a drill sergeant at heart. He lived on the next street over from Pinewood, and every evening as soon as the street lights came on you could hear the shrill blast of his whistle summoning his two children in from the Humewood playground. Don didn't envy the hup-two-three existence in that house.

To make matters worse, Harston affected a mirthless joviality. He was relentlessly hearty, and liked to address everyone by his or her nickname. Donald had foolishly let it slip that his father called him "Bunt," probably from watching him try to play baseball. Every time J.C. spied his pupil thereafter he would bellow "HELLOTHERE-BUNT!" His martinet methods were barely tolerable in the gym but in physics class, where Don had great difficulty grasping even the most basic principles, they reduced him to total panic.

There was only one way out, and that was to the pool hall. He played snooker every physics class for the rest of the year, and Harston never seemed to notice. The result was a resounding twenty-two percent on the final exam. It's a good thing Don Harron entered high school a year early, because it took him an extra year to get out.

He could have graduated in '41 without the physics credit, having done well in every other subject, but clung like a limpet to the laughable notion of a career in practical science. He returned to Vaughan Road for another year of physics, plus a commercial course in typing, shorthand and bookkeeping. The shorthand and bookkeeping were soon forgotten, but he did actually learn to touch-type without looking at the keys. Anyone who has seen his manuscripts can attest to the fact that he doesn't peek.

The best part of taking the commercial course was that he was the only male in a class of thirty-seven girls. Except for typing class, that is, where he was joined by another boy named Louie Libman. Their first lesson began with the word "if" in the centre of the keyboard. Having mastered that, they extended their range outwards, typing "if it" for a while, followed by "if it is." When they progressed to "if it is in," Louie let out a snort and Don collapsed in paroxysms of laughter. The hysteria may have been induced by the presence of the thirty-seven girls, who pretended not to understand what the fuss was about. The instructor Mr. Smith was not amused, and Harron was asked to leave the room.

Louie and Donald found one another terribly amusing, and cracked each other up as often as they could possibly get away with. The funny thing is, they're both still at it — making people laugh, I mean. Apart from the fact that they now get paid to do it, nothing has changed since typing class except Louie's name. As Larry Mann, he's spent most of his working life as an actor in Hollywood.

As for physics, Don had hopes of passing, at first. The dreaded J.C. Harston had left to join the air force, and his successor, Mr. Kerr, was a gentler soul. But the Angel of Mercy himself could not have explained physics to my father.

This time there was another way out, apart from the pool hall. He could join the Farm Service Force. As there was a war on, farmhands were hard to come by, so the F.S.F. was set up to recruit high school students. They could earn their academic credits by spending six months working fourteen-hour days in the field for twenty dollars a month. It would be much easier than trying to pass physics.

Lionel had reenlisted as a captain in his old outfit, the Royal Canadian Engineers, and his son was determined to do his part, with or without a uniform. The night Lionel left, Delsia and Mary sat sobbing in the living room, while Donald sat upstairs seething with jealousy. Half of those tears should have been his, and in two weeks the remaining "man" in the house would be leaving them as well, to do battle in the field as best he could.

He didn't have to look far to find a farm that required his services. His mother had cousins in the country, and Don had been to visit them. His Aunt Mabel had been widowed some years before, in one of those accidents that happen all the time in the dangerous business of farming. A whippletree broke while a horse was pulling a rope to lift a load of hay and caught her husband full in the groin. It was not Aunt Mabel who needed help, which disappointed Don, because she was a wonderful woman who had once cured his warts with a magic charm and some spit. Mabel had her son Morley to help her, a big husky fellow with a laugh like a steam engine on the blink. But Mabel's daughter Grace and her husband Charles

Hadden had only Charles' aged father to help out, so at the beginning of April, 1942, our hero set off for the Hadden homestead.

The Greyhound bus let him off in the village of Wick, Ontario, which turned out to be a general store. The only sign of life, apart from Charles Hadden who was there to meet him, was a dog sleeping under a tree. Don was immediately put to work driving a harrow over one of the fields. As Charlie Farquharson would say, it was a harrowing experience.

After three hours of this torture, it was time for chores. Don was so dizzy he could hardly stand up, and that was before he got a whiff of the barn. He found the smell overpowering, and was relieved when he could sit outside and breathe some fresh air in the rays of the setting sun. He was absolutely starving by this time, but when he asked about dinner, as discreetly as he could, they told him he had missed it. He almost cried.

"We have dinner at noon. This is supper." Whatever it was called, it tasted fantastic. The Haddens were on the "Beef Ring," a clandestine farmers' co-operative, which meant fresh steaks and chops every ten days. The only thing lacking was fresh milk. They produced lots of it, but shipped it all to the city.

After supper, Don was told that his time was his own until six o'clock the next morning. The room they gave him was very pleasant, and must have seemed huge compared to the cubbyhole he occupied at home. He settled down to read the book he had brought with him. Having finished *Work to Win* and *Strive and Save*, he had chosen *An Outline of History* by H.G. Wells for light summer reading.

He had gone to Sunday School all his life, plus Christian Endeavour classes in the morning before church (there is still Methodism in his madness), but a few chapters of H.G. Wells were enough to convince him that organized religion was nothing but cant and hypocrisy. Charles Hadden was the local Sunday School superintendent, but when his young farmhand refused to accompany the family to church that first Sunday, he merely shrugged and left him to mind the farm.

This was not a wise move. Left to his own devices, Donald threw himself into his new role of country squire with unbridled enthusiasm. Well, not unbridled so much as unbritched. As soon as he was alone, Squire Harron raced to the barn and hitched a pair of bewildered plough horses to an ancient buggy he had found in the driving shed. He had a wonderful time driving all over the property, but for some reason the horses kept racing faster and faster. He thought they were over-anxious to get back to the barn, not realising that the poor things were trying to get away from the buggy, which was banging against the back of their legs with every step. It seems he had omitted the hold-back and breech, or back-britching, which keeps them apart.

By the time the two horses entered the home stretch, they were in a total panic. They smashed straight through the barnyard gates and sent Don flying into the mud by the pigsty. Thanks to rickety gates and the Divine Providence Don no longer believed in, neither of the horses was injured. After they were combed and brushed and watered by their very humble groom, he tied the gates back to their posts as best he could with baling wire. The following Sunday found Donald in church with everybody else.

One job at which he was particularly unskilled was stripping cows. This involved finishing the milking by hand after the machine had drained the lion's (or calf's) share. Having only a very chaste lady fair in the city, whom he visited in courtly fashion once a month, and finding farmers' daughters not at all like the dirty jokes had led him to hope they would be, he was tempted to try the milking machine on an intimate part of himself. He changed his mind when he remembered the machine wouldn't stop until it had suctioned off three quarts.

Across the road from the Hadden farm lived a farmer named Lou Short. He had a son named Orville just like Charley does. So fascinated was Donald by this pair, and their speech patterns, that he would pop over for a quick chat in his spare time. Having abandoned H.G. Wells, his nights were spent mostly listening to the radio, or writing letters home on his prized possession, a Smith-Corona portable typewriter.

Despite his best efforts, Don continued to strip cows in the barn and girls in his mind without success. He doubts whether he ever earned that twenty dollars a month (Grace Hadden says he did), but just the same his pay went up to twenty-five dollars in August. It was threshing time, when all the farmers helped each other out. They would go from farm to farm pitching sheaves for ten hours a day, in addition to their regular chores. Don didn't mind because country hospitality, gastronomically speaking, surpassed his wildest dreams. Often there would be seven or eight different kinds of pie for dessert, and he thinks he tried every one of them.

Conversation around the dinner/supper table was rarely about the war. It centred around the essentials: the births, marriages and deaths of people they knew. Don, with his mouth full of pie, was all ears. It was here that he became permanently addicted to genealogy, as in "She was a Leitch on her father's side. He married a Rumball, you mind the Rumballs from Cannington. The Rumballs is cousins to us. The wife's Aunt Willena was a Rumball on her mother's side." And so forth. As the apple was to Newton, and the steam kettle to Watt, these pearls were a source of inspiration to young Harron. He collected them all carefully for future reference.

Saturday night was the big social evening. Don would either go to a square dance at the high school, see a movie in Sunderland or head into Uxbridge for a haircut or a tour of the local stores. He still remembers the Saturday night Charles Hadden bought a roll-top sweater to go with his peaked cap. The image stuck in his mind, next to the Leitches and Rumballs.

4

COLLEGE DAZE

BY September 1942, Don had saved a hundred and twenty
dollars, enough for his first term's university fees. The other
five dollars he frittered away. He was almost eighteen and had
planned on joining up, but his father insisted he go to university
for a year first. Lionel, who had progressed from captain to major
in the Royal Canadian Engineers, was evidently not as anxious for
his son to see action as he was himself. Major Harron had asked
to be sent overseas, but the powers-that-be had mercifully decided
he was too old for a second run at the front lines, and sent him
to Hamilton to train recruits instead. Dutzie was delighted to have
her Big Bum home on weekends.

Minor Harron compromised by getting a brushcut and becoming a private in the College Officers' Training Corps, as much a
part of campus life in his day as sit-ins and demonstrations were
in mine. The brushcut was a mistake: Donald was born with thin,
fine hair, and the result earned him the nickname of "Baldy" until
it grew back. My father still has a full head of hair, or rather his
own full, *thin* head of hair, and is pleased to note that the friend
who christened him Baldy now has nothing but a shine on top.

Abandoning all thought of the School of Practical Science, finally,
he chose Victoria College at the University of Toronto, and an
Honours course called Social and Philosophical Studies, or more com-
monly Soc and Phil, which had the widest possible curriculum to
suit his eclectic interests. He combined courses in geography and
anthropology with ethics and aesthetics.

42

In high school an essay had consisted of a composition that covered both sides of one page. Don was quite unprepared for the university version, which was much longer and required something called research. When he received his first assignment from Professor Richard Saunders on the feudal system he was rather worried. However, he looked up "System, Feudal" in the library's *Encyclopaedia of Social Sciences* and found just what he needed. He copied it out dutifully, word for word, and handed it in. When the essay came back marked A + , he began to think seriously of an academic career.

A week went by before the feces, or theses, hit the fan. Donald was summoned to Professor Saunders' private office, where the A to G volume of the encyclopaedia he had found so handy was sitting on the desk. "Dicky," as everyone referred to him, was shaking with rage. The angrier he became, the more pronounced became his lisp.

"Ever theen thith before?"

"Yes, sir, that's what I used for my essay for you."

"What elth did you uthe??"

"Nothing, sir. I thought that was good enough," replied the A + student.

Saunders exploded. "You thtupid dolt! You've committed plagiarithm! I have half a mind to have you exthpelled!"

There were plenty of goldbrickers around using the university to avoid army service, but the professor must have realised this wasn't one of them when Donald broke down and confessed that he had no idea how to write an essay, or do research. Such things had never been taught to him in high school, but he wanted to learn. Saunders let him off with a thtern warning.

Don tried out for the football team, having been a lineman in high school, but was told his five foot ten-and-a-half inch frame was too puny by college standards. He had to leave winning the Mulock Cup to larger pals like Frank Peppiatt and Keith Davey, which was a disappointment. He joined the water polo team instead, which he found to be a refreshing way to combine drowning with cardiac arrest.

He also signed up for the Victoria College Dramatic Society, hoping that here at least, a person with his professional experience could be sure of making his mark amidst so many amateurs. Earle Grey, the director not the tea, prefaced the auditions with a little speech about *vita* being *brevis* but *ars* being *longa*. The next production was Shaw's *The Devil's Disciple*, and Don tried out for the comic lead.

When the cast list was posted, it did not say "Harron – Left Outside," but close to it. He had been assigned a nonspeaking role which required no rehearsal, just his presence in costume on opening night. This was just as well, because something much more important cropped up: wheat, one of the biggest crops ever in the Canadian West, and hardly anyone to harvest it.

An emergency call went out for volunteers with farm experience to pile into trains heading for Regina, where they would be allocated to farms all over Saskatchewan. It was the same deal as the Farm Service Force earlier that year: the sweat of his brow in return for academic credits, and this time the pay would be an astronomical four to eight dollars a day. Don had his fees for the second semester to think of, so he signed up and boarded the train.

The carriages were Colonist cars, the kind that carried Clifford Sifton's immigrants out West before the First World War. At night they were made up into what were more like cribs than bunks, perfect for four-handed card games but impossible for sleeping. Don had never been out of southern Ontario before, so he spent a lot of time just looking out the window. As they travelled along the north shore of Lake Superior, the vast stretches of trackless forest overwhelmed him.

There was a stopover in Winnipeg, where he experienced the novel luxury of a hotel room with bath. When they reached Regina, he went with the rest of the lads to the local dance hall, called the Trianon, and then on to the Silver Dell, which looked to him like a real live nightclub.

His companions that evening were Ben Bramble, a friend from Vaughan Road Collegiate, and a new acquaintance from the train named Archie Buie. Archie was a flim-flam charmer soon to lead a dual life: as a conscientious objector when he was sober, and a paratrooper when he was drunk enough. They managed to pick up three girls who claimed to be debutantes. Archie turned to one of the girls and enquired, "What is that heavenly scent you're wearing, my dear?"

She replied simply, "Arrid."

The next day, Don and Ben Bramble were allocated to a farm outside of Chaplin, about seventy miles west of Moose Jaw. The farmer kept cursing the weather, which was perfect, and the crop, which was bountiful. Most of all he cursed Patterson's Saskatchewan government, which didn't help the farmers. His style of living is perhaps best exemplified by what they had for breakfast: baloney and mashed potatoes.

Don had worked hard on the Haddon farm, but it was nothing compared to a day of prairie field-pitching. Often when night came he was too tired to sleep. He can't remember that farmer's name, but he'll never forget the face. He describes the expression as that of a man squinting into a field of strong sunlight, pursing his lips in imitation of the north end of a chicken moving South.

It wasn't until years later that he realised what had stamped such an embittered expression on that farmer's face: years of drought with too many mouths to feed, followed by years of plenty with no one to bring in the crop. How anyone could contort his features like that *on purpose* is beyond me, but my father does it every time he puts on his Charlie mask, and people love him for it.

After Chaplin, the two boys were sent on to a German family near Estevan. They couldn't have been more different from the image Don had of the Hun he intended to do battle with. It was a friendly, close-knit family, with several strapping daughters. Don and Ben were made to feel right at home and worked merrily away for three days, until they were hit by a fourteen-inch snowfall. There was nothing to be done but pack up and go home.

Don arrived back in Toronto with less than fifty dollars, which meant he still had to come up with over seventy more for his second term fees. He applied for a job in the Post Office as temporary Christmas help, and resolved to keep an eye out for a second job to round out the holidays. In the meantime, there was the small matter of essays, which he now knew meant readin', writin' and researchin'.

At Victoria the big social event was the *Bob*, a tradition dating back to the 1880s when the college was located in Cobourg, Ontario. The original Bob was the college janitor, Bob Beare, who had played a few selections on his violin and distributed apples to the undergrads as a fitting end to the fall term. By the time Don arrived in 1942, the *Bob* had evolved into a satirical revue in which students lampooned the faculty. This was heady stuff to a respectful student, and he resolved to be a part of it some day.

Hot on the heels of the *Bob* came Don's début with the Vic Drama Society, in *The Devil's Disciple*. He was to appear as a Hessian officer in the trial scene where American patriot Dick Dudgeon is accused of treason by the British. They gave him a very handsome uniform — scarlet coat, tight white britches and high black boots — which almost made up for his lack of lines. The only fashion letdown was his perruque, grey rather than white, and devoid of curl. It made him look like Dame May Whitty.

Opening night went smoothly, he thought, until the director collared him after the performance. "My dear chap, you are sitting there like a bump on a log, while a man is on trial for his life! Can't you show any reaction whatsoever?"

"But, Mr. Grey, I'm supposed to be a Hessian, and Hessians don't speak English."

"Even a Hessian would be curious about a life-or-death situation. Do you speak any German?"

"*Ein wenig*, sir, from high school."

"Jolly good. Then ask, ask your fellow officers what is going on! Liven up the scene!"

On the second night, Don was given a new wig with tight platinum curls, and invited to use the make-up, something he had neglected to do the night before. He had never applied make-up in his life, but he picked up the brightly coloured sticks and set to work. By the time he was finished, and added the wig, he looked like Harpo Marx ready to lead the Parade of the Wooden Soldiers.

He sat very quietly in the wings until it was time for his entrance, and from that moment on he never shut up. Every time something was said in the trial, he would turn to his fellow Hessians and comment on the proceedings, not by muttering "rhubarb" or "*Was is dis''*, but loudly and at great length. Like Yosemite Sam, he was a Hessian with a sense of aggression. *"Was haben sie gesagt? Ich weiss nicht was soll es bedeuten, dass ich so traurig bin, ein Mär-chen aus alten Zeiten das kommt mir nicht aus dem Sinn!"* Thanks to Miss Richardson with the fabulous legs, he had memorized the first verse of *Die Lorelei*.

There would have been more of the same the next night, but Harron the Hessian was ordered not to return for the third and final performance.

He did a lot of acting in his other military role, as a College Officer in Training. The stiff posture and glazed expression he wore with his uniform, in order to look more professional, prompted people on the streetcar to ask if he were a zombie. He replied in the affir-mative with his best Boris Karloff imitation.

The training he found uninspiring at best. His fondest memory of his days in the auxiliary army is of a lecture on venereal disease. It was given by a wise, witty young officer named Graham Sander-son, a medical student whose father was Chief Librarian of the Toronto Public Libraries. Graham informed them that it *is* possi-ble to catch V.D. from a toilet seat, but it's a hell of a place to take a woman.

On the civilian side of the campus, Don made some interesting new friends. Ralph Hicklin, later the drama critic for the Toronto *Telegram*, introduced him to the writings of S.J. Perelman and T.H. White, the lectures of Northrop Frye and Marshall McLuhan, and the Ballet Theatre. Alan Brown, already a fine poet, was a lively character who left to join the RCAF. As a parting gesture, he pissed into an empty beer bottle and left it on the table in the King Cole Room for some unsuspecting mooch. He became a high-ranking administrator in the CBC, which Don says means doing the same thing from greater heights.

The Christmas break began, and with it a midnight-to-seven shift at the Post Office sorting mail. He enjoyed it for the first ten minutes, and after that began to understand why Canada Post has such labour pains with every delivery. He still wouldn't have enough for his next term's fees, so he and Ralph Hicklin got a job cleaning Western Technical School during the day. His most vivid memories of the holiday were the smell of Lysol and scrubbing the swimming pool with some utensil no bigger than a toothbrush. The rest was a blur, but he scraped enough cash together for a second semester.

With the second term came a chance to redeem himself with the Vic Drama Society. They were mounting a production of J.M. Synge's *Riders to the Sea* and were short a man. Don had read the play for his English Lit. option "as a matter of course," but he couldn't remember any male parts in it. He had forgotten about Bartley, the one in the casket.

"You mean, you want me to play a corpse?"

"Please, it's just for one night. It's the Inter-College One-Act Drama Festival."

"OK, what do I have to do?"

"Nothing. Just lie there."

They were asking the wrong guy. If there's one thing Don Harron can't do, it's nothing. When Pegi Brown opened the casket for one last look at her dear dead son, he pulled every funny face he could think of. Pegi, however, was a budding pro. Summoning up centuries of Irish suffering, she only gazed down at him with tragic disdain.

They won the prize, and this was not Don's only dramatic triumph in his freshman year. The Vic seniors organized their own one-act drama festival, with Ralph Hicklin and Jack Coleman starring in Reader's Digest Condensed versions of *Hamlet* and *Macbeth* respectively. It was decided as an afterthought to add a bit of Chekhov in the middle for comic relief.

The Proposal is a farce, in which a hypochondriac named Lomov is bullied by an oversized father into proposing to his daughter. Donald insists that his performance as Lomov was disgraceful: once let out of that casket, he lost control. At one point, he remembers spitting water between his teeth at the unsuspecting front row. He also insists that the Chekhovian interlude was never meant to be an official part of the competition. Be that as it may, when the three judges rendered their decision, the Victoria Drama award went to *The Proposal*, and its lamentable Lomov.

The announcement was made by the guest adjudicator (and distinguished poet) Professor Robert Finch of University College.

It was obvious from the look on his face that he had been outvoted by the other two judges, the Victoria College librarian Miss Honey and her friend from the U of T Bookroom. Don's face was no doubt familiar to both of them, as the earnest young freshman who took his research so seriously.

When Professor Finch was handed the award he was to present, his expression changed suddenly to one of smug satisfaction. Revenge was sweet. The dear ladies had gone to the trouble of preparing a Victoria Drama crest for the victor, felt letters just like athletes get, red and yellow to approximate the college scarlet and gold.

Don didn't mind, though. He keeps his trophy proudly on display in the bathroom to this day — and when people ask him what he did at university, he offers to show them the VD he got from Professor Finch.

5

AIRSICK OVER LONDON, PARIS AND BRANTFORD

HAVING fulfilled his promise to his father by completing one year at university, Don headed straight for the College Officers' Training Corps camp at Niagara-on-the-Lake. It was the summer of 1943 and he was almost nineteen, plenty old enough to lay down his life with the rest of the men. Right after training camp, he planned to enlist in the RCAF.

In the tent next to his were some of the finest minds to come out of Nazi Germany: Jewish refugees named Eric Koch, Emil Fackenheim and Arnold Warschauer, and Don's former Vaughan Road schoolmate Klaus Goldschlag. All four would make great contributions to Canada: Koch the writer, Fackenheim the philosopher (one of the most popular professors on the U of T campus in my day), Rabbi Warschauer and diplomat Goldschlag, who would return to Germany as Canada's ambassador. Back then, they had escaped from Hitler and put on khaki battledress, but were still officially classed as "enemy aliens" because of their German nationality.

He wishes he could recount the stimulating intellectual discussions he had with them, but there weren't any. They were all too busy coping with the demands of camp life and the complexities of Canadian slang. It wasn't long before even Don was tossing off expressions like "Getting much?" and "Where's the action?"

The "action" included long route marches, accompanied by a pipe band. Don really didn't notice the miles going by with the fife and drum to lighten his step. He also didn't notice the sun-

50

burn on his forearms, until he ended up wrapped in gauze with second-degree burns.

The other kind of action was more elusive. He kept hearing about a mysterious creature known as "the Badge Blonde" who would trade you her favours for the insignia on your cap. Don doubted this could be true: for a Peshawar Fusilier's cap maybe, but surely not for a lowly COTC. He soon learned that the thing to do was head for the border. In the States, they could pretend the initials stood for "Commandoes Overseas To China." In a Buffalo USO they were hailed as seasoned veterans in fact, thanks to Harron's arms being swathed in bandages. The girls even asked for a peek at his second-degree war wounds, but his delicate condition would not permit.

As soon as camp was over, Don and his laundry came back to Pinewood Avenue, and he and his pal Bill Bremner went straight to the RCAF recruiting offices. The service chiefs were crying out for air crew, especially now that the mass bombing of Europe was using them up faster than ever. Pilots in particular were at a premium, and Donald had high hopes of becoming one.

Bill, now Chairman and CEO of Vickers and Benson advertising agency, says he will never forget taking the RCAF aptitude test that day: "There were eighty questions and we had thirty minutes to complete the exam. After twenty minutes, feeling that I just might make it, I looked over and there was Don, finished, sitting there doodling and drawing."

They both passed the aptitude test, and went on to the medical. Don passed the "cough please" and night blindness tests with flying colours, but Bill was turned down. Harron had to hit the trail for Manning Depot alone. There, a few scant miles away, the same recruits were put through all the same tests again, and more. When he reported for his Harvard step test, his blood ran cold. He heard an all-too-familiar voice, the one like a loudhailer, calling "HELLOTHEREBUNT!"

It was his old physics and phys. ed. teacher, J.C. Harston. Don pretended to look around to see who was being spoken to. He was determined to pass the physical this time, and not even J.C. himself could prevent him. He noticed something was wrong, however, when the rest of the group were given uniforms and sent on to Lachine, Quebec while he was left behind, feeling very conspicuous in his green tweed suit in a sea of air force blue.

Finally, he summoned up the courage to ask the records people what was holding up his induction, and was surprised by their bluntness. It was his electro-cardiogram. "My what?" Don had visions of a winterized sweater.

"Your heart — it seems to be abnormally enlarged."

Like a dog wagging its tail upon hearing its name, the offending organ at once began pounding furiously. It kept him awake all night. The next morning he was told to report to stores for a uniform. "What about my heart?"

"Forget it. They had your cardiogram mixed up with someone else's." His heart immediately resumed its normal, quiet beat, and off he went to slip into something more suitable, in a becoming shade of blue.

Now that he was finally in the Royal Canadian Air Force, he couldn't wait to get out — for a few hours. The new recruits were officially quarantined inside Manning Depot, on the fairgrounds of the Canadian National Exhibition, for the first month of their service. Their only escape was forced marches along Lakeshore Blvd. at Sunnyside, where they would invade the donut shop for a quick dunk then march straight back again. This might have sufficed for social life, but Don's Vic 4T6 classmates were holding their annual dance, and Don had a date with a tall slim blonde named Mary Pat Fleming. He called her "Mary Fat Plumbing," which goes to show there's more than one way to win a girl's heart.

With the cunning born of desperation, he figured out that if he put a pair of fatigue pants over his walking-out uniform, no one would suspect that he was trying to sneak away. He did just that. As night began to fall, he hid the fatigue pants in a bush beside the CNE Automotive Building, and strode calmly out of the Princess Gates. He took a streetcar to the Royal York Hotel, and had a marvellous time. At about four o'clock in the morning, he decided it was time to get back to the sheep pen. (This is not air force lingo. His bunk was in the sheep pen of the CNE Coliseum.)

He took a taxi back to the Exhibition grounds, as close to his pen as he could get, and strolled quietly in the back way. He almost made it. Suddenly a voice cried out: "Halt! Who goes there?" It sounded incredibly loud in the silence of the night, but also very high. Don realised he was dealing with an even newer recruit than himself.

"What?"

"Halt and identify yourself!" came the squeaky reply.

"Aw, cut the shit will you, kid?"

"Er . . . what?"

"Look, I've been on the town and I'm tired and I want to go to sleep, so keep it quiet, huh?"

"Uh . . . oh . . . okay. Pass, friend."

The following day, Don retrieved his fatigue pants from the Automotive Building bushes, just in time for his daily close-order drill session. The corporal in charge of moulding the raw recruits into some kind of formation had a wit as sharp as the crease on his trousers. He would conclude each session by casting his eyes heavenwards and soulfully intoning, "Father, forgive them, for they know not what they do."

On this particular day he seemed to be scrutinising Don with unusual intensity. Harron had always suspected the corporal was omniscient, and now he was sure of it, as sure as if he had "AWOL" ("Absent Without Leave") stamped on his forehead. At the end of the drill session Don was told to remain behind, just as he had feared. The corporal's eyes seemed to burn into him. He almost confessed on the spot, but a question from the corporal intervened: "What the hell kind of knot you got in your tie?"

"A Windsor knot, sir."

"A Windsor knot, CORPORAL," the corporal corrected. "What the hell is a Windsor knot?" Don was happy to explain that the Duke of Windsor did an extra circuit with his tie to make the knot bigger. The corporal's face softened with envy. "Teach me how to tie one of them, will yuh?"

Next stop was the Initial Training Centre, to begin the long hours of study and testing to determine which part in the aircrew would be his to play: pilot, navigator, bomb-aimer, gunner or flight engineer. Before reporting to the ITC in Victoriaville, Quebec, he was granted a week's leave and headed straight for New York.

It was not only his first trip to New York, it was his first trip anywhere on his own, except to pick crops. Officers had to pay, but for the lowly "A.C. Deucey" (Aircraftsman Second Class) like Donald, tickets to Broadway shows and even fine restaurant meals were absolutely free. And there was no charge for staying at the old J.P. Morgan mansion on Madison Avenue, which had been converted into a hostel for overseas servicemen, including Canucks.

He went to see three musicals, including *Oklahoma* which he claims was a bit disappointing because the chorus girls were so wholesome, but it must have made an impression on him because two of his funniest musical satires are based on it. Even more exciting than Broadway were the free passes to radio shows, especially Fred Allen's *Sal Hepatica Hour*. Like a kid in a candy store, or a new dill in brine, Don Harron was in his element.

The only letdown of his week in New York was a visit to the famous Stage Door Canteen. He didn't recognise a single celebrity, although the place was supposed to be full of them. Back in Toronto, however, he walked into the Active Service Canteen on Adelaide Street and recognised a real star right away. He'd never seen her before, and didn't get to meet her until sometime later, but he adored her from that night on.

The show was a bunch of skits from a local revue called *Town Tonics*, and the star was Jane Mallett, a tiny lady with a big smile, a delicate wit and the dirtiest laugh you ever heard in your life. She made fun of all the rich people Don had ever known (admittedly not many, apart from Uncle Tom Hunter and his friends), but she did it in a way that would make them laugh at themselves. Don was utterly enchanted.

Ending his leave on a high note, he headed for his posting in la belle province. His resolutely Protestant upbringing had led him to believe that all Catholics, especially French-speaking Catholics, consigned him to Hell, but the local inhabitants seemed quite harmless. They seemed friendly, in fact, and it wasn't long before Don was trying out his high school French on them. Being a dutiful son, he wrote home a lot, so his first shopping expedition was to buy stamps. *"Y a-t-il des timbres de poste?"* he ventured.

My father is a whiz at accents, so they must have known what he meant. They were probably just stunned to hear a *maudit anglais* airman make any effort to speak their language. The look of vague disbelief on their faces was replaced by broad grins as Don proceeded to act out in mime exactly what he wanted. When Marcel Marceau had finished licking and affixing the invisible stamps and posting his invisible letter, the guy behind the wire mesh said, "Sport — you wan' stamp?"

Flushed with this success, Don asked one of the local girls to a dance. A dark-eyed beauty with a sophistication the other girls lacked, she told him her name was Fluff, just Fluff. This didn't bother him until her father opened the door and he had to ask for his date. Her father didn't say anything, just grunted and went back to the kitchen to resume the conversation he was having with some friends, leaving Don alone in the parlour. He couldn't understand what they were saying, but mindful of the bitterness that surrounded conscription in Quebec, he assumed that the heated exclamations were aimed at him.

By the time Fluff finally appeared, he was a nervous wreck. She didn't speak, just gave him a look that said "Let's get the hell out of here!" and they did. Her presence at the dance seemed to attract quite a lot of attention. Now he saw her as the outsider, the Mata Hari among the British military, piquant in a childlike way, yet brittle in a way that was not at all childlike. Don was definitely intrigued. He was beginning to think that maybe, just maybe, he was going to get all the way to second base that very night.

Judging by all the nudge nudge, wink wink he was getting from his friends, they thought so too. He kept buying her drinks, which she kept drinking. He began to worry about her rate of consumption, but she showed no sign of becoming drunk. He tried his hand at conversation in what Charlie calls the "Garlic langridge," but she wasn't interested in talking. She seemed more concerned with her surroundings than her partner on the dance floor. She was particularly impressed that the commanding officer was gracing the proceedings with his presence. Many other eyes were upon the commander too, monitoring his alcoholic intake. Commander Dawes was known to order fire alarm drill at 3:00 a.m. when under the influence.

Second base began to look awfully far away. Don didn't even try anything in the taxi on the way back to Fluff's place, but when he asked the driver to wait, she looked puzzled. As he escorted her up the front steps, she tried her hand at conversation, incredulously: "You doan wann to phoque?"

Several thoughts raced through Don's mind. Perhaps he had misheard her. In the best English tradition, he pretended not to hear and kissed her goodnight. In the best French tradition, she kissed him back. "*Je vais ski demain!*" he protested. Fluff replied with a Gallic shrug and a knowing smile: Mata Hari saying good-bye to Walter Mitty. She turned to open her door, and he dove into the cab.

Back at the barracks, a self-appointed committee was waiting to see how he had made out. He assumed an air of smug, silent superiority.

"Get it?"

"Everybody else has!"

"She's the town bicycle. Anyone can ride!"

"Did you take a safe along?"

"Better go sick parade tomorrow and check for a dose!"

Don ignored their taunts, sauntered off to the washroom and brushed his teeth fifteen times with Listerine.

Initial Training was over, and he was ready for Flying School. Not, alas, to become a pilot. He claims it was his left-handedness that disqualified him, and nothing to do with his performance on the Link Trainer, which resisted all his attempts to fly it.

Instead, he was assigned the role of Bomb-Aimer. They don't mince words in the RCAF. The Americans call their death-droppers "Bombardiers," which is what the Canadian artillery calls their privates. Anyway, Bomb-Aimer it would be, and his next stop the Number Five Bombing and Gunnery School in the town of Fingal, south of London, Ontario. On his last night in Victoriaville, the base movie theatre showed a stirring piece of propaganda called "The Purple Heart." It was the story of an American bomber crew shot down over Japan and put on trial as war criminals.

Since it was a wartime film, the Japanese all acted like Mongolian devils. Don couldn't help identifying with Farley Granger as the brave young bombardier who was scared inside. He couldn't help identifying at the end, either, when a Dr. Fu Man Chu type chopped off Farley's hands for aiming those bombs. Don's wrists twitched all night.

Once settled in at B & G Fingal, he thought he'd better log some flight time before his first trial bombing run. A Harvard trainer went up every night to check weather conditions for the next day's training operations, so he hitched a ride. Mentioning that he had never flown before was a big mistake: by the time the pilot had run through his repertoire of acrobatic stunts — fortunately not many — the entire contents of Donald's evening meal lay cradled in his forage cap.

The cap was the only receptacle he could find. It was also the only cap he had, but that was all right. Getting the newness out of their uniforms and equipment was a top priority with the new recruits. By the time Don had finished scrubbing his cap with Listerine it looked like a seasoned veteran of at least thirty or forty bombing missions.

Some of the instructors had completed their tour of operations, sixty or seventy missions over enemy territory. To Don, they seemed to have a distinctive aura, a dash and flair that separated them from the rest. They also looked bored out of their flat caps most of the time. It was called Flying School, but B & G featured 10 percent flying and 90 percent classroom work. Don found it gruelling, tougher than high school finals or university. A sense of urgency is created when the subject changes from philosophical studies to how to make your life last longer and shorten someone else's.

Don wasn't bored. His spare time was spent listening to all the different accents around him. Fingal was part of the Commonwealth Air Training Plan, and he could study British and Australian dialects to his heart's content. There was even the odd Texan who had put on RCAF blue before Pearl Harbor and decided to stay, foregoing the magnificent olive-drab sports jacket and buff-coloured slacks of the U.S. Army Air Corps.

Don's nocturnal hitch-hiking on the Harvard trainer continued, the only progress being that of his wedge-cap from Listerine to Lysol to Dettol. His first official flight was on an Anson Mark II, and when he climbed down into the bomb bay, he was instantly overcome by claustrophobia. He can't remember how well he scored in dropping practice bombs that day, but his aim into the long-suffering wedgie was not great. He eventually came to terms with his infirmity, by bringing along a barf bag and a bottle of air freshener.

One day, after a particularly lengthy mopping-up operation (inside the bomb bay, not enemy territory), Don emerged from the plane only to run smack into another. Or rather, it ran smack into him. Perhaps overcome by prolonged exposure to air freshener, he had failed to notice that a large and very loud winged object was sneaking up behind him. Had he been tall enough for the football team his career would have ended right there. As it was, the leading edge of a wing merely removed some of his scalp as it taxied down the runway.

He reported to the MO (Medical Officer), who had to cut some hair off the crown of his head to clean up the wound. This left him looking like a Franciscan monk, which is certainly one side of his character. Fortunately the wound was not deep and he emerged without fracture or concussion, not even a headache — until he walked out and found his Squadron Leader waiting for him on the other side of the door. "Come to my office. We'll have a chat."

"What about, sir? I'm feeling fine."

"Look a bit pasty to me. Ever get sick up there?"

"Uhh . . . yes . . . once in a while." (About five times out of five.)

"Better get it into your records. Otherwise, if nobody catches you till you get overseas, they'll peg you as LMF."

"LMF?"

"Lack of Moral Fibre. Send you home with a dishonourable discharge. Now that we know it's just a weak stomach, we'll expect it in combat."

On his next practice run, Donald did not throw up. He would have liked to, but he couldn't because he was scared stiff: not of being branded LMF, which only mildly terrified him, but because the pilot checked in tighter than a bull's arse in fly time, as Charlie would say. Don saw this before he got on the plane, and knew it was his duty to report the pilot immediately, but decided that discretion was the better part of valour — or as he put it, "better faint-hearted than fink." In other words, he thinks he took the easy way out by opting for the death ride instead of causing any unpleasantness. A true Canadian hero.

He began to think better of this on the plane, when the Anson took off like a hot rod, leaving more rubber on the tarmac than on the treads. It was too late, of course: he didn't know how to use a parachute. The rest of the bombing run remains a blur in his mind, but the landing he will never forget. He swears they touched down on one wheel, bounced forty feet in the air, then landed on the other.

Another bombing run that remains permanently etched in Don's brain is the one where he got the wind wrong. What he wrote down was a 27 mph west wind. The speed was right, but it was an east wind. He didn't know it at the time, but his practice bomb fell fourteen miles off target, near the little town of Drumbo, just west of Paris, Ontario, landing in a pile of manure. He might never have found this out, more importantly his superiors might never have found this out, had not a farmer been filling his wagon from the pile at the time.

The victim must have known, perhaps from bitter experience, that he could get compensation from the government only if he could prove damage. It was a hot, humid August day, but farmer, horse and wagon set off immediately for Fingal, forty miles away, just as they were, with one side of each completely covered in crap. Not one smidgen would he scrape off until the Air Force admitted (it could scarcely be denied) that the man's person and property had been violated. Don decided that with citizens like that farmer around, there was no way we were going to lose the war. He was also very glad he didn't have to face his accuser in person.

By the time AC2 (Aircraftsman Second Class) Harron passed out from Bombing and Gunnery School, he was only throwing up three times out of five. Next stop was Navigation School at Crumlin (not Kremlin) just east of London.

Before being taken over for the war effort, Crumlin had been a private airport. It had kept some of its civilian services, including the cafeteria, which seemed the height of luxury after months of Mystery Meatball, Fish Eyes in Glue and Green Apple Quick-Step Pie at Fingal. However, the man in the next bunk died of food poisoning a week after they arrived, and Don never ate at the cafeteria again.

The moment of truth was fast approaching. None of the ACs knew whether they would get their commission as officers. This was not just a formality. Some army officers had surrendered their commissions to meet the urgent need for aerial cannon fodder, and ended up as air force sergeants for their pains.

Yay or nay, the tailors measured all the men for officers' uniforms. AC2 Harron yearned for the flat cap and greatcoat, hoping against hope they would choose him in spite of his weak stomach and poor aim. They did. Obviously his marks in the classroom and his ground-work counted for more than his emissions in the air.

Commissioned by His Majesty, and outfitted by His tailor, nineteen-year-old Pilot Officer Harron put on his new dream duds. First thing he did was pull the wire out of his cap and give the crown a swift kick. He put on his greatcoat, threw the glorious white scarf jauntily around his neck, donned his cap, and strode proudly out to greet the day like Errol Flynn in *Dawn Patrol*.

Not fifteen yards outside the hut, he received his first salute. It came from a Warrant Officer Second Class, a grizzled veteran of World War I bedecked with ribbons, who snapped his arm straight from the shoulder and turned to face his superior. Pilot Officer Harron returned the salute limply, lowered his eyes in shame and slunk straight back to the hut.

6

ON THE BRINK

THE last stop before going overseas would be Maitland, Nova Scotia, for commando training. But first, there was a two-week leave, which he spent in New York again. Now that he was an officer he would have to pay his own way, but he didn't care. His pay had gone up from $1.30 a day to $6.25. He felt almost rich, and this might be his last chance to see the bright lights of Broadway. It might be his last chance to see anything.

The play that made him itch to tread the boards again was *I Remember Mama*. He observed the young actor slouching and stammering his way through the juvenile role and thought, "God, I could do better than that . . . that . . . what's his name?" He consulted his program. It was some guy named Marlon Brando.

There was one blow to his ego, however. He threw his Dawn Patrol scarf over his shoulder and strode as dashingly as possible into the Barbizon Hotel for Women to pick up his date. He gave the receptionist his Baron von Richthofen look and asked her to ring the young lady he would be escorting that evening. "Miss Allardyce," said the receptionist into the phone, "there's a West Point cadet down here to see you." He felt more crushed than his flat cap.

His leave over, it was time for Pilot Officer Harron to head for the Maritimes, mercifully by train. It stopped at four o'clock in the morning in St. John, New Brunswick, where he and his fellow officers were turfed out to catch the ferry to Digby, Nova Scotia. From there, they took another train up the Annapolis Valley, and landed in the red mud next to Cobequid Bay.

I don't know what Maitland is like now, but back then it was nothing but a mess hall, a dormitory and a gymnasium. Commando training consisted of twenty-mile route marches between breakfast and supper Monday to Friday. The commandos' evenings were devoted to knocking themselves and each other out playing floor hockey. Saturdays and Sundays were spent wandering around Amherst looking for a good time. Don confesses he became a weekend Catholic, crossing himself in church on bended knee because the girl's mother was a great cook.

Other memorable moments from Maitland included watching a drunken young officer spend twenty minutes trying to hang his trousers on a hanger, then tying the legs in a knot to make sure they didn't fall off. Don was much more impressed by the officer who whistled cheerily on his way to the washroom in the morning, carrying his towel on the handy rack provided by his erect penis. In order to make a good impression on his mates, Donald made sure he kept his copy of *The Brothers Karamazov* carefully concealed between the covers of a comic book.

Now officially commando-trained, he went back to Toronto for a quick leave-taking before reporting to Lachine, Quebec for his overseas posting. Feeling like Robert Taylor in *Waterloo Bridge*, he made arrangements to say a heroic farewell to three different girls in the same evening. It might be more accurate to describe the arrangements as heroic.

He took one girl to the opera at Massey Hall, to see Ezio Pinza as Mephistopheles in *Faust*. He took the next girl to dinner at the Old Mill, with flowers and champagne. The parents of the third girl were out for the evening, so with her the choice was obvious: a four-hour necking session with Frank Sinatra (on the turntable) for inspiration.

After all that preparation, his stay in Lachine was brief and anti-climactic. As 1944 wound down, so did the demand for airmen in Europe. They were saving the rest for Japan, in case of need. To Don's chagrin, his unit was put on indefinite leave at the last minute and sent home. The flight just before his did get away, and spent the spring and summer in England as excess air crew — the lucky stiffs. (As opposed to the *unlucky* stiffs who went earlier, and never came home.) Don went back to Toronto, all dressed up with nowhere to go.

The most heroic engagement of Pilot Officer Harron's military career was his attempt to report back to Manning Depot in Toronto for the Air Force Reserve. It was the morning of December 12, 1944, the day Torontonians still refer to as The Great Snowstorm, because we're not used to Tierra del Fuego-type blizzards. The wind was howling, the sky was black as night and looked to remain that way, and the snow, falling thick and fast, was already up to his thighs.

A normal person, even in the phoneless Harron household, would have thought to go to a neighbour's and call in first, before attempting to report in person. This did not occur to Donald because he is not normal: he is pathologically punctual. On and on he trudged through the darkness, lifting a knee to his chin with every step, the only moving object apart from wind and snow. Then, suddenly and miraculously, a streetcar appeared. There was one transit driver as crazy as Don Harron in the city of Toronto, and they found each other.

He arrived at Manning Depot only half an hour late, but there was no one to report to. The few stranded souls he found on duty told him to go home and try again when the city had dug itself out and the streetcars were running again. Now his only problem was how to get back to Pinewood Avenue.

It was night by the time he turned back, mainly because he was in no hurry to leave the Depot. He had met up with a wag named Dunc Chisholm. Dunc was also a WAG (Wireless Air Gunner) with two tours of European operations to his credit, and a lot of funny stories to tell about his experiences. He confessed his greatest ambition was to get into showbusiness. Don confessed that he'd been there already. He told Dunc radio was a cinch — at least, it had been when he was a star ten years earlier. He didn't even blink as he said it.

Together, the two of them were going to take radio by storm — as soon as the snow cleared. Dunc figured the teen market was the coming thing so they mapped out a series of half-hour radio shows with the title *It's High Time*, even more appropriate for today's teen market. All they needed was a sponsor, and that would be a cinch too, because Dunc's father knew Jack Brockie, the legendary P.R. man for Eaton's Department Store. Brockie was in charge of Eaton's famous Christmas parades, and the man who wrote their clever ads on the back page of the *Evening Telegram*.

About four days later, the Dunc n' Don show rolled into Brockie's office. Both were wearing brand new grey flannel suits with a fashionable slight drape (twenty-five inches at the knee, eighteen at the ankle). Both had their Air Force Reserve buttons proudly pinned to their lapels. Jack Brockie didn't buy *It's High Time*, but Harron did land a job as a result of the visit. This was because Brockie's assistant turned out to be Bill Bremner, who had evidently been going places while Don was in the air force.

Eaton's hired Don to make two celebrity appearances, both in his grey flannel suit: one at an Easter kids' party on the fifth floor of the main store, the other at a Bunny Hop for disabled children to be held in Casa Loma. It felt so good to be back in the spotlight again.

Brimming with confidence, Don put a notepad and pen for signing autographs in his pocket, and pulled on a grey felt balaclava which matched his suit perfectly, contrasting nicely with the pink lining of his long, floppy ears. He put in his buck teeth, picked up his bunch of fresh carrots, and prepared to make his big entrance. Bugs Bunny was ready for action.

The action consisted of making children laugh. He signed page after page of autographs, each bearing a cartoon self-portrait and the forged inscription, "Love, Bugs." For several hours of this, Eaton's paid him fifteen dollars, the same fee Basil Tippet had paid him for a chalk talk nine years earlier. I guess he didn't mind, because he's still at it. The only difference, over forty years later, is that his costume is even more outlandish, the inscription reads "Yer frend, Charlie Farquharson" and his fee, as honorary chairman and mascot of the Easter Seal kids, has gone down to zero.

Easter 1945 was over all too soon, and it was job hunting season. Until they decided to unleash him on the unsuspecting Japanese, the RCAF was paying him not a cent. He tried his hand selling vegetables at a farmers' market, boasting to all passers-by that the corn he held in his hand was a special hybrid variety — until a customer informed him that hybrid corn is only fit for cattle.

He tried selling shoes in Eaton's Annex, a step down from the bargain basement and relegated to an adjacent building. Working with him, selling shoes with "composition" soles (i.e., composed of layers of paper), were future Attorney-General of Canada Allan Lawrence and future TVOntario host Elwy Yost, king of the vintage movies.

One day, Don was trying to sell a pair of composition-sole shoes for $2.98. The lady and her little boy waited patiently while he searched the stockroom for the proper size. Eventually he emerged empty-handed and, bending over the customer to break the news at eye-level, said disconsolately, "I'm sorry, Madam, but I have checked our stock and I am unable to . . ." Suddenly, he lunged forward and shouted "FINDYOUSIZESEVEN!!!"

Don swears that kid's feet never touched the ground once: his mother grabbed him and fled in terror for the nearest exit. What had happened in mid-sentence was that Allan Lawrence had passed behind him. Unable to resist the invitation presented by Donald's posterior, he had given him a swift goose right where it counts.

Don was not above paper soles; he didn't mind shifting muck, slopping pigs or cleaning out a swimming pool with a toothbrush; he had even clerked in the civil service. But there were limits, and the next job proved to be beyond them. Delsie phoned her brother Tom at his insurance company, and before Don knew what hit him, he was a filing clerk at Smith, Mackenzie, Hall and Hunter.

By the third day he was so stupefied with boredom that he abandoned his desk and spent the afternoon poring over forbidden files. These were the secret records of all clients suffering from venereal disease, and there were many pillars of society among them. Don has never revealed the content of those files, although what he read remains fixed in his mind. The next morning he announced firmly and without explanation that he was leaving and would not be back. He had seen the underside of life, and was in no mood to be trifled with.

There were more odd jobs after that, but Don hardly noticed

them. He had more important things on his mind. Ralph Hicklin, who had already introduced him to Perelman, White, Frye and McLuhan, invited him to come and see an evening of one-act plays being performed in a small barn behind someone's house at Bathurst and Ridelle.

There was no admission charge, and the actors were unpaid. The plays were *Fumed Oak* by Noel Coward, *Saturday's Children* by Maxwell Anderson, and *Mooney's Kids Don't Cry* by a new playwright with the unlikely name of Tennessee Williams. Don enjoyed them all. Afterwards, a lady with a cultured voice stood up and gave a critique of each piece. She was firm but fair, and stressed the need for stage experience to break habits picked up in the less demanding medium of radio drama.

During the coffee and biscuits which followed, Hicklin took his friend Harron over to meet her. He mentioned that Don was on indefinite leave from the air force. Her eyes lit up. She leaned forward, scanning his face. "Do you act?"

"I used to, years ago."

"You don't look that old."

"I was a child. It was radio."

"Radio is what keeps actors alive in this town. But theatre is where you learn. Do you know *Charley's Aunt*?"

"Never met her." (In fact, Bill Bremner says Don unsuccessfully attempted to direct a production of *Charley's Aunt* at Vaughan Road Collegiate.)

"It's a play we're getting ready to take round to Veterans' Hospitals. Lots of men's parts. Tryouts are next week. Be there." It was a command, not a request. In any case, it would never have occurred to him to refuse. Dora Mavor Moore had that effect on people.

Don was relieved to see a lot of women but very few men at the audition. He was given the part of Jack, "room-mate of Charles, his friend." He realised later that "his friend" is a theatrical term meaning "a really boring part." Jack provided a sort of tragic relief, in sober contrast to his chums Charley and Lord Fancourt Babberley (played by Jack Benny in the movie), the one who gets to dress up as Charley's aunt. Don didn't mind. He felt privileged to become a member of Dora Mavor Moore's Village Players, and all within a few days of meeting her. He was not privileged to dress up in drag until some time later.

Don't let the fact that Mrs. Moore's troupe worked without pay fool you into thinking that they were amateurs. They were all skilled performers, and the only really professional theatre company in Toronto. Most of them made their living in radio (this was the Golden Age of sound without pictures) while honing their stagecraft with Dora. The big box office attractions in those days were always imported — never homegrown — touring companies from the States and Britain.

Babberley was played by Jack Medhurst and Charley by Vernon Chapman, both seasoned professionals. Vern adopted a comic walk which Don still believes is a foolproof way to get laughs: short, very rapid steps with absolutely no movement of the arms. Try it some time.

Two actresses were cast as Charley's real aunt, to accommodate the fact that both were in great demand for radio shows. One was Bernard Braden's beautiful wife Barbara Kelly. The other aunt from Brazil-where-the-nuts-come-from was Jane Mallett, who had won Don's heart for life when he saw her in *Town Tonics* at the Active Service Canteen.

Spettigue, the comic ancient, was played by Bud Knapp, who in Don's opinion was one of Canada's finest radio actors, second only to John Drainie. In fact, the only member of the cast who didn't overawe young Harron was the fellow playing his father. It was his erstwhile partner from The Great Snowstorm, Dunc Chisholm.

About ten minutes into the first rehearsal, Don wanted to run away and hide. Dora told him to wait until everyone else had gone. She then ushered him from the barn into the living room of her house and spent the evening patiently instructing her new pupil in the basics of stage movement. In one night, he learned how to walk, turn around, sit down and stand up again without rearranging the furniture, something over twenty years of practice in real living rooms had failed to teach him.

Rehearsals went much better for him after that, which was a good thing because under Dora's watchful eye there was no question of escape. They did *Charley's Aunt* in several hospitals, plus the Active Service Canteen. Don would still rather have been in uniform than in costume, but it made him feel that he was at least trying to do his bit for the war effort. The laughter of servicemen is still his favourite sound, and he's travelled from Cyprus to the North Pole just to hear it.

The Village Players did a series of plays that summer in the barn, and Don was in every one of them. Dora must have been pleased with his progress, because she cast him in J.B. Priestley's *They Came to a City* as the romantic lead opposite Barbara Kelly. Barbara was cool and blonde; Don was dark-haired and scared to death.

He received his first rave review in Federico Garcia Lorca's *The Shoemaker's Prodigious Wife*. Lorca is best known as the author of tragedies like *Blood Wedding* and *Yerma*, and as a martyr of the Spanish Civil War, but this piece is a surrealistic comedy. Don played the part of an eight-year-old boy. The program notes neglected to mention this fact, however, and Rose Macdonald's review in the *Telegram* declared: "Donald Harron is superb as the idiot."

The next production was an evening of one-act plays. In William Saroyan's *Hello Out There!* he played a young man accused of rape, about to be lynched by the mob outside his jail cell. The director was a young radio actor named Herb Gott, who had lost both arms in a train accident when he was fourteen. Herb was trying to explain to Don how to react to the mob clamouring for his blood, and said, "My hands, when I had hands, used to sweat. . . ." His tone was matter-of-fact, but its effect on Donald was both electric and profound.

His performance in *Hello Out There!* caught the attention of Fletcher Markle, who was known as Canada's Orson Welles. His real name was Bill, but everyone agreed that Fletcher suited him much better. He took Don to meet Andrew Allan, the dean of Canadian radio drama, with the result that young Harron appeared on the final show of the *Stage '45* season. In the 1940s, the Golden Age of radio, the *Stage* series was as important a part of Sunday night as *The Ed Sullivan Show* would be in the television age to follow.

You might think that Don Harron, having risen so far so quickly, had stardom firmly fixed in his mind, but he considered it a long shot at best. He loved acting with the Village Players but it didn't pay, and he couldn't see himself landing more than a couple of radio jobs a month. Even at $35 each, that wouldn't add up to a living.

He got a couple of jobs modelling for advertisements, including posing for Kellogg's Corn Flakes as a forensic scientist staring earnestly at a beaker. He was sure he wouldn't get any more modelling work, because he didn't have "many good angles" to his face, so he didn't pursue it. Either no one bothered to tell him how gorgeous he was, or he didn't believe them.

He wasn't sure quite what to do. His burning ambition was to be a cartoonist, probably to please his father, but couldn't convince himself he could make a success of it. Nor could he think of anything else he'd be good at. However, events on the world stage solved his dilemma, at least for the moment. With the dropping of "The Bomb" (in fact, "Bombs") on Japan, his services as a Pilot Officer were no longer required. Not only that, paid university tuition plus $75 a month living allowance was available to all veterans. To a young man with no money and an insatiable curiosity, it was an opportunity too good to be missed.

It felt good to sign up at Victoria College again, even though he hadn't decided what course to take. Back in '42 he had picked Social and Philosophical Studies because it was a catch-all course that let him roam around the syllabus to his heart's content. This was 1945, however, and being almost twenty-one, Don felt some sort of specialization was called for.

Unable to make up his mind, he went to seek the advice of a family friend in the Bursar's office. When Dean Maxwell asked him what he wanted to do with his life, he lied and said he didn't have the faintest idea. This would seem to make guidance counselling a pointless exercise, but Don kept mum because Cartooning wasn't on the syllabus.

Dean was stumped at first, but it didn't take him long to find the answer. "Philosophy," he said. "You can't go wrong with Philosophy." In other words, if you Don't Know, you might as well Not Know along with the greatest thinkers of all time. This seemed reasonable enough, so Donald signed up for Philosophy with an English or History option.

When he reached home, he found his ninety-five-year-old grandfather lying at the bottom of the stairs. His parents and sister Mary were out and his grandmother, perplexed beyond imagining, had placed a pillow under her husband's head and was standing vigil over him where he had fallen. Suddenly promoted to head of the family, Don called an ambulance and sat down beside his grandfather to wait, while his grandmother busied herself making tea and sandwiches, any little task she could find.

Don had long harboured mixed feelings about his grandfather. Apart from reading the Bible and retrieving road apples, it seemed to him that Christopher Hunter had not done a stroke of work in fifty years. Young Donald, who had earned his own spending money since he was ten, refused to make excuses for his grandfather. As far as he was concerned, the only "allergy" his Bampa suffered from was an aversion to sweat and toil.

He had never been openly hostile, but showed his contempt in various little ways. Because his grandfather stood, or rather sat, for everything Tory, Don took great delight in standing up for socialism. (At school, where all his friends were Liberal or CCF, he took equally perverse delight in playing the staunch Conservative.) When Bampa Hunter listened to church services on the radio, Don would deliberately find noisy things to do around the house. But none of that mattered as they sat together waiting for the ambulance.

The old man obviously knew his time had come and rose to the occasion, spiritually speaking. The only comfort he wanted was his Bible. In his eyes was the look tragedians aim for in death scenes. The look told Don that once the ambulance took his grandfather away, he would never come back.

The ambulance arrived at last. When the attendants picked up the tall, gangly figure, they hinted that his hip was probably broken. Fortunately, his wife was too deaf to catch the remark.

Don only vaguely remembers the ambulance ride and all the questions he couldn't answer at the Emergency admissions desk. The next thing that remains in his mind is what his grandfather looked like a week later, lying flat on his back with a pin in his hip, barely able to recognise his visitor. Don thought he was prepared for the worst, but was shocked all the same. The proud, patrician head of the family who had towered over him all his life was now a shrunken, emaciated near-corpse.

Christopher Hunter died on September 11, 1945, in his ninety-seventh year, a week before Don's twenty-first birthday. Florrie Hunter never made it to the funeral. When her husband was taken away, she took to her bed and never got out of it again. She died five and a half weeks later, on October 22nd, at the age of 81. It seemed to the family that they had hung on until the war was over, until the future seemed safe for their children and their children's children, then quietly passed away.

Don had always been his grandma's boy, the second-greatest object of her devotion. Even in her eighties she had continued to fuss over him and spoil him with brown sugar sandwiches. He loved her deeply, and felt utterly bereft. By this time he was back at Vic after a two-year absence and had started to study, act and entertain in earnest. Work has always been his solace and his refuge, and he gave himself up to it with ferocious concentration.

7

THE HICK FROM VIC

THE academic year 1945-46 was an exciting time to be a college student. The University of Toronto campus was packed with returning servicemen and women. After six years of war, the world was being given another chance to make good. Everyone was ravenous for knowledge, it seemed. Unlike in my jaded era, hardly anybody skipped lectures. In fact, if you weren't in the lecture hall at least ten minutes early, you were lucky to get a seat.

Donald now belonged to the Victoria College class of 4T8, instead of 4T6. I attended their fortieth anniversary reunion celebrations on June 3, 1988 and discovered that to the class of 4T8, Charlie Farquharson is really "The Hick from Vic" in disguise. It was agreed that while they all have different memories of college days, the one image that remains fixed in everyone's mind is of Don Harron wearing buck-teeth, a Dawn Patrol scarf and a pair of red longjohns, leading the fund drive for Dutch War Relief. "We think of him as *ours*, you know," one of them confided. I understand — I think of him as mine, too.

In my day it was unfashionable to join a sorority or fraternity, but in my father's day it was practically compulsory. Don is by nature a loner, not a joiner, and found the initiation rituals excruciating. The first ordeal was to stand in the lobby of Lowes' Uptown movie theatre on a Friday evening and shout "Get your program here!" To all takers he was required to solemnly proffer a piece of toilet paper, dip a knife into a jar and slap some peanut butter on the offending sheet before handing it over.

72

His final task made him feel like a Visigoth about to sack Rome. He and another would-be Brother in the Bond were blind-folded and driven to an unknown destination. They were dropped off on a deserted sideroad with a brush, a can of red paint and a sealed envelope. Their instructions were to paint the score of that day's football game in three-foot-high letters on the chapel of rival McMaster University. College football had been cancelled by the war, and had just started up again. The first exhibition game had been 31-0 in U of T's favour.

It was an act of vandalism for which he can never forgive himself. Afterwards, they kicked the can of paint down a small ravine and hightailed it back to the highway. They got a ride back to Toronto with a couple of salesmen who envied the two boys their chance to go to university and get some of that higher learning.

At the time, he says his motives were culinary pure and simple (well, simple anyway): the fraternity provided a hot meal at lunchtime to its members. The campus was so packed, he remembers furtive forays to Macdonald's Drug Store after the ten o'clock class on Bishop Berkeley's concept of Idealism. He and his friends would dash over and stuff themselves with doughnuts as they earnestly discussed the Bishop's revelation that nothing is real, everything is but a magic lantern show in the eye of the beholder. If they'd waited until twelve o'clock they wouldn't have had a hope of getting a seat at Macdonald's. *That* was reality.

Soon after this Don tried to pledge a black friend of his named Arthur Bell, and in typical Canadian style was ever so nicely, ever so gently rebuffed. Forty years later, he's still getting mail from that fraternity, but has yet to answer one of their requests for money or even good fellowship.

Fortunately there were plenty of other extra-curricular activities, even if they didn't include hot lunches. The Vic *Bob* had evidently suffered the fate of indifference during Don's absence, so he offered to write the first half and his high school buddies, Ben Bramble and Bruce Quarrington, agreed to write the second.

The *Bob* he saw in '42 had featured hilarious and daring take-offs on such august figures as Canon Cody, chancellor of the university, and the college principal Dr. Walter T. Brown. Don felt the

1945 *Bob* should celebrate the return of the troops, the ones now invading campuses, so he wrote a one-act farce loosely based on the Gene Kelly-Frank Sinatra film *Anchors Away*, about two Canadian sailors returning to civilian life as college students.

He was well into writing his *Anchors Away, Eh?* before he faced the fact that he had to have songs to go with it. Undeterred by his inability to sing, play, read or write a single note, he wrote the lyrics and then set them to music, usually something highly derivative, by humming in the ear of his accomplished pianist Lorne Watson. Someone who saw the show later told him that another songwriter had stolen one of his tunes and changed the lyrics. Don let George Gershwin keep the credit for composing *Bidin' My Time*.

Another song Harron wrote for the '45 *Bob* is still sung at Vic reunions. It's called *Do It Up Brown*, after the college principal, and used to make its author writhe in shame, until he persuaded them to cut the infamous lyric "Old Dr. Brown knows how to brown-nose." He claims the ringleader responsible for its continued popularity is his friend Jack Pearse, who played one of the sailors. Jack looks hardly older today, forty years later, with the same impish grin and ears that threaten to carry him aloft in a stiff breeze. He and his wife Helen run an enormous summer camp called Tawingo, which Don insists is just an excuse for Jack to inveigle young innocents into community singing. I know it's true because I went to camp there. He did not, however, teach us *Do It Up Brown*.

Don himself, in his red flannel underwear, a white wig and buck teeth, appeared briefly in the '45 *Bob* in the title role — as Bob, that is, the spirit of old Bob Beare. He describes his performance as neo-Danny Kaye-cum-Mortimer Snerd. It was devoid of historical accuracy, and it was a big hit.

As the fame of "The Hick from Vic" spread across Queen's Park to the other colleges, Don came to be known as "The Campus Cut-up," a title conferred upon him by "Eros," author of a witty column in the *Varsity*. Eros was in fact a University College undergrad named E. Ross Maclean, one of the few men on earth more addicted to puns and alliteration than Harron himself. The Campus Cut-up became a favourite topic in his column.

After the *Bob* was over, Don missed the thrill of working with a live audience. Hoping they had forgotten his Hessian excesses and ill-gotten VD, he went back to the Vic Drama Society and auditioned for a part in Thornton Wilder's *The Skin of Our Teeth*.

The Skin of Our Teeth was the most popular-but-still-intellectual drama of the day, which encapsulated the history of mankind like an expressionistic Classic Comic. Don was given the part he had hoped for, Henry the juvenile delinquent, played by Montgomery Clift on Broadway.

The first act is quite farcical, and Don enjoyed getting huge laughs from an audience which obviously recognized The Hick from Vic. Henry doesn't appear much in the second act. The third act takes place against a post-war landscape of nihilistic destruction, and no doubt in other productions Man's struggle to begin again is taken quite seriously. Unfortunately, when Henry made his dramatic appearance in Act III as Cain the fascist menace, with the mark on his brow to prove it, Don's appreciative audience burst into howls of laughter.

Friends and fraternity pals congratulated him on his success, but he knew he had failed. Trying to wear both masks, the comic and the tragic, is terribly difficult. Don learned this the hard way that night, and has been learning it the same way ever since. He finds this easier than trying to choose between them.

As the college year drew to a close, The Campus Cut-up began to feel lonely. He had lots of dates, but no steady girl. This occurred to him one night at a college dance where other men had partners to clutch and kiss, while he made them laugh as the jovial M.C.

It was spring, when students turn into rutting beasts just as they should be finishing up their essays and swotting for their final exams. Like Flower and Thumper, it was our young hero's turn to become twitterpated at last. The occasion was the Miss Victoria College '46 beauty contest. It was held downstairs, while in the college chapel upstairs the well-known miler Glen Cunningham was giving a speech to the Student Christian Movement entitled "I run for Christ." Don was the Master of Ceremonies as usual, and the head judge was Canada's most admired literary scholar, Dr. Northrop Frye.

Dr. Frye made a joke about not being allowed to judge the other parts of the body, and everybody laughed. Don made a reference to events on the floor above, explaining to students who might be in the wrong place that this was a beauty contest, that he was the M.C. and that he was not running for Christ. Nobody laughed except Frye.

Next came the parade of female flesh, demurely clad from head to toe in the New Look: broad hairband, cascading tresses, ''Sloppy Joe'' Shetland sweater, mid-calf length skirt and perhaps an inch or two of skin followed by the inevitable bobby socks and saddle shoes. Hardly revealing, yet one of the contestants had to be practically dragged onto the stage by her handlers. She was obviously petrified, and remained staring steadfastly at her saddle shoes. Don's heart went out to her in her shyness.

She was dressed in green skirt and twin set, setting off her cascading tresses, which were a glorious shade of red, the kind Clairol can't buy. All Don could see of her face was a patrician nose and a mass of golden freckles. She was slim and fragile, like a cowering Audrey Hepburn. When the judges rendered their decision, she was Frye's choice for Miss Victoria College 1946. It could have been out of compassion, or it could have been that Dr. Frye has a keen eye for pulchritude. It could also be that he was taking his job as head judge seriously: Gloria Fisher, in second year Modern Languages, was one of the most scholarship-laden students on campus.

Frye was outvoted by the other two judges, probably a couple of spoilsports who insisted on seeing a contestant's face. Gloria Fisher came in third, but she had Frye's vote and that was enough for Don. A meeting was engineered by Jack Pearse, who was dating Gloria's room-mate Helen Hulse. Don was afraid they'd have nothing in common, the shy scholar and the campus cut-up, but to their friends it was as obvious a match as Anne of Green Gables and the class clown Gilbert Blythe.

He couldn't get over how quick she was to put herself down in every way. She was ashamed of her beautiful face, her delicate figure, even her ears which no one could see, and freckles were her life-long sorrow. She even hated the name Gloria, so her friends called her ''Fish.'' Her family called her ''Gogie,'' which rhymes with ''Hoagy'' as in Carmichael.

Her father was a poor country doctor and home was a little town with the forbidding name of Gravenhurst, which Don instantly dubbed "Grave n' Hearse." She had escaped the local high school on a scholarship to Branksome Hall, the swank private girls' school in Toronto, and thence to Vic on three more. Her ambition was to become an interpreter and live in Europe.

She seemed very eager to hear about what Don was studying, so he invited her to come to one of his lectures. This happened to be Gloria Fisher's idea of a hot date.

Soon they were attending Frye's course on the English Bible together. They would discuss each lecture for hours afterwards, and he was stunned by how much better she understood them than he did. (She would deny this, of course.)

In his memoirs a few decades later, Don was still wondering which came first: "Love me, love my subjects, I suppose. Or was it the other way around?" He didn't know that by the time little Gloria was twelve years old she had read every book in the Gravenhurst Public Library. The qualities she looked for in a man were all in Don's head. The fact that the prince was handsome was an unexpected bonus.

The rest of the term sped by with only a trickle of radio jobs to distract Don from campus activities and Gloria. Then, just as final exams were looming, he was flooded with offers for live broadcasts. One show was on the eve of his main Philosophy exam, but it was a big part, it was good money and it was Leacock. He couldn't say no.

The hard part was not so much dashing between lectures and rehearsals, exams and broadcasts: studying scripts at school and textbooks in the studio didn't faze him a bit. The hard part was getting home at night to cram for a final and discovering he'd left the textbook behind in the studio. On the main Philosophy final, he says he had to bluff his way through Kant's *Critique of Pure Reason*, using all the charm he could muster plus a couple of puns for good measure.

Suddenly it was all over: exams written, parts performed, the school year ended and Gloria whisked back to "Grave n' Hearse."

Don took a summer job at the Ontario Department of Education, where he had worked briefly before joining the air force. The work was tedious but undemanding, and they agreed to give him time off if any radio work came his way. He still maintained his connection with the Village Players but was keeping a low profile in hopes of having his weekends free, should he be invited to visit his "freckled sprout" in her native habitat.

Back in 1946, CBC radio was not the pristine service we know today. It carried a lot of American programming, and paid advertisements. Don was offered a regular spot as the "Lifebuoy newsboy," doing the commercial cut-ins to sell soap on the popular weekly series *Big Town*, starring Edward G. Robinson. All he had to do was shout "Wuxtry! Wuxtry! Get yo' Lifebuoy here!" and the announcer did the rest. For this, he would be paid twice what he was earning at the Department of Education. Soon after, he landed a running part in a radio soap opera. Evidently he was to be spared a summer of drudgery after all, and gave up his job at the Department of Education without regret.

Things did not work out as he had planned, however. The Lifebuoy commercial cut-ins were done live, like everything else on the air, and had to be timed precisely with the transmissions from New York. Unfortunately the announcer in question was the wild and witty Alan MacFee.

A notorious prankster, who happened to be between suspensions at the time, MacFee read the livestock reports just before the 6:30 news, and in between the canners and cutters would slip in the names of minor members of the Royal Family. There was something about Don's "Wuxtry! Wuxtry!" that reduced him to helpless fits of laughter. Don tried valiantly to keep a straight face, but it wasn't long before they couldn't be trusted in the same studio without collapsing in hysterics. Not being on staff, Don was fired. Alan was suspended soon after, but that was for attaching a hose to the exhaust pipe of his car and mildly asphyxiating a CBC producer. They eventually moved him to late night, where he could do less damage with his one-man *Eclectic Circus*.

As for the soap opera, Don never cracked up on the air, but he couldn't help making fun of the scripts in rehearsal. Unfortunately his caustic comments were overheard by the big boss, Colonel Rai Purdy himself. Purdy had been commander of the Canadian Army

Show before becoming chief of (future Lord) Roy Thomson's radio/TV operations in the U.K. He had popped in from overseas to see how things were going, and was not amused. By the time Don was fired by phone the next day, they were already holding auditions for his replacement.

After flunking out of commercial radio, the non-commercial side of government radio, the home-grown stuff, came to his rescue. He was hired by Andrew Allan for a *Stage '46*, by Fletcher Markle for a series of thirteen original radio plays, by Bernard Braden for a thirteen-week situation comedy series, and for a documentary series called *Summer Fallow*. *Summer Fallow* was about farm life, and its attendant problems. It provided young Harron with his first chance to try out that rural accent he'd been playing with.

Both Markle and Braden were alumni of Andrew Allan's *Stage* crew of actors, writers and actor/writers who took the airwaves by storm in those days. Allan was a great teacher as well as a great director. Working with him and his crew was more than a career opportunity to Donald, it was a great honour:

> "I was never more than a denizen of the outer rings of this bright constellation, but the atmosphere of purpose, of the importance of letting people in this country know what a fascinating bunch they are, has never left me."

I received a phone call recently from an actress who performed on *Stage '46*. Marcia Diamond had heard about my biography-in-progress, and tracked me down to tell me this story:

Just graduated from the drama department of the University of Minnesota, she decided to do what all young actors should do (and probably would if they could get a work permit): stretch her wings in foreign lands. A summer in Toronto, with its international reputation for radio drama, seemed like a good place to start.

She was thrilled to get a part on *Stage '46*, but terrified at the prospect of working with so many seasoned veterans, all total strangers. They seemed to be a tight-knit group, and apart from asking if she had her ACTRA permit, ignored her with their undivided attention. Just as she was saying to herself, "Yankee, go home!'' a young man with a friendly smile walked up, shook her hand and said, "Hi, my name's Don Harron. Who are you?" He took her by the arm and proceeded to introduce her to every member of the group. Marcia Diamond has never forgotten his kindness — and she's still living in Toronto.

Right after his first *Stage '46*, Don paid his first visit to Gloria in "Grave n' Hearse," and was astonished to discover that the rural purgatory of Gloria's description was more like Paradise on earth. Like Leacock's beloved Orillia to the south, Gravenhurst was (and still is) a beautiful little town on two lakes, right in the heart of cottage country.

The Fishers lived in a ten-room yellow brick house with acres of garden and a magnificent view of Muskoka Bay. Gloria's father, if not poor, really was an overworked country doctor — in Don's words, "the most beloved man in Muskoka, one of those dedicated souls who would get up at three in the morning and drive along country roads to attend to the needs of his patients. You'd think he'd have been discouraged when after driving twenty miles in the middle of the night he was shown a four-year-old boy and told: 'Lookit him, Doc! Ain't he bow-legged!! Kin ya fix that?'"

Gloria's mother was a cheerful and resourceful soul who "looked like Mae West and talked like Carrie Nation." Both children, Gloria and her adorable kid brother Mac, had inherited their red hair and freckles from her. During the Depression, when Martha Fisher acted as a kind of Lady Bountiful to the whole town, she combined extreme frugality and subterfuge to keep up her standards of dress. On shopping trips to Toronto she would buy the most fashionable hats at Eaton's and Simpson's, take them home to Gravenhurst, copy them and send the originals back for a refund.

She was also a superb cook. When he returned, reluctantly, to Toronto, Don wrote to:

> "Gog" (rhymes with "Vogue")
> c/o Dr. M.M. Fisher
> Gravenhurst Ontario
> (where Chocolate Cake is made)

> > > > Sat. Nite
> > > > Far from "home".

. . . Your family were wonderful to me, darling. I felt completely at ease with them — (especially when they took away
those embarrassing knives and forks from the table when we
were eating).

The P.P.S. reads:

One of the biggest thrills I've ever had was walking thru
the streets of that wonderful little town with you. - Honestly
darling, I have never felt such complete happiness in my life
before.

It wasn't long before another letter ended: "P.S. — Marry me."
I know that's what he wrote because I have his letters in front
of me. I found them in Gloria's doll clothes trunk. On the back
of one envelope, she had written "Mum, save this for me." Which
her mother did, carefully preserving it in the basement of the yellow
brick house along with her rubber band, twine and used wrapping
paper collections. The small green trunk contained only letters,
mostly from Don, handwritten in green ink and postmarked
Toronto.

In those primitive times before automation and postal codes,
letters mailed with a four-cent stamp before the last pick-up at
7:50 p.m. could be counted on to reach Muskoka the following day.
They may have been written in green, full of jokes and puns and
cartoons, often in a dialect remarkably similar to the Charlie Farquharson of today, but they were passionate love letters coming from
Donald Harron, and Gloria Fisher knew it. Some of them were
stained with her tears, some with her lipstick, before being consigned to her private archives.

In them Don revealed trials and tribulations never mentioned
elsewhere. Actors are never in short supply, and young actors are
a dime a dozen. This means they can be ignored, forgotten, lied
to or taken advantage of with impunity by those who hire them.
Don considers these facts of life not worth whining about, but I
want my children to know what they'd be letting themselves in for
if they decide to follow in his footsteps.

After Lifebuoy and the soap opera slipped through his fingers, a part in *The Soldier's Wife* radio drama was taken away from him without a word of explanation. They gave it back to the actor he had been hired to replace, saying only that it had nothing to do with his ability. Two days later, he almost landed a real live motion picture called *Bush Pilot*. The producers couldn't make up their minds between him and Frank Perry for the role, so they decided — literally — to toss a coin. Don threw heads, and was out on his tail.

"I'm not taking the Soldier's Wife brushoff lying down," Don announced in his next letter to Gloria and promptly collapsed. He spent a week flat on his back with a bad cold and fever. The next green missive begins: "I'm all better now. – Spent Sunday afternoon sitting in the sun up at our Barn Theatre while everyone else slugged scenery about as I re-cooped."

Lionel Harron's all-time favourite expression was "I can't stand sitting down." This has always been true of his son. The letter reveals that Don wasn't just sunbathing while recuperating. It was the first week of June and, tired of waiting for the exam results to see if he had passed, he had decided to take a chance and get started on the required reading for his third year course. He did this every summer, and by the time classes began at the end of September he had read every book on the list. By his sickbed, he also kept some light reading — *The Cambridge History of English Literature*.

On his second trip to Gravenhurst he stayed as long as he could. Gloria drove him to the depot to catch the last bus Sunday night. Someone had an early edition of *The Globe and Mail* at the ticket counter, with the U of T exam results on the back page: Don had tied with a girl from Trinity College for first place in his course.

Gloria scored I,2 (like A–) in Modern Languages again, but was planning to switch to Philosophy and English, which would mean giving up her scholarships. Don blamed himself for this (he should have blamed Northrop Frye), and he was sure it would confirm her parents' suspicion that he was a bad influence, a barbarian at their gates.

He needn't have worried — the Fisher family adored him. In any case, Murray and Martha didn't know a thing about their daughter's scholastic situation until some time later, when they received a very large bill in the mail for her residence fees and tuition.

Don chose his moment of triumph to wonder if choosing philosophy hadn't been a big mistake. His reasoning was that philosophy teaches you to generalize, which is a deadly habit for an actor. However, the Department of Veterans' Affairs, unlike the Department of Fishers' Affairs, would never grant him the luxury of starting over.

The reluctant philosopher kissed the scholarship shredder good-bye, and caught the bus back to Toronto. He resigned himself to his fate, and resolved to make the best of a bad situation. This Don refers to as his "Pollyanna attitude." I call it turning a laurel wreath into a crown of thorns.

8

NEW PLAYS AND OLDER WOMEN

NOWHERE in his memoirs does Don Harron mention how he spent the rest of the summer of '46. He was looking after his mother, who was very ill, and taking care of the house. Lionel had to hold down his job at the Department of Highways and his sister Mary was working at the Royal Bank, so Don took a self-taught crash course in cooking and cleaning.

He also continued to do the reading for his courses, and began work on the '46 *Bob*, which he had agreed to write all by himself (including music and lyrics) as well as direct. And he kept writing to Gloria:

> I finally did all the washing in the house and I'm a beaten girl. . . Don't think I'm grumbling about my plight. It's been my fast pace that has helped put Mother in bed. . . Besides I may as well add to my store of knowledge in the household arts and come a little closer to my ideal Renaissance man.

This was followed by the confident proclamation, postmarked July 23rd, 1946:

> I'm going to be a wonderful cook for you. I sit at the dinner-table, grin shyly at Dad and say: "Er — this meal is very good isn't it?" He either a) burps if he likes it, or b) says "Say, don't they have anything but hamburg on the meat counters these days?" Oh well — Dad's not in love with me the way I hope you are.

84

The doctor had ordered two weeks of complete rest in bed for Delsia, to be followed by a month-long convalescence in the country, alone, without the family. The thing I found odd about this was that six weeks of quiet isolation seemed an unlikely prescription for Delsia's symptoms, which my father described in his letters as a bad cold, high blood pressure and skin troubles. Seeking a second opinion, I naturally turned to my Aunt Mary, Don's sister, who was there at the time.

"Didn't you know?" she replied matter-of-factly, "Mother suffered from clinical depression."

I was absolutely stunned. "But Grandma was so cheerful and so funny!" She was, too. Delsia was a born clown. Like Robert Morley and Zero Mostel, she combined a large girth and a broad sense of humour with the most delicate, graceful movements. "She was always the life of the party!" I said.

"I know," replied Aunt Mary, "and when it was all over, she'd lock herself in her room for three days."

After phoning my sister Mary to let her know that the blues are hereditary in the Harron family and not something of our own invention, I confronted my father with this information. He was surprised. "Depression?! Really?? I never knew that." Then he looked puzzled, for a minute.

He lived with the woman for almost a quarter of a century, and looked after her with devotion to the end of her days. How could he fail to notice his mother's periodic trips into the black pit of despair? Your guess is as good as mine. And they ask me why I call this book *A Parent Contradiction. . .*

There was another mother figure in Don's life, one who commanded almost as much loyalty. Physically, she and Delsia Hunter Harron were remarkably alike, but Dora Mavor Moore was made of much sterner stuff. She was plagued by debts, but never doubts, as far as anyone could tell. Donald always speaks of her in reverent tones.

Privately, in his letters to Gloria, he sounded almost afraid of Dora. She gave her All to the Theatre, asking nothing in return, living the most spartan existence, and expected her Village Players to do the same. Acting was a privilege, and you paid for it by performing a variety of off-stage chores: sets, props, costumes, promotion. One night she phoned and gave Don a shopping list of corporations to contact for financial support.

By the end of August, his letters began to acquire an uncharacteristically peevish tone: "The VPs give me nothing but richly embroidered and slightly jaded cultchah." Almost eight weeks of house-husbandry were beginning to tell. Self-pitying drudges like me, equipped with modern conveniences, will understand the bitterness of a Renaissance man with dishpan hands.

On the evening of August 28, 1946, Don was summoned to an all-important top secret meeting of the Village Players. He found at least sixty people crammed into Dora's historic old house on that historic night. Mavor Moore was there, on a brief stopover between the army and the U.N., the only one of Dora's three sons to take a lively interest in the performing arts. Peter Mews was back from the Army Show and a transcontinental tour with a pop trio. Bill Needles, the Hotspur Don had heckled so shamelessly in high school, was there to lend his calm objectivity. Everyone present was a veteran of Dora's war, her crusade to create world-class theatre in her own back yard.

As you might expect, the meeting started on time and Mrs. Moore came straight to the point: the Village Players had been offered a permanent home, a real theatre. (The Barn, like most of Canada, was too hot in the summer and impossible in the winter.) The theatre being offered was a small lecture hall in the basement of the Royal Ontario Museum — no windows, no wing space, no backstage washrooms and no free rent, but it meant the chance to become a professional company. Actually, the phrase Dora used was "professional but non-profit." It also meant putting on a play every two weeks, and that would mean a full-time commitment for a paltry fee.

There was a mixed reaction to the proposal. Those hoping for a career in the theatre, mostly the younger element, were solidly in favour. Most of the older members, who had regular jobs and family responsibilities, looked stricken. For them, it would mean the loss of a very satisfying creative outlet, and Don's heart went out to them.

There were two notable exceptions to this generation gap: Dora, her eyes shining with excitement, saw the opportunity to run a full-time professional company as her dream came true. She was an enlightened despot, however, and let her players decide the issue by a show of hands. (Not a secret ballot — Dora Mavor Moore was no fool.)

She must have been surprised when one of her brightest young stars raised his hand with the "nays." Although Don Harron hadn't been with the company very long, and his absences had been frequent, he was obviously one of those who would benefit most from the change of status. As for the new location, the Museum is conveniently situated at Avenue Road and Bloor, right across the street from Victoria College.

Don voted for amateur status mainly because he didn't want to see Dora get hurt. As a child, her father's circle of friends included writers like Tolstoy, Yeats and Shaw. To her, "professional" theatre did not mean "commercial" theatre in any sense of the word. He was sure her love of Goldsmith, Ibsen and Shakespeare, pitted against Broadway musicals like *Oklahoma* and *High Button Shoes* at the Royal Alexandra Theatre, would mean financial disaster.

The "yeas" won the vote, and the Village Players were reborn as the New Play Society. Don is convinced that the Moores agreed on the name because Dora thought of it as a new society to put on plays, and Mavor saw it as a society to put on plays that were new. But it was Dora herself who said "There can be no Canadian theatre without Canadian plays." And there *weren't* any OLD Canadian plays, at least not in English, back in 1946.

Don wrote to Gloria: "Mrs. Moore is risking her frilly shirt on this venture and I can't let her down." However, he made a private pact with Dora: if she would only cast him in shows for which she really needed him, and let him skip rehearsals when he had radio broadcasts, he would work for free. He also told her he would not be in the Victoria College production of *The Taming of the Shrew*, which she would be directing in the fall.

She agreed, and both parties carried on as if the discussion had never taken place. Dora's productions are the only exception I know of to my sweeping statements about his perfect punctuality and attendance, perhaps because she was like a mother to him.

Dora promptly cast him in the title role of the New Play Society's

first production, Synge's *Playboy of the Western World*. I should
mention that the play takes place in a remote Irish village, and
Synge's hero is called a playboy because the locals think he has been
adventurous enough to kill his father.

The first act went very well, despite opening night jitters which
made everyone's brogue as thick as Irish stew. At the first intermission, Don drank a silent toast with Peter Mews, Bill Needles and
Vern Chapman. Being thirsty as well as in a festive mood, he succumbed to temptation and gulped down a whole glassful of 7-Up.

That was a big mistake and ran contrary to his carefully planned
strategy. Have you ever wondered what goes through an actor's mind
during an inspired performance? Well, I can tell you what was uppermost in Don Harron's thoughts on that triumphant opening night:
he had to pee, very badly.

Knowing there were no backstage washrooms, he had been restrict-
ing his liquid intake all day, until that fateful 7-Up. During
rehearsals, he had already devised a contingency plan for the end
of the second intermission. Don suffers from what is known as "the
Harron bladder," a weakness he claims to have inherited from his
grandfather Hunter as fitting punishment for his disrespectful
behaviour.

Act Three begins with the Playboy's groupies (all the girls in the
village) looking out of the pub window to watch him compete in
a race. This was Don's first time offstage since the beginning of
Act One, apart from intermissions when the washrooms out front
were full of theatregoers. His escape route was through the Museum
cafeteria, deserted at night, to a door which led to the lobby.

He had four minutes, and he could have made it if everything
had gone as planned. First, he had to wait doubled-up behind the
lobby door while a couple of accursed stragglers extinguished their
cigarettes. When he tore into the men's room, he was surprised to
find no urinal, only a washbasin and a cubicle, which was occupied.

There was no time for niceties, so he turned on the water,
unzipped and was about to pee into the sink when the toilet flushed,
the cubicle door opened and an elderly woman emerged. She didn't
scream, she didn't utter a sound, but the look on her face turned
him to stone.

The woman went (probably for a taxi, a cold compress and a couple of aspirins) but Don didn't go, although Lord knows he tried. Nothing happened, and his four minutes were up. As he left the washroom, he noticed that the door beside it was marked "Gentlemen."

When the Playboy burst onto the stage, supposedly having won the race, the villagers gave him a tumultuous welcome indeed. They'd been wondering what the hell had happened to him. The sweat on his forehead and the wild look in his eyes were totally convincing. You could feel the intensity in the back row. It was a performance dripping with realism.

He found out later that some actors put themselves in just such a predicament on purpose. James Dean held off shooting the ferris wheel scene with Julie Harris in *East of Eden* until he was ready to burst. As the cameras rolled, he played each take with mounting dramatic tension.

Fortunately for Don, opening night for a New Play Society production was also the second-last night. Dora was not one to dwell on past successes. As agreed, he would not be in the next production, *Oedipus*, because it was time to put on the *Bob*.

Don had two major problems with the '46 *Bob*. Too busy being an Irish playboy to hold many rehearsals, he had trusted his leading actors to learn their lines. Jack Pearse did, Alan Beckett didn't. The other stumbling block was finding a venue, because the traditional Hart House was unavailable. I suspect Don didn't realise you have to book ahead.

In desperation, he ended up phoning Massey Hall, and to his amazement they said yes. It was the first time the *Bob* had been performed off-campus since 1887. According to Don the first half was a fiasco, but the audience loved it. The author/composer/lyricist/director/prompter had wisely not written a part for himself. Alan Beckett still didn't know his lines, and seemed to take fiendish delight in speaking only if Don hissed the lines at him. After a while Alan pretended not to hear them at all. Don Harron's inadvertent onstage appearances as an overworked prompter earned him the kind of spontaneous standing ovation few actors ever experience.

The second half of the show was completely different, a parody of Italian opera entitled *La Traviesti*. It included all the biggies like the quartet from Rigoletto, *O Sole Mio*, the sextet from *Lucia* and several radio commercial jingles.

The *Bob* was a riotous success, but a letter promptly appeared in the *Varsity* complaining about the poor script and lack of originality. Don had expected complaints about his efforts as producer and director, but this cut him to the quick. He swore off producing and directing for life and announced that he would have nothing more to do with the *Bob*, suggesting sarcastically, as he tossed the torch aside, that the smart-aleck critic give the '47 *Bob* a try.

However, there was no time to sulk. Mrs. Moore, without batting an eye, had cast him in two productions at once: *Ah! Wilderness* for the New Play Society, directed by Andrew Allan himself, plus *The Taming of the Shrew*, to be directed by Dora at Vic, which he had already refused to do.

When he protested that she was asking him to perform a physical impossibility, Dora said "I only want you to play the Lord in the Prologue. After that you can go off to your other rehearsal." The fact that he was also trying to attend classes, do radio shows and draw a series of cartoons for the college magazine didn't even enter into the discussion.

Don had never seen *The Taming of the Shrew* performed, and he never got to see it by being in it. Right after the Prologue, he would whip off his grey beard and dash across Queen's Park to be a sixteen-year-old boy in turn-of-the-century Connecticut.

Ah! Wilderness is a sunny comedy, not the wrist-slitting torment we associate with Eugene O'Neill. Andrew Allan had brought some of his top radio performers with him. Bud Knapp played Don's father, and Tommy Tweed was superb as his drunken uncle. It is the only time Don remembers seeing the veteran actor/writer in front of a live audience instead of a studio microphone. Andrew must have forced Tommy into it with all the clout at his disposal ("You'll never act in this town again, Tweed!") and it was well worth the effort.

Don's sweetheart was played by Sandra Scott, who happened to be dating the director, so the kissing scenes were extremely chaste. The young hero also tussles with the town hooker, played with great flair by a preacher's daughter from Kentucky named Beth Caddy, and the effect was electrifying.

On opening night, Beth placed the tip of her tongue in Don's ear at a critical moment. After eight months of courting a redhead whose mother had convinced her that French kissing made you pregnant, Don went into shock. He sat transfixed, unable to remember his lines. Finally, the realisation that Beth must be getting wax build-up brought him back to reality — or rather, from reality back to theatrical illusion.

The first season of the New Play Society, 1946-47, was a dazzling, daring and eclectic mix by any standards. It included Maugham's *The Circle* with Jane Mallett, Bernard Braden and Barbara Kelly, a Chinese-language production of *Lady Precious Stream* complete with interpreter, which played to packed houses, and Dora's staging of the Coventry Nativity play, using the original medieval script of course.

During the second half of the season Don was studying for exams instead of taking part(s), but he went to see every production. They put on Gogol's *The Inspector-General, Mr. Bolfry* by James Bridie (whose real name was Dr. Osborne Mavor — a cousin of Dora's), and their first play that was actually new, *The Man in the Blue Moon*. It was written by a brilliant young mathematician from Vancouver named Lister Sinclair and starred Don's favourite radio actor, John Drainie.

Another daring project was an intellectual musical about religion by poet Ronald Duncan and composer Benjamin Britten. It is hard to estimate how many tickets were sold to unsuspecting tourists, lured to the museum's basement by signs bearing arrows and the show's title: *This Way to the Tomb*.

Don did appear in one more NPS production that season — William Saroyan's *The Time of Your Life*. The director was Fletcher Markle, who had cast himself in the leading role. (Shades of Citizen Kane, sneered his detractors, because it was true.) Fletcher had assembled a very distinguished cast, including Lorne Greene as a longshoreman, Mavor Moore as a drunk and CBC producer Frank Willis as an Armenian philosopher who constantly repeated the same words of wisdom: "No foundation . . . all the way down the line."

Don was cast as Harry, the dancer who wants desperately to be the funniest comedian in the world, and succeeds only in being touchingly pathetic. Unfortunately, his dancing was not meant to be pathetic — Harry had been played by Gene Kelly in the original production.

Don kept avoiding the issue in rehearsal, saying "Just let me mark it here. . . I'm working on a few steps." In private, he was tearing his hair out, until he took Gloria to see Lionel Hampton's band at the Palace Pier, and found what he was looking for.

There, amidst all the white folks doing their best, was a black couple dancing in a different way. Don knew immediately that Harry should boogie like that, and watched them like a hawk all night. Most of their acrobatics were beyond his abilities, but that still left him something to work with.

At rehearsal the next day he started to groove his hips in a slow bump-and-grind, as if screwing his body into the floor. The pianist, Wray Downes, coaxed him along with skill and patience. It was weird, but it worked. *The Time of Your Life* was a huge hit — both nights. Charlie Farquharson is still doing a Down Home version of the same dance.

The final production of that first season was imported. Mrs. Moore was determined to show her complacent Anglo actors what style is all about, and invited Les Compagnons de Saint-Laurent from Montreal to provide a demonstration. Don barely understood a word they said, but Jean Gascon and his troupe performed Molière with such skill, such daring and such obvious enjoyment that it didn't matter.

Again Don had been swamped with radio work just as final exams began. This time he found the history exam quite difficult. It turned out he was in the wrong building, and had just written the Honours paper instead of the much simpler Pass Option he had studied for.

With appalling predictability, he came top in his course, although he didn't find this out until after the inevitable collapse in bed fretting over the results.

After a holiday in Gravenhurst, Don returned reluctantly to the city in search of radio work. Apart from a second season on *Summer Fallow*, the pickings were slim. His hopes were riding on getting work in New York instead, because Fletcher Markle was down there directing the *Studio One* series for CBS. In his letters to Gloria the previous summer, after descriptions of lavish dinners in expensive restaurants as guest of the Markles, the last mention of Fletcher had been that he'd borrowed Don's savings, 150 bucks.

He had made up his mind that Gloria's birthday would be the perfect time to slip the engagement ring on her finger. Already it was June, and he only had until February 21 to save up.

As the green ink flowed northward for a second summer, there was still no word from the master in New York, although Don received second-hand reports: "Fletcher wants me to come down, but I guess he's too busy to write." This turned out to be true in more ways than one.

He did receive a summons from Mistress Moore, however, telling him that an American film company was coming up to shoot a movie in August. Not only would she see to it that he got a part, she also happened to know they were urgently in need of a script — something commercial and corny. Dora had Harron pegged as the right man for the job.

Finally the call came from *Studio One*. Don would be recreating his role as the young hero in *Ah! Wilderness* with a bevy of American stars, including Everett Sloan and Anne Burr. Don flew to New York as fast as the train would carry him. Fletcher and his wife Blanche took him to Toots Shor's, where he had his first taste of blue-blood rare roast beef and a cold potato soup that was so good he tried to order "Vicious Sauce" again the next day.

Over dinner, Don told them about the film script he'd been working on: the central character is a baby-faced seventeen-year-old who lies about his age and becomes an RCAF fighter pilot. During the Battle of Britain, he distinguishes himself in the air and is seduced by his Wing Commander's wife while on the ground. He returns to Canada and goes to university, but finds he can't make it with co-eds because he's hooked on older women. After a string of lust affairs, he finally falls for a girl his own age. This time it's romantic love, in fact he worships her purity, but the girl turns out to be a nymphomaniac, has her way with him and tosses him aside. In despair, he drives his brand new sports car off the end of a dock to a watery grave.

Don didn't have a title yet, so Fletcher gave it the name of his long-abandoned novel, *There Was a Young Man*, and announced breezily, "We'll work on it over the weekend." Don thought he was joking.

He wasn't. It just so happened that 20th Century Fox had already paid Markle to write a movie. It was due in two weeks, but he'd been too busy with other projects, including an affair he was having with Don's leading lady on *Studio One*, Anne Burr.

Spending the weekend at the Markles' house in Scarsdale, Don pulled out his *Ah! Wilderness* script and began to go over his lines, but Fletcher grabbed a notepad and wrote down *There Was a Young Man*. They worked on it most of Sunday night.

Back in New York City, Don stayed at his friend Hedley Rennie's studio, using his typewriter to write *There Was a Young Man*. They worked at a furious pace, Don doing the writing and Fletcher keeping tabs on his progress while pursuing his "other projects." To Gloria, Don wrote: "I don't know why you say I'm doing Fletcher a favour."

Fletcher made a lot of contributions to the story line, however, like "Good! Good! I like it, I like it, but those older women he has affairs with, he'll have to murder them as well."

Don protested that his hero was not a psychopath, just a mixed-up kid with a Distinguished Flying Cross and Bar. "I don't make the rules, it's the Hays Office!" Fletcher explained. "You can't commit a sin on the screen without being punished for it, and according to the Hays Office the only suitable punishment for adultery is death. The kid's suicide takes care of his side of the punishment."

"What about the nymphomaniac who drives him to suicide?"

"We won't have her go all the way, maybe just a cockteaser."

Writing scripts in the Land of the Free was like walking through a mine field. Between rehearsals and re-writes, by the time *Ah! Wilderness* went on the air Tuesday night, Don was far too tired to be nervous. By Wednesday night, Fletcher seemed to think Don's work on the screenplay was completed. He would "polish it" himself, but first he had to get going on his next *Studio One*, starring the reigning queen of the radio soap operas, Mercedes McCambridge.

The next morning, Don caught the train back to Toronto. It never even occurred to him to make the rounds of New York agents and casting directors. He arrived home dead tired and flat broke, but not discouraged. He'd held his own on American prime time, and the $50 from the radio show had almost covered his expenses.

Just for the record, *There Was a Young Man* never was, Fletcher and Blanche were divorced, and the next Mrs. Markle was Mercedes McCambridge.

9

SPRING THAW

DON arrived home from New York just in time to help his parents pack. Fat was whisking his darling Dutzie off to her girlhood stomping ground, Camp Billie Bear. Don was left to look after the house and his nineteen-year-old sister Mary. I'm sure she thought it was the other way round. Either way, without parents to take care of and worry about, they had a lot of fun.

Don spent a lot of time hanging out with a fellow clown named Jackie Rae, whom he remembered seeing in vaudeville at Shea's Hippodrome, when he was a child star with golden curls and a little white suit. Jackie had to earn himself a DFC and Bar in the Battle of Britain to live down that little white suit. In the summer of '47, he was playing disc jockey on a series called *Hot House* and producing a new CBC/NBC series called *The Wayne and Shuster Show*.

Jackie invited Don to attend the first broadcast. Afterwards, they tuned in a rival network to catch another new comedy team, Dean Martin and Jerry Lewis. Johnny Wayne turned to Frank Shuster and said, "Those guys aren't going to last, because you know what? We're cornier than they are!"

Jackie seemed lonely with his wife and kids in England for the summer, and though Don wouldn't have admitted it, with Gloria and his parents in Muskoka, he was feeling pretty lonely too. He invited Jackie to come and stay at Pinewood for a while, a gesture which probably saved his life.

On Sunday July 27, 1947, Don made his first (and last) appearance on *The Wayne and Shuster Show*. In his letter to Gloria the next

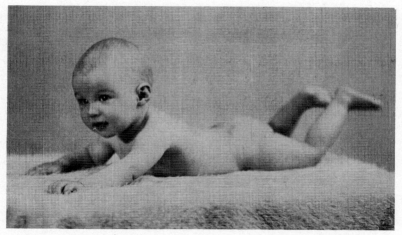

Don Harron made his debut on September 19, 1924. Eleven long years went by before anyone actually paid him to perform.

Delsia Ada Maude Hunter married a graduate engineer named Lionel William Harron. Their son Donald Hugh contemplated a career in practical science, which made everybody laugh.

Little Donny at his grandparents' place in Dunbarton, Ontario, carting a load of bear.

He Ain't Done Right by Nell at Vaughan Road Collegiate in 1941, with Larry "Long Distance" Mann (seated) and Don Harron the villain in the plaid suit.

Don still in civvies, with father
Lionel, mother Delsia and sister
Mary Isobel, at Pinewood
Avenue (1942).

(TAKEN FROM LIFE
AT THE TENDER AGE
OF 21)

Lionel and Don—in his father's footsteps at last (1943).

The Hick from Vic (1945).

DA GEET FAT
GEEOLE DA VAT
VAT SAY!!

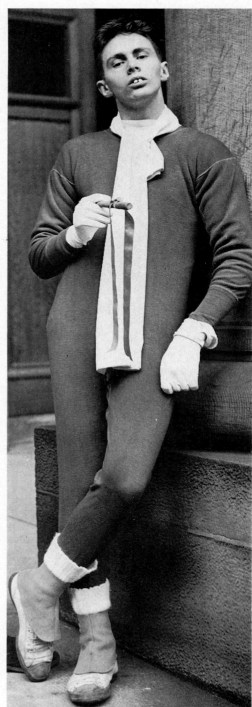

All these self-portraits of "a failed cartoonist", as Don Harron describes himself, were found in letters to his first wife Gloria, written 1946–48.

Mavor Moore says that Harron's career took off in radio "once Andrew Allan discovered that marvellously hooded voice." Don is seen here with mentor Fletcher Markle, another alumnus of Allan's talented *Stage* crew at CBC.

The Seventh Veil at the Prince's Theatre in London, England (1951) with Martha's godmother Ann Todd, whom Don describes as "the most beautiful woman I have ever seen."

Rural philosopher Charlie Farquharson was born the year after Martha, in *Spring Thaw '52*, and became an instant favourite on CBC-TV's *The Big Revue* later that year.

Henry Fox

CBC Archives

The birth of Canadian television, September 8, 1952: Harron chewing his nails (far left) and Mavor Moore studying his script (extreme right). The most memorable moment for Don was when a 19-year-old musical genius (middle, in white gloves) leaned over and whispered a few lines from *Spring Thaw '52* in his ear: Glenn Gould was quoting Charlie Farquharson, and his accent was pretty good, too!

Don Harron was the first Canadian to appear in a starring role at the Shakespearean Festival in Stratford, Ontario—as Bertram in *As You Like It* (1953). "It was a manly performance, also one of delicacy and restraint," Globe and Mail critic Herbert Whittaker recorded at the time, a performance "we think not many young actors could give."

Don's other role that year was Lovel in *Richard III*.

day, he reported that the show had gone well, and that having Jackie as a house guest was ''a million laughs.'' On the Saturday, he'd tuned Lionel's mandolin to sound like a ukelele, and the local gang had sat around the living room singing campfire songs. ''Then Jackie showed everyone his appendix and we all went to bed tired but happy.''

In his Wednesday letter he said that the following Monday he and Jackie would both be on the radio, Jackie on CJBC and Don on CBC, doing *Timber Lodge* at 8 p.m., then straight into *Summer Fallow* (his third season) at 8:30. Right after that, the two of them planned to hop into Jackie's jalopy and head straight up to Gravenhurst for a few days of sun and fun.

The next morning, July 31, Don woke up in agony. The nagging pain he'd been nursing in his gut for weeks had turned into something much more serious. He decided it must be food poisoning, and took a laxative. After this brilliant move, he collapsed. Jackie found him and immediately began going through the doctors in the yellow pages.

Dr. A-something breezed in, a handsome devil with white hair and a deep tan. He prodded Don's abdomen, Don hit the ceiling, and Dr. A called for an ambulance. The patient gasped, ''Is it food poisoning?''

''Food poisoning? Let's just hope your appendix doesn't burst before we get you on the table!'' Don was pretty frightened, until the ambulance drove off and the siren scared him half to death. As soon as they arrived, the hospital staff rushed him to an operating room, gave him a shot in the rump and cut him open. He watched the whole thing in the shiny lamp reflector above the table.

Dr. A stopped by his bed the next morning to tell him he was fine and would be home in three days. Lionel and Delsia couldn't be reached by phone, but Don called Gloria as soon as he was able, to tell her that he couldn't make it up to see her just yet, but not to bother coming down. She caught the next bus, of course, and came to visit him every day in hospital. After his release, she went to see him at Pinewood and found him in extreme pain, which was worrying because it didn't make sense.

Don couldn't remember Dr. A's name, so Gloria phoned her

father, who located him through the medical directory. Dr. A showed
up just long enough to announce that Don had contracted pleurisy.
"Don't just lie there, get up and walk around the garden, and keep
walking as long as you can." He gave Don a shot of sulpha and
departed, probably to work on his tan.

The more Don walked, the more it hurt. As the pain worsened,
so did his temper. He remembers telling his beloved to get the hell
out of his house, at which point she marched to the phone and called
her father in Gravenhurst a second time. It was an unheard-of extravagance, but the doctor's daughter smelled a rat, and it was Dr.
A's diagnosis.

She described the symptoms and Dr. Fisher said, "It can't be
pleurisy. I'll get Kinsey at the Western." Dr. Kinsey (the chest
specialist, not the sexologist) arrived in a matter of minutes and
declared the problem to be a pulmonary infarct. Don tried to laugh,
but the pain prevented it.

Pulmonary infarct meant blood clots in the lungs. Not only was
exercise the worst thing for it, the sulpha caused a violent reaction.
Dr. Kinsey rushed Don straight back to the hospital, where he
received an injection in one or the other of his buttocks every three
hours for weeks on end. This experience gave the expression "I can't
stand sitting down" a whole new meaning.

Lionel and Delsia came back from Muskoka as soon as they got
the letter about their son's appendix operation. They arrived to
something much more serious, of course, and cancelled the rest of
their holiday to be near him. In his memoirs, Don wrote: "Part
of it I felt was guilt because they hadn't been around when the
appendix attack happened. I saw no reason for their guilt but I used
it."

Pencilled in the margin, I wrote "YOU MORON, THEY JUST *LOVED*
YOU!!" Honestly, if you don't talk back to your parents, they'll
never learn anything.

Old school chums, now medical students, took to congregating
in his hospital room. The conversation inevitably reverted to shop
talk, so Don would go back to reading Toynbee's *A Study of History*.
He never complained. The more his buttocks came to resemble dart
boards the more frayed were his nerves, but he saved his frustra-

tions to vent on his nearest and dearest. One day, he swears he threw his entire family out of his room.

The director of Hart House Theatre, Robert Gill, came to his bed of pain to offer him the lead in an upcoming production, Cocteau's *The Infernal Machine*. Don said yes, but Dr. Kinsey said no, nothing strenuous for three months. Gill promptly offered him the lead in Maxwell Anderson's *Winterset* later in the season.

The play is based on the Sacco-Vanzetti scandal of the 1920s, and the role of Mio is a kind of latter-day Hamlet. Burgess Meredith's performance in the original Broadway production had been hailed as a milestone in American acting. Don jumped (figuratively) at the chance.

The hospital set him free in September, his favourite time of year. It was a thrill to walk across the campus, drinking in the sunshine, but he couldn't help feeling left out of things. The New Play Society was doing J.M. Barrie's *What Every Woman Knows*, and down the road at Hart House, Murray Davis was playing young Oedipus instead of him.

Worse was yet to come. Those fools at Vic had actually allowed the upstart who'd criticized his *'46 Bob* to write and direct the *'47 Bob*. Don went to see it, and found an old-fashioned minstrel show just like his parents used to do, complete with banjos and burnt cork. He was appalled, but at least he had the satisfaction of knowing that smart-ass Norman Jewison was never going to make it in showbusiness.

Don turned his attention to high verse drama. Despite all his success with the New Play Society and in radio drama, the guffaws and knee-slapping which had greeted his Cain-the-fascist-menace in *The Skin of Our Teeth* still burned in his memory. With *Winterset*, he was going to shatter for good all attempts to typecast him as the college buffoon.

Act One ends on a dramatic high, as Mio decides to confront the judge who condemned his father to death. To illustrate the passion behind this decision, the young man lights up a cigarette, takes one puff, rips it out of his mouth, stamps on it, and heads for the judge's house as the curtain falls.

Don hadn't smoked anything since the cedar bark of his youth, and kept forgetting to bring matches to rehearsals. He remembered them on opening night, but when he struck one with a flourish on the bottom of his shoe, nothing happened. He was wearing rubber soles. Undaunted, he bent over and struck it again, this time on the floor of the stage, stood up and inhaled so deeply that shreds of tobacco poured down his throat.

No smoke, though. My father is far-sighted, and the stage manager informed him afterwards that he'd held the match at least three inches from the end of the cigarette. Perhaps this was just as well, because he also missed it by a mile with his foot when attempting to extinguish it. The really funny part was that nobody laughed.

He did hear snickers when he least expected them, though, at the tragic climax when little Miriamne and her beloved Mio die in a hail of bullets. Don was so upset he refused to take a curtain call. When the applause persisted, Robert Gill told him to stop being so unprofessional, so a very sullen Mio took a perfunctory bow.

The next night, he attacked the end of Act One armed with a Ronson lighter. It worked, which was unfortunate because this time he overcompensated and burned off most of his right eyebrow. The cigarette emerged unscathed.

Again nobody laughed at his sharp, wheezing intake of breath, the complete absence of smoke under the street lamp, or the shreds of Golden Virginia between his teeth. At the very end, however, the snickering was louder than the night before. Don began to suspect that his leading lady, Joyce Bochnek, was doing something twitchy during their death tableau.

On the third and final night, he was allowed to forego the cigarette. He chewed gum instead, and at the moment of decision spat it out. Without thinking, he stamped on it, and this time his aim was true.

As the final curtain fell to faint snickers and thunderous applause, Don was totally confused. He had made a complete fool of himself all three nights by the lamppost, yet you could have heard a pin drop. Why did they mock him in death?

The answer was revealed when the cast pictures were developed: Bob Gill had staged the ending so that Mio and Miriamne fell in exactly the same position, side by side like a pair of gazelles jumping a fence. Neither one was aware of the other's unconscious mimicry, and none of the onlookers had thought to point it out to them.

Don's first chance to play a villain came in Lillian Hellman's *The Little Foxes* at the New Play Society. He says the best part was the review by Augustus Bridle. Don's favourite critic had been quoted in the *New Yorker* magazine's "Dept. of rich, warm, soft, beautiful prose" and was always good for a laugh, but this time he outdid himself.

Commenting on the black members of the cast, Kay Livingstone and Don's friend Arthur Bell, Mr. Bridle wrote: "The Negroes . . . Kathleen Livingston and Arthur Bell . . . are both so excellent you'd think them actual Negroes." There was no mention of who did the make-up.

Don's next assignment was the first *All-Varsity Revue*. He had suggested Jackie Rae to direct, but that Norman Jewison character had been chosen instead. At their first meeting they eyed each other warily. It took them all of two minutes to become life-long friends, because they both love to laugh and take their work so seriously.

Don's part in the *Revue* was brief but dramatic. He persuaded his friend Royce (now Senator) Frith to sing *Laura* while he wreaked havoc with props and sound effects à la Spike Jones.

Harron and Jewison performed together soon after, at a U of T pep rally for a football game against Queen's University. Norman played a coach, and Donald a big (thanks to extra padding) dumb football player, wearing a Queen's sweater with a large Q on the front. He was flanked by players wearing a 4 and a 2, so that when they stood together on the field, the message read "4 Q 2." Ah, college days.

There was a distinct chill in the air whenever Don went near the New Play Society. Dora might have been offended that he'd given his all to Hart House in *Winterset*, and for free. Or perhaps what bothered her was his annoying habit of skipping rehearsals whenever he had a radio show. In this case, the temptation was purely economic: each half-hour broadcast, with four hours of rehearsal, paid $22.50. Dora's plays, with two performances and three weeks of rehearsal, paid fifteen bucks. Still, he accepted Dora's money, so in all fairness he owed her regular attendance.

Whatever the cause (I suspect he was studying), the New Play

Society got along without Don Harron for the rest of the season. The only big problem that second year was a new play, a stage version of Hugh MacLennan's *Two Solitudes*. The script failed to materialise at the last minute, and a replacement had to be found. With a fighting spirit worthy of his mother, Mavor Moore lost no time in salvaging the situation.

Grabbing a script from Tommy Tweed, a title from Andrew Allan and performers from all over town, Mavor threw together a topical revue. Dora, Shakespeare and Sophocles had to sit on the sidelines — it was time to send in the clowns. I don't know about Shakespeare and Sophocles, but Dora sat stony-faced through every rehearsal.

Tommy Tweed's script was about attempts to unionize a department store. It already had a wonderful title, *It'll Never Get Well If You Picket*, but Mavor expanded the scope, adding sketches and musical numbers. Drawing from an idea tossed off by Andrew over lunch one day, he chose the perfect title which had nothing to do with the plot and everything to do with being Canadian: *Spring Thaw*.

The cornerstone of his cast was the one person who had done it all before, and all by herself — Jane Mallett. From Army Show days he recruited Connie Vernon and Peter Mews, both of whom had been working in department stores since being demobbed. He also hired Drew Thompson, Eric Christmas and a couple of eager students from Lorne Green's Academy of Radio Arts, Alfie Scopp and Gerry Sarracini.

That first *Spring Thaw* had a love story as well as the thin thread of a plot. For his heroine, Mavor netted the canary from Bob Shuttleworth's orchestra, a stunningly beautiful soprano named Frosia Gregory. Frosia had done some troop show work with Anna Russell, and her infectious laugh set the perfect tone. For his hero, Mavor chose a handsome young man named Don Harron.

It was right before his *final* final exams, but how could he resist? In the mad scramble to mount this last-minute production, the cast was infused with a team spirit just like in those Garland and Rooney movies: "Hey, gang, we can do it! Let's put on the show right here!" Don vividly remembers Mavor taking him through the changes of a skit while the opening night patrons were settling in their seats.

Mavor had never even seen the sketch. There hadn't been time to rehearse it. It was a solo number called *Flicker Flashbacks*, in which Don did a quick-change act in the flicker of a strobe light, hasty impressions of silent screen stars like Charlie Chaplin, William S. Hart, Lon Chaney, Harold Lloyd, Theda Bara and, for Canadian content, Mary Pickford. It had been a big hit on campus, so what the heck.

Advance sales were so brisk, *Spring Thaw* opened on April Fool's Day 1948 to an extended run — three whole nights. Not only was it very funny, they were making jokes about Yonge Street and Eaton's instead of Broadway and Macy's. By the third night they were turning customers away and were already planning a sequel, *Spring Thaw '49*. Dora Mavor Moore still didn't understand what all the fuss was about, but she knew the box office receipts would help her through another season of Shakespeare and Shaw.

Because of his top marks the previous year, Don had spent his senior year on a scholarship which required him to live in residence. This placed him at a stone's throw from the Museum Theatre, Hart House, his girl and the U of T reference library. Weekends, he went back to Pinewood with his laundry in one arm and Gloria in the other.

Dutzie fed the lovebirds three meals a day, never asked them to lift a finger and never complained. Gloria could hardly be blamed for taking all this tender loving care for granted. *Her* mother not only provided the same three-star service in Gravenhurst, she took the train down to Toronto every week to pick up her daughter's dirty clothes and deliver a neatly pressed and folded pile of clean ones.

Final exams began the Monday after *Spring Thaw* closed. This time, despite having so little time to study, Don ended up with the Regent's Silver Medal, the Sanford Gold Medal in Philosophy, and the offer of a steady job lecturing in English Literature at Trinity College.

He turned it down, as he turned down the chance to be a Rhodes scholar. He had made up his mind to leave the sheltered groves of Academe and take his chances in the cold, cruel world of full-time showbiz.

Gloria had just completed her junior (third) year of the Philosophy and English course, and they planned to marry as soon as she graduated. This meant that Don had twelve months in which to build his career to the point where he could support a wife and start raising a crop of redheaded children, referred to in his letters as "rusty moppets."

As if by arrangement, he and his mother were incapacitated on alternate summers. It was Dutzie's turn, and skin troubles really were the problem this time. The pain of phlebitis and varicose veins had been getting worse, but she never did anything about it. Don decided that he wouldn't be able to enjoy the summer until his mother was taken care of, so without telling her, he booked an appointment with a specialist. A month later, she had surgery on the veins in both legs.

The hospital sent her home with strict orders to rest with her feet up. Unaware of the great culinary strides her son had made since the summer of '46, Dutzie hobbled in the door and was horrified to see him boiling spare-ribs and broiling potatoes. That first day home from the hospital she sat in the kitchen with her feet on a camp stool, peeling vegetables and conducting operations.

The phone rang. Don was surprised to hear from Earle Grey, who had not called since throwing him out of *The Devil's Disciple* in his freshman year. There was no time to reminisce, however. Earle and his wife Mary Godfrey were doing a series of Shakespeare's plays in the open-air quadrangle at Trinity College. Opening night of *The Taming of the Shrew* the night before had been marred by a drunken actor in a minor role. The Tailor had only one short scene and they were absolutely desperate. Could he come down right away?

Don was in the process of refusing, on the grounds that he had to keep the home fries burning, when he felt a firm maternal grip on his arm. The look in his mother's eyes said, "Please, Don, for the sake of your family, do what you do best and leave the potatoes to me." He went.

Earle suggested Don play his lines with a slight stammer, to emphasize his nervousness. Earle and Mary ran through the stage business with him, which consisted of the Tailor measuring her ample bosom and waist, and her knocking him on the pate for his pains. (This is not in the script.)

Two hours later he had learned his eight lines and was on stage in costume, make-up and a blond wig that made him look like Danny Kaye. This resemblance to the master of double-talk, plus permission to stammer, proved too hard to resist. Every part of his body twitched in sympathy with each syllable, with the result that "You bid me make it orderly and well, according to the fashion and the time" sounded more like "Da geet gat geedle da veet vot flan san da gooble da geenble da vee," or thereabouts.

Poor Mary Godfrey and Earle Grey didn't know what to make of it, but the audience lapped it up. It was largely a college crowd, most of whom recognized the Campus Cut-up. Thus with his parting gesture to the University of Toronto, standing in the quadrangle of the college where he could have been a lecturer, Don restored the buffoon image he had worked so hard to tear down.

10

TRAUMA AND TE DEUM

IN the fall of 1948, Dora Mavor Moore offered six of her actors a whopping thirty dollars a week to form the core of a permanent company for the New Play Society's third season. This was thirty dollars more than "The Old Lady of Threadbare Street" paid herself. Lloyd Bochner, Toby Robins, Robert Christie, Glen Burns and Bill Needles all said yes. So did Don Harron.

This did not prevent him from taking every other job he was offered. His constant stream of excuses and mock illnesses must have turned Dora's hair grey, if it wasn't already. His excuse to himself was that he needed to build a nest egg for his redhead.

The only other regular job he had that didn't interfere with his NPS schedule took place early in the morning: Schools broadcasts. One morning a bleary-eyed Donald Prince of Denmark cried, "I do not set my life at a Finn's pee!"

He was delighted when the department of education asked him to write for a series they were planning on *Roman Family Life*. He submitted a sample script, *Roman Manners*, and was summoned to a meeting at the CBC with the head of the department, a rumoured ex-distributor of porno films, and the producer, a sinister black-haired beauty straight out of the Addams family.

The gentleman told him his script "simply wouldn't do." The lady said the dialogue was "just a little too Lister Sinclair-y." Don, who placed Sinclair just below Shaw on his list of icons, and not just alphabetically, told them he considered that a compliment.

Ex-Porno King and Vampire Queen wanted changes. He pressed

them to be more specific. They hemmed and hawed, and hawed and hemmed, until finally the E.P.K. stood up and said, "Look, just take it back and make it duller." Don thinks he threw it away in disgust.

On air, he was asked to be the voice of Orange Crush for Harry "Red" Foster's series about the RCMP, *Men in Scarlet*. On the first day, the normally mild-mannered and mellifluous Harry "Red" stormed out of the control booth to set him straight: "Never, EVER say the name of our sponsor that way! It's not O-range Crush, it's just plain Ornjcrush. Got that? ORNJCRUSH — say that over several times and never forget it!!"

The New Play Society did Shaw's *You Never Can Tell*, with Don and Toby Robins playing the twins. He dyed, or rather glooped up, his hair with lamp black to match her raven tresses. I don't know if the effect left as indelible impression on the audience as it did on his pillowcase.

The big theatrical event of the '48/'49 season was a new Canadian play, Morley Callaghan's *To Tell the Truth*. The action takes place in a bar run by a young flute-playing "poet who lives his poetry." Don was the obvious choice for the part. The other leads were Lloyd Bochner as the gangster and Dianne Foster as the whore-with-the-heart-of-gold with whom he is in love. One matinée, Lloyd accidentally tore Dianne's bra off when he was only supposed to rip her blouse. Don immediately stepped in between her bared breasts and the wide eyes of the audience, and said the first old joke that came into his head: "Gee, lady, if yer gonna drown them two piglets, wouldja gimme the one with the blue nose?" How gallant.

The production was so successful that two weeks after closing at the Museum Theatre it re-opened at the Royal Alexandra, the first Canadian play in its forty-two-year history. The main excitement backstage at the Alex was the persistent rumour that the show was going to Broadway. No fewer than three big New York producers had come up to see it. Monday's *Evening Telegram* dispelled all doubts with the headline: BROADWAY WILL SEE *TO TELL THE TRUTH*.

In smaller print, the paper reported that the producer was looking at Jimmy Stewart and Margaret Sullavan for the leading roles, not

Harron or any other member of the Canadian cast. The taste of Toots Shor's rare roast beef turned to ashes in his mouth.

Don turned his attention to new challenges, principally *Spring Thaw '49* and his impending marriage to Gloria Fisher. At the time, the former seemed the more daunting prospect of the two, because there were past glories to live up to.

The second *Thaw* dispensed with even the thread of a plot, and ran to packed houses for two whole weeks. Peter Mews and Connie Vernon spawned a *Thaw* tradition with their hilarious spoof of John Weinzweig's ballet *The Red Ear of Corn*. Performed with cabbages, it was called *The Red Choux*.

Don the author contributed two sketches that year. Were I dependent on the Harron archives, this section would be a blank but Mavor Moore, bless him, donated his papers to York University, and many of my father's sketches were among them. I couldn't find *News by Television*, but I did find part of his trilogy, *The Rump Drama Festival*.

A take-off on the Dominion Drama Festival, it presented three condensed versions of the same play: *Macbeth* by The Old Play Society, *Mac and Beth* by Doughty's Mellow Drama Company, and *Mac Bat* by Les Misérables. Northrop Frye fondly recalls Mac Bat crying *"Je t'aime! Je t'adore!"*, and a door being slammed off stage.

On the strength of this, Don was asked to write two radio series for the CBC. The new head of network programming was Bud Walker, who had been the announcer when Harron was a boy-hero-adventurer on the *Lonesome Trail*. Don's first assignment was to write a show with Lister Sinclair and Eric Christmas.

Eric had been one of the highlights of both *Thaws*. He could make audiences scream just by pointing to an exit sign stage left, asking "Do you know what this reminds me of?", then solemnly pointing to the same thing stage right. It was Eric who came up with the title for their half-hour weekly news satire, *Keep in Touch*.

The first joint effort by Christmas/Harron/Sinclair was more like a Goon Show for Ph.D.s, and it went over like a lead balloon. Lister bowed out gracefully: "As W.C. Fields once said in *My Little Chickadee,* there is an Ethiopian in the fuel supply, and it appears to be me. I henceforth resign to let these splendid chaps do what nature has obviously ordained them to do — split the ears of the groundlings with laughter.''

Eric, who had kept pretty quiet up until then, quickly revamped *Keep in Touch* into a situation comedy about the triumphs and tribulations of a Cockney immigrant, a situation he knew something about. Eventually, he and Don discovered they worked better and faster the more they were apart, and ended up writing shows on alternate weeks.

This arrangement conveniently allowed for a work-free honeymoon. The week before the wedding he left his script on the streetcar, and had to reproduce all thirty-two pages from memory. This is every writer's idea of Hell. On the eve of his wedding Don did not have a stag party, the usual rite of passage: he was at home frantically trying to re-write the script. He finished it about half-past ten and delivered it by streetcar to the main CBC building on Jarvis Street.

When he awoke the next morning he was filled with apprehension. He wondered how his redhead was feeling. He worried about how his parents would manage, without him there to clean out the eavestroughs (''Dad gets dizzy in Cuban heels'') and shovel the coal. He worried about the crease in the pants of his new grey flannel suit, and he was right about that. Dutzie was pressed into service, and headed for the ironing board. Lionel was outside polishing his brand new car, his first set of wheels in twelve years.

Don had decided to blow his hard-earned nest egg on a British Vanguard for his parents. Lionel smashed it beyond repair a year later, and never drove again. He kept renewing his license, in a spirit of optimism I suppose, but Don wisely spared him the opportunity to do further damage.

They made it to the church on time and without mishap. Actually it was Hart House Chapel, a tiny place which could only hold the immediate family, which is probably why they chose it. ''The groom is not supposed to see the bride before the actual ceremony,'' Don recalls, ''but there she was waiting outside the chapel with her parents, her gorgeous titian hair a mite too tightly curled . . . I think this was the last time I can remember that she was ever on time for anything.''

The wedding reception was a quiet supper at the Old Mill with

family and close friends, no speeches or toasts. He remembers one
of his actor friends whispering to another: "I think it's a very pleasant
match for a *first* marriage."

They were bundled onto the train for Manitoulin Island in a blizzard of confetti. He was twenty-four, she was twenty-two, and they
were both virgins. After a three-year engagement they set about the
task of deflowering each other, and their relationship never recovered
from the experience.

Back in Toronto, Gloria paid her first visit to a gynaecologist who
assured her that she was not abnormal, she just had an impenetrable
hymen. The problem was rectified by a very minor operation. Gloria
says that she was so stricken, and Donald was so sorry for her, that
they didn't even talk about it. Even today, after all these years, he
wouldn't give her away. (I did, just now, because she told me to,
urging all maidens to get a check-up before losing their heads.)

In his memoirs, my father writes about this traumatic experience
with gallant affection:

> My first wife has always been a highly receptive audience for
> my inanities and a very compatible companion. What was
> lacking in bodily contact, we made up for with the mind, and
> the end of the honeymoon returned two people to Toronto
> who had cried a bit, laughed a lot, and found that they actually
> liked each other very much.

They set up housekeeping over a drugstore that was sublet from
Mavor and Dilly Moore, who were at the United Nations for June,
July and August. In addition to *Keep in Touch*, which lasted five
months, Don had begun work on the second radio series gleaned
from his *Thaw* work: *Boddy Gimby's Hoedown*.

Bobby was still one of the *Happy Gang* stars, which guaranteed
good ratings. The producer of this country variety show was Jackie
Rae, who was crazy about that rural character Don brought back
from the farm in '42. He'd become as adept at reproducing the
accent as Don, and suggested they work up an act.

Don chose the name Harry Shorthorn for himself, partly inspired
by Lou and Orville Short across the road from the Hadden farm.
For his comic foil, dubbed Luther Duckett after an actual farmer,

Jackie cast an American impressionist named Dick Nelson. Together, they provided continuity between musical numbers. Harry would say, "By swinjer, that was purtier'n a pink pig at market time, played with lotsa jinicker."

His partner would echo his sentiments: "It was a regler wham-snapper of a ring-tail snorter of a rang-dang-doo!" This was a far cry from lecturing in English literature, and Don loved every minute of it.

Mavor came back from the U.N. with a new play under his belt to begin the New Play Society's fourth season. A third *Thaw*, without question, was planned for dessert at the end. In between, there would be new plays by Andrew Allan, Harry J. Boyle, John Coulter and again Morley Callaghan, as well as Dora's friends Shaw, Goldsmith, Ibsen and Shakespeare. Not only would it be a lively and successful season, it contained seventy percent Canadian content and didn't hurt a bit.

Don was asked back at the same thirty dollars a week, and accepted with pleasure. He was also asked to get out of Mavor's apartment, which at least put an end to his friends' teasing about breaking into the pharmacy downstairs for more condoms. To save money they took a flat behind a dentist's office, where they had to share their bathroom with the dentist and his patients during office hours.

The bathroom was not soundproofed, and it didn't take them long to discover that the dentist and his receptionist were using it after-hours for their extra-marital affair. Their activities caused Mr. and Mrs. Harron much amusement, tinged with envy.

At the Museum Theatre, the same basic company assembled for rehearsals, including Lloyd Bochner, Pegi Brown, Bob and Margot Christie, Toby Robins and Don Harron. For his expressionistic play *Who's Who*, author/director Mavor Moore appropriately added two guest stars, big names in broadcasting: Lorne Greene, "the voice of Canada," and old pro Alex McKee, one of the busiest radio actors around.

Alex was so convincing playing a member of the audience pro-testing the action on stage that one night they actually had to stop the play, to convince a real member of the audience that McKee was a fake and should be allowed to continue his disruption.

In one scene, Don's character had to change from a young man in his twenties to the same man in his seventies, in a matter of seconds. He asked Alex how to do it. "Just relax all your muscles. That's all age is, getting to be relaxed about everything."

During intermission on opening night, Mavor Moore had to be rushed to the hospital with an acute attack of appendicitis, and was operated on at once. He never did get to see the whole show. The following day, Don announced to the rest of the cast that Mavor was the only author in history to have had two openings on the same night.

There was a new critic in the audience on that eventful evening. The *Globe and Mail* had lured Herbert Whittaker from Montreal to review plays and write a column called *Showbusiness*. His piece in the *Globe* the next morning proclaimed young Harron "a genius," but Don doubts if anyone except the cast read the theatre page that day. The cruise ship S.S. *Noronic* had burned in Toronto harbour with heavy loss of life.

The next Canadian play was Harry J. Boyle's *The Inheritance*, about conflict between generations on an Ontario farm. It was adapted from his radio play *The Macdonalds of Oak Valley*, with Frank Peddie recreating his role as the head of the family. To Don, he was the embodiment of all those Scottish crofters thrown off their farms by English landowners to make way for herds of sheep (because, as Charlie Farquharson was later to say, "Yiz kin skin a sheep morn once.")

John Drainie played the elder and Don the younger and more rebellious of the two sons. For the first and last time, he tried to use the rural accent he was so fond of in a serious context. In the *Toronto Star*, Jack Karr reported that "As the chief protagonist, Don Harrison, the rebellious son, plays his part in a workmanlike manner but seldom alleviates his surliness with any feeling of warmth." Don swore off the accent, cold turkey, and stayed on the wagon for over two years.

Thanks to their work together in *Spring Thaw*, Don was invited to share the limelight with Jane Mallett in a Montreal nightclub. He would follow Jane in his first-ever, one-night-only appearance as a stand-up comedian; or at least his first without a Wolf Cub uniform and chalk in his hand.

Don put together a bunch of topical material with some, he thought, witty political references. Jane's all-Canadian clubwoman character, as familiar in Westmount as in Rosedale and every other establishment enclave, had the audience in convulsions. Don received polite applause. He wasn't sure where he'd gone wrong, until Jane told him he needed a mask, like she had, a comic disguise.

Back home in Hogtown with the New Play Society, it was time for him to tackle one of the Biggies for any young dramatic actor: Oswald Alving in Ibsen's *Ghosts*. He was determined to show the world what a great idealist dying of inherited syphilis he could be. There is no doubt that he managed to communicate this to the high school students who filled the front rows on opening night. They had decided on an out-of-town opening and travelled to Orangeville, twenty miles from Toronto. In the tragic closing moments, just before Don was about to deliver the famous last words, "Give me the sun, give me the sun," one young theatre-goer cried out, "Jeeziz, look at that Oswald — he's goin' *nuts!*"

Ghosts was followed by Andrew Allan's *Narrow Passage*. Don was delighted that Andrew would be directing — their first stage work together since *Ah! Wilderness* — but not so pleased with his part. He was beginning to feel typecast. Herbert Whittaker's review confirmed this: "As the sensitive, hag-ridden musician, Don Harron played with what we have come to recognize as this young actor's flair for presenting the highly-strung and desperate."

Nineteen-fifty began with *Heartbreak House*, his favourite Shaw play, but Mavor Moore had other plans for him: "It's time you directed, Donald my boy, and I have just the thing for you. John Coulter has written the most important Canadian play to date. It's about Louis Riel and those two rebellions he caused."

Directing *Riel* was definitely not typecasting. Don felt flattered, and terrified, and tried not to think about the Vic *Bob*. The only thing he could remember about Riel were from Cecil B. DeMille's movie *Northwest Mounted Police* and his own second form (Grade 10) textbook. His history courses at university hadn't included marginal countries like Canada.

DeMille had portrayed Riel as a slavering Mexican bandit with a Gatling gun, substituting tuque for sombrero. The textbook had very little to say, none of it nice, but Riel's picture appeared on the page opposite Sir John A. Macdonald's. Don remembered it because he had pleated Sir John A.'s picture like a *Mad* magazine fold-in, so that he appeared to be thumbing his nose at Riel. After reading Coulter's play, he thought this seemed pretty accurate.

Don had met John Coulter at the Arts and Letters Club, and had been so fascinated by his Ulster accent that he'd used it on CBC radio, performing in Tommy Tweed's adaptation of Paul Hiebert's *Here Lies Sarah Binks*. Coulter grew up in Belfast, and he saw Riel's execution of Thomas Scott, and the subsequent execution of Riel, as an Old World conflict spilling over into the New and splitting it in two for almost a century.

The easiest part was the casting. Coulter wanted Don to play Scott, even though it was his professional début as a director. Don chose Mavor Moore for Riel, even though Mavor still had his job at the U.N. in New York. Robert Christie was such an obvious choice for Sir John A. Macdonald, and so good at it, the role became a permanent part of his career.

E.M. "Moe" Margolese (not a gangster) was to play the kindly Archbishop Taché. He pulled out at the last minute to take a more lucrative Ford Radio Theatre job. (So maybe he *was* a gangster.) Seething with rage, Don turned around and handed the part to an eager little guy who had been hanging around playing walk-ons. His name was Les Rubie, and he turned out to be a wonderful Archbishop. If you watched television in Ontario in the '80s, his face is familiar to you as the kindly grocer in Lottario commercials, more interested in promoting gambling than selling produce.

Perhaps the most inspired piece of casting was Herb Gott for the key role of Riel's defense attorney. As far as Don knew, the radio actor who had directed him so sensitively in Saroyan's *Hello Out There* had never appeared on stage, probably because he had no arms. Don was sure that with flowing courtroom robes and a convincing performance, this fact would go unnoticed. He was right.

His biggest challenge appeared to be fitting twenty-eight scenes and almost as many characters onto the Museum Theatre's twenty-foot box that served as a stage — but then they had already managed as much if not more in *Spring Thaw*.

Adapting comic techniques to tragic business, he restricted the cast to fourteen actors, most of them playing more than one part. Scenes would occur either upstage or downstage, in relentless succession. He wanted to reverse the scenes in Act One and de-emphasize the role of Louis Riel's mother, but Coulter said he would prefer to see his work as he had written it. Authors are like that.

From the moment rehearsals began, Don lived and breathed *Riel*. Gloria, her mother's daughter after all, spent her time cooking his meals and transporting them to the theatre by streetcar from the western end of the line, twice a day. At the end of each evening rehearsal, she would take him home and put him to bed. After breakfast, eaten in situ, he was off to the theatre and she to the kitchen.

His biggest problem was holding onto his Riel, who was hardly ever there. Either Mavor really was forced to commute to New York on urgent U.N. business all the time, or the Moores were taking fiendish delight in giving ''The-Dog-Ate-My-Homework'' Harron a taste of his own medicine.

Don began to despair of Mavor ever learning his lines. When he didn't even show up for the dress rehearsal, Don threw a tantrum.

Just as Mavor had been living up to his role as Riel by continually skipping the country, Bob Christie now assumed command with the authority of Sir John A. Macdonald. He had been a very patient prime minister until that moment, but now he let Don have it. He told him to stop fretting over technical details and allow the cast to get on with the job of suppressing their own panic.

Opening night was immediately preceded by a four-foot (all-right, maybe a three-foot) snowfall which paralysed the city but did not prevent several veterans of the Second Riel Rebellion (1885) from attending the show. Even Mavor managed to show up.

The lighting plot worked just fine, thanks to a lot of overtime put in by Sir John A. Don says the worst part of the evening was his own performance as the fanatical Thomas Scott, ''a slice of pure Smithfield ham.'' His Ulster accent, under stress, became even thicker than the accent of the playwright he was imitating.

Much of the stress came from watching Mavor, who had a firm grip on his character but only a vague recollection of the words.

Don spent all his time off stage hiding under the raised platform where Riel would meet his end. From this vantage point in the scaffolding, horizontal and in costume, the Ulster fanatic fed the Métis rebel his lines.

Both Moores had surprises for Don that night. At the last minute Dora had recruited four choirboys from St. Michael's Cathedral to close the show with a *Te Deum*, as Riel was being hanged in full view of the audience. It was the perfect touch, and Jimmy Arnold, Frank Busseri, Connie Coderini and Bernie Toorish gave a magnificent *a capella* performance.

As the lights dimmed, the pure sound of their young voices died away. While the audience applauded, the soon-to-be-famous quartet burst into a bluesy rendition of *Tell Me How Long the Train's Been Gone* — what The Four Lads would call a "big finish."

Mavor Moore delivered an even bigger surprise than his mother: in spite of everything, he was magnificent.

In the *Evening Telegram*, Rose Macdonald described his Riel as "one of the best-rounded and most convincing performances of his career, retaining the centre of the stage without elbowing out the other characters." Perish the thought — he needed all the prompters he could get.

Rose objected to the hanging scene, however, as betraying "a delight in horrid details." Along with most of the other actors, brief honourable mention was made of Donald Harron, who "also directed." Don felt as though he'd just had quintuplets, and that was all it said — "also directed."

John Coulter's New York agent Monica McCall was far more appreciative. She was reported elsewhere in the *Telegram* as saying: "It is absolutely magnificent what that group is doing in Toronto. I do hope you people appreciate it! I can't tell you how surprised and excited I was at the Museum Theatre Friday night. And the size of that stage! They're marvellous, absolutely marvellous!"

Nobody has ever persuaded Don Harron to direct a play again, despite the fact that his labour pains on that snowy night in February 1950 resulted in the birth of a new cultural industry — the Riel business. Coulter's second act, the courtroom trial based on actual transcripts, continues to be performed every summer in Regina.

Books, plays, operas and ballets are still being written about this fascinating, enigmatic figure. He has no rival in Canadian mythology — except, of course, for Anne of Green Gables.

11

A QUESTION OF ROYALTY, AND A STERLING RECEPTION

DON didn't know it, but when he married Gloria, he also acquired his first business manager. Martha Rome Fisher had built her dream house (and especially garden) out of more than cutting corners and clipping coupons, although there was a lot of that. She was new to showbiz, but she was shrewd.

Her son-in-law appeared in nine out of ten New Play Society productions that season, and directed one. She'd read the reviews, so she also knew his *Spring Thaw* sketches had been big hits in '49. They were counting on him to provide more of the same for *Spring Thaw '50*, due to run for three weeks, and Martha wanted to know how much he was going to make in royalties.

Being paid for writing a bunch of skits hadn't entered Don's head, and paying for them certainly hadn't entered Dora's. When he presented his demands, "her usual Churchillian presence, stern but loving, turned positively Stalinesque. I was the actor who gave her more trouble than any other by furtively accepting other work, coming late to rehearsals, and on one occasion arriving for an opening five minutes before curtain time . . . and so on."

Only the prospect of facing his mother-in-law empty-handed made him stand his ground. He was caught between not just any old opposing forces, but a couple of truly formidable mothers. Don and Dora settled on two dollars per major sketch per performance, plus fifty cents for blackouts.

Blackouts are brief moments in a pool of light, which allow the rest of the cast a few seconds for scene and costume changes. Here is a typical Harron blackout, based on a pre-Ms. Clairol commercial:

"In Jail"
Two prisoners are seen in prison garb, in jail. A guard passes them. Prisoner One says:
"Does he, or doesn't he?"

It was highway robbery, but Mrs. Moore coughed up the four bits.

In the meantime, it was still winter. There would be three more plays before *Thaw,* beginning with *King Lear.* The Museum Theatre was a tiny space in which to create a blasted heath and they only had ten days in which to rehearse. Don suggested they combine the evil sisters, Goneril and Regan, into one wicked case of Goneregan. Dora dismissed his whining: "All Shakespeare demands is two boards and a passion!" She cast him as Edmund, the two-timing Bastard. Mavor, though of tender years, would be King Lear, and no messing about with world affairs at the U.N. His mother was directing.

Mavor was a great inspiration at the first rehearsal. But, coming back from New York for the dress rehearsal, he managed to lose his voice — entirely. Just to be on the safe side, he whispered his way through the dress, which would have been all right except the rest of the cast kept doing the same, to Dora's despair.

Don was not amazed that Mavor managed to give a masterly performance on opening night, because he was always at his best when things were going wrong. The amazing part was that he also knew his lines, perfectly. He could even invent more lines, and in iambic pentameter, when the occasion demanded it. The mad Lear was supposed to mistake a stool for his daughter Regan, and give it a good talking-to, but it wasn't there. It was in the wings, under the stage manager's rump. Mavor turned to his Fool and said, "Arise and bring me yonder joint stool, Fool, and you and I shall jointly sit upon't!"

After *Lear* came a new play by the previous box-office winner, Morley Callaghan. Don played a character who only appeared in Act One of *Going Home,* which allowed him to skip several rehearsals and spend more time at home, writing his sketches for *Spring Thaw*. One evening when his mother-in-law came to dinner, Gloria burned the roast and stormed off to the bedroom, slamming the door behind her. "She was the most understanding of creatures when I did anything wrong, which was often — but if she made a mistake, look out."

Don and his mother-in-law were left alone. They ate Campbell's Cream of Tomato soup while Martha dished out some food for thought: "Why don't you two go to London? It's time you went to the Old Country."

"What for?"

"Well, to see some high-class theatre, for goodness sake! Isn't that part of your job, to find out what the best ones are doing?" He'd never thought of it.

He booked passage to England the very next day. Bunny (Bernard) Cowan, the smooth announcer on *Front Page Challenge*, ran a travel agency on the side. He arranged for them to leave New York on the Cunard liner S.S. *Georgic* two days after the New Play Society ended its season. Gloria was in heaven.

In the meantime, Don was in *Spring Thaw '50*. He revamped his mock opera from the '46 *Bob, La Traviesti*, around a hot political topic: the suburban municipalities were being dragooned into amalgamating with the city of Toronto to form a Greater Metropolitan monster.

The villain of the piece, bandit and ne'er-do-well ("politico") Taranna, presents the hapless villagers (Yetobico, Leah-Side, Longebranchi, Swansi. . .) with a twenty-four-hour ultimatum to join forces with him. The strongest among them, Zcar-borro, calls his bluff: "Amalgamati??? Esta baloni!!"

As Taranna's unruly hobby horse takes him back to his castle in Citi-hallo, the villagers sing *Benvenuti tutti frutti* (or "Divided we stand, united we fall") to the tune of the *Toreador Chorus*:

"What is the score, please, tell us what's the score?
Don't shoot the bull, we've heard it before."

Zcar-borro replies:

> "This . . . tyrant has our backs against the wall,
> Don't be a slave to City Hall!!
> For if you do my friend, 'twill be the end,
> 'Twill be the end of all."

The village flirt and general run-about, Teetisi (as in Toronto Transit Commission), is determined to win Zcar-borro away from his true love, the fair Mimi-co. She goes to visit Taranna, who is in the dark, except for a candle: "Citti-hallo camera obscura! Faulta della Hydro . . ."

Teetisi rings the bell. "Ah! La Bella della phone!" cries Taranna. Together they sing the terrifying "Aria of Death," the *Todmorden*. (Northrop Frye was delighted to see his pupil had graduated to triple puns: not only does Todmorden contain both the German noun for death, and the German verb "to murder," on the TTC it was the end of the line.)

When Zcar-borro and Mimi-co announce their engagement, Taranna and Teetisi offer the lovers a toast. Their attempt to poison Mimi-co and slip Zcar-borro a love potion backfires, of course. Teetisi gets the poison, which puts her out of commission for good, Taranna is transformed by the love potion into somebody you'd wanna amalgamate with, and all ends happily.

In the process, librettist Donaldo Harroni and composer Carlo Tisdallo (Charles Tisdall) managed to cover not only the *Toreador Chorus*, but *La Donna è Mobile,* the *Habañera* from *Carmen*, the *Soldier's Chorus* from Faust, the *William Tell Overture*, the sextet ("Set 'em Up") from *Lucia*, the quartet from *Rigoletto,* and for a beer-stained finale, the *Anvil Chorus* ("Labattsa").

One night in Diana Sweets, which was the traditional après-theatre hangout as it had been the après-lecture hangout in college days, Don met a guy who looked like a movie gangster but said he was in "ennuhtainment." The more they talked, and laughed, and talked, the more he realised that this guy would be perfect for the press agent in a sketch he was working on called *The Hollywood Version*.

It took a bit of persuading. Lou Jacobi was a stand-up comedian, appearing at stags and smokers, and social director of a Jewish resort in Muskoka. (Five years before, it had been a German prisoner-of-war camp.) He said he hadn't "acted sideways" in fifteen years, meaning facing a fellow actor in a play, as opposed to telling jokes to the audience.

Don convinced him to at least come to a rehearsal and meet the director. Lou ended up in several sketches besides *The Hollywood Version*, including Don's *Honesty is the Best Politics,* and *T.V. or Not T.V.* It is impossible to tell from the program who played who in *La Traviesti*, because the "Perpetratori" are listed as "Dorothia di Lammermour", "Lotte Traubel (Mezzo-Barracuda)" etc., conducted by "Sir Malcolm Magnesia (agitato con gusto)."

Don wrote a solo number for Pegi Brown called *A Private Schoolgirl Has to Have Her Public*, with music by Lucio Agostini (not a pseudonym). He did this not only because she was gorgeous and talented: he also found her difficult to perform with. It was her unnerving habit of never looking into someone's eyes on stage, always at their hairline. It made Don feel like there was a fly crawling across his forehead. He begged her to stop, but she couldn't. In fact, she kept looking up until she married a British aristocrat and retired young.

During rehearsals for *Spring Thaw '50,* Don learned that he had a much more disconcerting habit of his own. Jane Mallett pointed it out to him, and the rest of the cast confirmed the horrible truth: when Don was appearing in a sketch he had written, he mouthed everyone else's lines along with them. They begged him to stop, but he couldn't.

Don swore to Jane never again to perform with her in anything he had written. Fortunately *The Great Canadian Play*, featuring Don and Jane as The Man and The Woman in scenes from the quintessential Russian play, British play, American play and Canadian play, was written by *Saturday Night* columnist Margaret Ness. It was great fun — except for the ten seconds in which he had to change from his Noel Coward tux to his torn Tennessee Williams T-shirt. The Russian peasant and Mountie outfits were easy, and Jane was divine.

This third *Thaw* was such a big hit everyone agreed to extend the run for another two weeks. All except Don Harron, who had a ship to catch. He wanted to stay, but he'd already paid for the tickets.

No doubt it was with mixed feelings of sadness and trepidation, tinged with relief, that the cast waved goodbye to their lip-synching leading man. Jack Medhurst, Ted Follows and Eric House took over his roles, and *Spring Thaw '50* went on being revived until the end of the year.

The night before the S.S. *Georgic* steamed off to Liverpool, Don and Gloria arrived too late for a Broadway show and settled for a nightclub called Le Ruban Bleu. The suave compère, Julius Monk, gave a long and effusive introduction to a hot new act. The Four Lads bounded onto the stage, and the Harrons almost hit the floor. It was the same four choirboys from *Riel*. They had a joyous reunion at a less sophisticated place called Hamburger Heaven after the show.

After a couple of hours' sleep, the Harrons boarded the *Georgic* from a pier on Manhattan's West Side. One of the luxury liners in her heyday, the sister ship to the Britannic had served as a troop ship during the war. Don claims she spent five years at the bottom of the Red Sea before he and Gloria sailed on her.

Bunny Cowan had also neglected to mention that they would be billeted in separate cabins with three strangers each. In any case, both became violently seasick. Gloria retreated to her bunk with Sir Thomas Browne and thoughts of death for the first couple of days.

Don divided his time between eating in the dining room and vomiting into the Atlantic. Since it was a British ship, there were five meals a day: breakfast, elevenses, lunch, tea and dinner at eight, not counting the hot beef bouillon served on deck at all hours. He consumed Canadian quantities of each, which kept him pretty busy.

His most vivid memory of their last day on board is of getting up at five in the morning to catch a glimpse of the green hills of Cobh through the swirling Irish mist. They docked in Liverpool at Whitsuntide, and found the populace on holiday. However, they managed to get their steamer trunks and themselves to London and the Charing Cross Hotel, which is right on top of the railway station of the same name. Don could have sworn that the trains were coming straight into their room.

He bought the *Evening Standard* and looked up the theatre listings. Under the ''A''s was the Aldwych, where Bernard Braden was appearing in *A Streetcar Named Desire* with Vivien Leigh, directed by her husband Laurence Olivier. And it was just down the Strand from the Charing Cross Hotel.

On their way to the theatre they stopped off at Forte's for a snack, perhaps because it looked like a giant British version of Fran's Restaurant in Toronto. He ordered a malted milk, expecting a shake, and was treated to a steaming cup of grey lumps in water called ''Horlick's.'' So they headed for Tennessee Williams country, where they at least spoke the language.

To their amazement the production was bizarre and seemingly interminable. Vivien Leigh's Blanche Dubois sounded Irish, while her sister Stella's ''Suthin'' accent was pure minstrel show. As Mitch, the modern version of ''Jack, his friend,'' Bernie sounded convincing enough but looked almost a foot shorter than Stanley, played by Bonar Colleano, whose accent was pure Brooklyn.

Don doesn't know a sharp from a flat, musically speaking, but he has perfect pitch when it comes to accents, and this cacophony was sheer torture. For Bernie's sake they stuck it out, and went backstage afterwards wondering what to say, apart from, ''*You* were great. Uh . . . how are Barbara and the kids?''

The production was a big success, and there were hordes of visitors backstage. In Bernie's dressing room they met Vancouverite Doug Haskins, who had been very popular on late-night Toronto radio with a one-man mixture of comedy and social commentary. Doug said he wasn't feeling well, and departed. Braden then introduced the Harrons to his other visitor, Daniel Mann, who looked Don over and asked him if he was American. ''No, Canadian,'' Don replied.

''What's the difference?'' said Mann, not waiting for an answer. He added, ''Be here at 10:30 tomorrow morning — I'd like to see you,'' and walked out the door. Bernie explained that Vivien Leigh was leaving the company to make the film version of *Streetcar* with Marlon Brando. Mann had come to re-direct the production with a new Blanche Dubois plus a few other replacements, including the young paperboy who has a two-minute scene with her.

Bernard, ever kind and generous, took Don and Gloria out to

a sumptuous supper at a private club, where Barbara joined them. At the table Bernard told the Harrons about his successful BBC radio show, *Bedtime with Braden*, and Don told the Bradens about the latest *Spring Thaw* and the sketches he had contributed. Bernie disappeared to make a phone call, and about half an hour later Bonar Colleano, star of *Streetcar*, turned up. He too had a radio show.

Working with Eric Nicol (''Canada's funniest writer,'' according to Don) and England's funniest writers, the brilliant team of Dennis Norden and Frank Muir, Braden had created a new, relaxed style of radio comedy. Bonar was going to star in a thirteen-week radio series, deftly titled *The Bonar Colleano Show,* and he was hoping for some of that same magic.

They came right to the point: on Braden's recommendation, Colleano had brought Doug Haskins over from Toronto to write his scripts. Things had not worked out, and the series was due to begin in three days' time. A typewriter and stack of paper were sitting idle in Bonar's hotel suite — could Don come over right away?

They sped off to Bonar's suite at the Grosvenor House and Bonar went to bed, leaving Don on his own to turn straw into gold, while Gogie fell asleep on one of the many sofas.

The Bonar Colleano Show was a situation comedy about a dashing young leading man, played by guess who, leading the life of a dashing young playboy in contemporary London. His sidekick would be played by another Canadian, Paul Carpenter, who had been a hit on the BBC series *Riders of the Range*. The only thing missing was laughter.

Don threw in every joke he could think of, including sight gags. He knew it was radio, but *Spring Thaw* was still fresh in his mind. At about 9:30 a.m. he woke up Bonar and handed him the finished script. Bonar dropped it on the floor by his bed and went back to sleep.

Don felt a cold coming on. All he could think about was a hot lemonade and a warm bed. But back at the hotel there was a message from Bernie Braden reminding him to be at the Aldwych at 10:30 to meet Danny Mann.

He splurged on a taxi, but when he saw almost a hundred young men lined up at the stage door ahead of him, he wondered why he'd bothered. The line didn't move for fifteen minutes, then the door opened and a stage manager, with Daniel Mann beside him, called out "Hands up all of those who are Americans!"

Don remembered Mann's comment the night before, and decided to be a brazen imposter. He looked around, and saw only two other hands in the air. He felt ashamed in the face of so much dumb honesty, especially when the stage manager said, "Okay, you three inside. The rest of you can go home."

The first to audition was Lyndon Brook, who had already made his mark on stage and screen. He was also the son of two British stars of stage and screen, Clive Brook and Diana Wynyard, which rather belied his claim to American blood. So did his accent.

Next was a real American, who was so good that Don was sure he would get the part. By this time Don had a fully developed head cold, and during his audition he had to concentrate on not sniffling. But perhaps the congestion gave his voice a deep, resonant quality, because he was offered the part at £12 a week.

He walked back to the hotel in a daze and found another message from Bernard Braden. It said that Bonar Colleano loved the script and was offering a thirteen-week contract as co-author at forty guineas a week.

Between *Streetcar* and the radio series, Don would be making £54 a week in a country where the average weekly income was less than ten. And he'd been in Britain for less than twenty-four hours. . . .

12

BACK DOOR BUSINESS

FOR the itinerant artist, those really were the good old days. On their second morning in London, Donald joined British Equity for a fee of three or four pounds, which permitted him to perform in the play, and Gogie found a flat for five pounds a week. You couldn't get an Equity card and a flat in London today even if you had a high-powered immigration lawyer, an estate agent in love with you and a lot of money.

The flat was in St. John's Wood in a handsome house surrounded by a garden. It did not come equipped with "ev mod con", as in the classified "adverts": they would have to share "k & b," and their two large furnished rooms needed a coat of "distemper." Gogie handed over fifteen pounds for the decorating and five pounds for the first week's rent.

At the first rehearsal Don reported all this to Bernard Braden, who said, "You can't possibly live in St. John's Wood; in London a good address is everything" and immediately arranged for the Harrons to move into his old digs in Chelsea. Kissing their twenty pounds and St. John's Wood goodbye, they found themselves living in a tall red brick Victorian house at 34 Lower Sloane Street, just off the King's Road. There they had one room (a bedroom, not a "bed-sit") and they still had to share "k & b."

It was 1950, but Britain had its war debts to repay and bomb-damaged cities to rebuild. Wartime rationing was still in effect and included petrol, sweets, eggs, butter and meat. Luckily, the Harrons' landlady was having a carnal relationship with the local butcher,

127

who came to dinner every Sunday and brought a "joint" with him. Don and Gloria were invited to partake of this under-the-counter treat, usually lamb or roast beef.

At rehearsals of *A Streetcar Named Desire* the phrase "method acting" was never spoken, but Don knew that Daniel Mann was of the Group Theatre School like Lee Strasberg, Harold Clurman and Elia Kazan, who would be directing the Hollywood version.

Perhaps over-anxious to make a good impression, Don was giving his all to the role when Mann interrupted: "I just want to time this scene to see how long it runs, so don't give me any acting, just repeat the lines." It seemed like an odd request, but he complied. When he finished, Danny said, "That's exactly how I want you to play the part." It was an acting lesson Don will never forget.

The new Blanche Dubois was Betty-Ann Davies, a British actress and thoroughly nice person who made Don feel very much at home in their scene together. A pleasant surprise was the new Stella, a Saskatchewan girl named Frances Hyland. She had graduated with high honours from the prestigious Royal Academy of Dramatic Art, and was under contract to H.M. Tennant, the most successful management firm in the West End. Some time later, Don found out that Franny, playing one of the leads, was on salary at £10 a week, while he walked away with £12 as a glorified walk-on. This lesson in freelancing was not lost on him.

One member of the original cast who stayed on was a young Israeli named Theodore Bikel. Don liked him immediately but would have befriended him anyway because Braden and Colleano took delight in making him the victim of fiendish practical jokes. They probably kept on doing it because Theo bore their slings and arrows so cheerfully. He was also extremely busy having affairs with two gorgeous women. Both were frequent backstage visitors, almost but never quite at the same time. Harron dubbed him "a Bikel built for two."

The producer introduced himself the first day, very simply: "Hello, Mr. Harron, my name is Beaumont." It was "Binkie" Beaumont himself, already a theatrical legend, known for his impeccable taste in clothing and casting. Don was horrified to hear himself saying "Oh, I've heard of you!" Binkie wanted to know if Don would go on stage a day earlier than the rest of the replacement cast, because his predecessor was leaving to do a film. If so, would he please come and meet Miss Leigh, who was waiting in her dressing room.

Don was greeted by that face, those eyes, and a hearty handshake. Her accent was *teddibly* County, the one normally worn with pearls, tweed, cashmere and stout walking shoes. They began to run through the scene together, Vivien Leigh in a curious neo-Irish brogue (not in the film), and he in his drawl from deepest Southern Ontario.

Short but sweet, it is one of the best two-minute scenes ever written. Blanche Dubois is revealed as a "genteel nymphomaniac" when the paperboy comes collecting for the *Evening Star*. She contemplates seducing him on the spot, then reconsiders. When they finished the scene, Vivien Leigh remarked, "Jolly dee, bang on!" and that was that.

Don was sent upstairs to a cubbyhole, henceforth his dressing room, to prepare for his London stage début. The scene went well, except that the audience laughed when Blanche called him a "young prince out of the *Arabian Nights*." Miss Leigh was offended by this reaction. She began muttering under her breath, and at first Don thought she was sending him out for cigarettes. Then he realised it was not "Kents! Kents!" but something much more obscene on her exquisite lips.

Don was dying to meet her husband, but all that he saw of Laurence Olivier was a shadowy figure in the back of a limo, waiting at the stage door to whisk his leading lady away after her final performance.

Elsewhere in the West End, at the Paris Cinema on Lower Regent Street, the first live broadcast of *The Bonar Colleano Show* went off swimmingly. Reaction in the popular press was enthusiastic, but Don suspects this had less to do with his skill than with Bonar's talent for hobnobbing with the columnists. Either way, Donald had twelve more scripts to write.

He also had a co-author, Doug Haskin's ex-partner George Wadmore. George was a charming fellow, considered a Young Hopeful by the British Broadcasting Corporation, and Don learned a lot from listening to his funny stories. What he didn't get from George, at all, was copy, and sometimes he was still writing the script after the broadcast started.

Now, it's one thing to write in the safety of your room, quite another with a cinema full of actors, technicians and live spectators (not to mention the folks at 'ome) hanging on to your every word. Even more intimidating, Don couldn't help measuring himself against the writing team working for Bernard Braden. Nicol Norden and Muir managed to be brilliantly funny for *Breakfast with . . .* every week, and another series called *Take It from Here*.

In retrospect, he realizes he should have trusted his instincts more, used his eyes and ears and taken advantage of his unique position as an outsider, living and working in the locale where the series was taking place. Instead, he ran in desperation to the bookstores for tattered copies of *Captain Billy's Whizbang of Humorous Hits and How to Hold an Audience*.

Bonar's way of helping was to drag Donald and his typewriter along with him on his late-night rounds, to witness a real playboy in action. One of Bonar's chums bore an astonishing resemblance to actor John Mills, and they took advantage of this fact to lure eager shopgirls to another friend's house, equipped with a two-way mirror on the ceiling of the master bedroom, and fixed seating in the attic. In the kitchen below, Don, with *Cap'n Billy* beside him, would pound earnestly at the keys.

Don got a bit more writing done at the Aldwych Theatre, between his scene with Blanche Dubois and curtain call, when he would have to troop out and share in the applause. However, his dressing table was so tiny it could barely hold a typewriter, let alone a copy of *Cap'n Billy*. Feeling trapped, he would escape downstairs for a breath of fresh air at the stage door.

The streetwalkers were looking for payers, not players, and treated the actors as fellow professionals. Many of them were French, former "Piccadilly commandos" who had done active service with their backs to the wall during World War II. These seasoned veterans never talked about sex; they talked about money and how they planned to spend their retirement in the South of France.

One of the ladies was a gossipy exception to the rule. She told Don all about the kinks and quirks of her distinguished clients. He was surprised to learn that the formative experiences of viscounts and baronets gave them a taste for bondage, discipline and the downright peculiar.

Don had never had a nanny or been to a "public school" (which in Britain means the opposite, of course), and couldn't see being paddy-whacked for pleasure, or paying to watch a naked girl in a see-through raincoat scrub the floor. One distinguished gentleman was said to particularly enjoy being kicked in the testicles by a girl wearing nothing but a hat with a veil and a Swiss watch.

His own sex life seemed awfully Presbyterian by comparison. This was brought home to him by Henry Miller. He found a copy of *Tropic of Cancer* in Bernie's dressing-room, which was much bigger than his own and had a comfortable couch. As Bernie spent far more time onstage than he did, it seemed only natural to sneak in there for what he thought of as a pornographic read. He couldn't imagine asking Gloria to do any of it.

Things could have been worse. Colleano's Canadian sidekick on the show, Paul Carpenter, was a very likeable fellow. He was married to the daughter of impresario George Black, but Pauline had just left him, taking the furniture with her. Paul discovered this by accident: returning home at two or three in the morning, too drunk or too tired to put on the light, he threw himself into bed and crashed onto the bare floor.

Unfortunately this was not the part of being a West End playboy that Bonar Colleano was interested in presenting, although it's much funnier. Don tried writing at home. The pounding of the typewriter far into the night was music to Gloria's ears, but not to his landlady's or co-tenants'. So, instead of going home after *Streetcar*, he would head over to the BBC's Aeolian Hall on New Bond Street. The night watchman would let him in just before midnight, and let him out again four or five hours later.

On his way home he always saw a few hookers still on the street, hoping for a last fare before turning in. One night (morning) he felt so depressed about his scriptwriting that he decided to seek oblivion in the arms of one of these women. Standing in a shadow, he spied a head of red hair and a full-busted silhouette in a brown corduroy suit.

"Short time, dear?" was hardly a promising beginning, but writers are a desperate breed.

"How much?"

"Ten bob, dear. No kissing."

Yum. He followed her up a laneway with the money in his hand, wondering what the hell he was doing. She led him into a miserable little room with a daybed that seemed to have lost its legs, and held out her hand for the money.

After paying, he turned around to find somewhere to put his clothes, and heard the most ungodly sound behind him. He looked back and discovered that the poor old thing had fallen instantly asleep. She was snoring loudly, the ten-shilling note clutched tightly in her gnarled fist.

Seeing her in the light for the first time, he recoiled in horror. She was almost a carbon-copy of his landlady, "Ginger" Ewen, a redheaded Margaret Thatcher with more teeth and less chin. Thank God she was asleep. He practically ran all the way home.

Meanwhile, Gloria was getting so fed up with the real Ginger and her constant chatter that when she wasn't trooping reverently through art galleries and museums, she would pretend not to be home. Ginger would knock and Gloria, curled up with Northrop Frye or Stendhal, would ignore it. Undeterred, the sonorous landlady would carry on a one-sided conversation from outside the door.

The fogs of November rolled in, Gloria was morning-sick (my fault), and the Harrons discovered that their enthusiasm for all things English did not include the English winter. They were tired of running out of pennies to feed the gas meter, and of having to sit right in front of the fire to get warm, toasting one side at a time. George Wadmore explained that this was part of being British — "red on the front, blue on the back and white with rage inside."

They stuck it out for a few more weeks at their chic but uncomfortable address, then moved to Park West, an ugly modern block of flats on the Edgware Road not far from Marble Arch. Equipped with all mod cons at last, they sat in centrally heated comfort and looked out at the beautiful old terraced houses across the street.

Assured of a steady income from the Tennessee Williams play and the radio series, Don signed a six-month lease. But soon afterwards *The Bonar Colleano Show* came to an abrupt end: in true playboy style, Bonar smashed himself to death in his sports car. And *A Streetcar Named Desire* was ending its London run. Don was worried — he would soon have a family of three to support — but

Bernard Braden assured him that there were many opportunities for Canadians to play Americans in the West End.

Bernie introduced him to a top agent, Olive Harding, a warm, motherly, straightforward woman who took him to lunch at Prunier's and introduced him to a non-alcoholic cocktail called a "Pussyfoot." She told him to write brief chatty letters to all the theatrical management companies in London, asking for an appointment. There were thirty-two of them, and to his amazement he received thirty-one cordial invitations to pop by.

In the meantime, Olive arranged for an interview at famous Shepperton Studios at Walton-on-Thames. It was an hour's journey by suburban train, so he caught an early one to make sure he would be back in time for *Streetcar*. There, another motherly lady interviewed him in a friendly manner about his theatre career thus far. After a brief absence to take a telephone call, she returned to her desk and eyed him with renewed interest: "Tell me, Mr. Harron, do you dance?'

"Well, yes, sort of. . . . How do you mean?"

"What I really mean is, can you move your head and arms in time to music?"

This was a relief. He felt he could manage any dancing that didn't involve feet. "Sure, I guess so."

"Then would you go on the set now? They're waiting for you."

Before this startling bit of news had a chance to sink in, a pale young man appeared and whisked him away. He was dressed in a ruffled clown shirt and Raggedy Ann wig, with purple patches on his cheeks and purple bee-stung lips, and shoved onto a soundstage.

There in front of him was Moira Shearer in a diaphanous tutu, talking to Sir Frederic Ashton. They were filming *The Tales of Hoffman,* a follow-up to the success of *The Red Shoes*. As Don stood open-mouthed beside the pale young man, another young chap came running up all out of breath: "Derek, I'm terribly. . ."

Derek wasted no time: "You're late, you're late, you silly thing. Too many drinkypoos I shall wager."

"Late? Ten piddlyfucking minutes!"

"Never mind, we have another dancer to take your place. So off to London with you, Tardypants!"

Don swears he was about to intervene on behalf of the one with the hangover when Derek turned around and goosed him up a ladder. There were six round holes in this ladder, five of them filled with bottoms. Don's was shoved into the sixth, and he was given one stage direction: "Do exactly what the others do."

For the rest of the day Sir Frederic, as the hump-backed jester Kleinzack, kept jumping out of a huge papier-maché tankard, then doing a pas-de-deux with the lovely Moira to the strains of the *Tic-Tac Polka*, conducted by Sir Thomas Beecham.

At lunch Don tried to communicate the importance of his making it back to the Aldwych before seven. It's hard to be taken seriously in a Raggedy Ann wig. They said he wouldn't be kept much past five, but would have to be back bright and early the next morning. He made it both times. Later when he saw the film, he couldn't tell which set of purple cheeks were his, but at least he had the satisfaction of having been a member of the Sadler's Wells Ballet for two whole days, and was seven pounds richer for the experience.

Don spent the next few weeks being interviewed by all the theatrical magnates who had answered his letters. They were all extremely polite and gave him a cup of tea, sometimes even a piece of Dundee cake or a Peek Frean biscuit, but no job offers.

Fortunately, Olive came through with a BBC audition for a ninety-minute television drama. It was a prestige production written by British Labour M.P. Christopher Mayhew about the United Nations, so there were lots of parts for foreigners. Don was cast as an American under-secretary of state.

This would be his first on-screen appearance anywhere. There was still no such thing as Canadian television, although in Toronto you could pick up the Buffalo station, if you were prepared to climb on the roof to adjust the antenna for the privilege of watching Milton Berle in a snowstorm.

Like radio, TV was live, a situation doubly fraught with peril. One of the leading roles was played by a stage actor in his late seventies, who gave the young players a lesson in quick thinking they will long remember. He kept muddling the lines in rehearsal, but assured the director he would be "all right on the night."

He was, too, until his big confrontation scene with the Russian representative. Without warning, he lapsed into silence in mid-speech. Obviously, he had forgotten his lines. His lips, however, kept right on moving in impassioned eloquence. The rest of the cast stood open-mouthed in amazement, and nobody said a word.

Finally the Russian, Arthur Young, interrupted his tirade. Young ad libbed a paraphrase of what *supposedly* had just been said, and got the scene back on track. The old actor, who never lost his composure for a second, was able to complete the scene as rehearsed.

At the BBC switchboard, it was pandemonium. You have to pay an annual license fee to watch television in Britain, and irate viewers wanted to know why they were being short-changed by a picture with no sound. After the broadcast, all the actors crowded around their ancient colleague to congratulate him on his coolness and daring.

There was no part for Harron in the West End after *Streetcar* left town, and there was rent to pay, so Don left Gloria in centrally-heated comfort and joined a provincial repertory company in the seaside town of Brighton. The Dolphin was a converted cinema right next door to the prestigious Theatre Royal. It survived in that seaside resort on the overflow from its neighbour, and by offering light comedies at cheaper prices — six shillings for the best seats, one (shilling) and six(pence) to perch in the Upper Circle.

Don's first role at the Dolphin was the romantic lead in the sturdy old American farce, *Separate Rooms*. Playing his sardonic older brother, the one who gets the funny lines instead of the girl, was Hal Thompson. Don recognized him, but not because they were both born in Toronto. It was from an old Marx Brothers movie, where it had been Hal's turn to play the romantic lead. Don asked him what it was like to work with Minnie's boys, and Hal replied, "Biggest pains in the arse you ever saw!" Don concluded that his big brother liked getting the lion's share of the laughs, and kept his distance.

Repertory theatre is great training and very hard work, rehearsing days and performing nights to produce an uninterrupted series of plays in rapid succession. With such a schedule, Don couldn't commute from London; he would have to find digs in Brighton.

He had heard many gruesome tales about theatrical digs, the kind of lower middle-class home desperate enough to house and feed *that* sort of total stranger. One Irish lady refused actors on the grounds that "the moment they're done eatin' yiz out of house and home, they're all upstairs to their beds and at it loike knoives!"

Don wasn't. He was alone in his bed at Mrs. Bone's. Her idea of an evening meal consisted of macaroni and cheese and three kinds of potatoes, but at least she wasn't sadistic like some he'd heard of. He gave her a free ticket to *Separate Rooms:* she confessed she nearly laughed twice, and had to hold herself both times.

On Sunday morning he would catch the train to London, Gloria and central heating in every room. Her cooking, though still fraught with peril, had begun to take on a new allure, but her housekeeping was becoming a little too spotless. Having nothing else to do, far from family, friends and now husband, he worried that she was becoming an intellectual recluse.

Mondays, it was back to Brighton and Mrs. Bone. His only punishment was to be miscast a second time in a leading role. The play was Terence Rattigan's successful wartime comedy *While the Sun Shines*. The part, a big bombardier with a Texas accent, had been played in the original production by Bonar Colleano.

Playing opposite him, and towering over him from a great height, was Leslie Howard's son Ronald. At one point Don was to leap across the stage clad only in a towel. Having acquired the native British colour (off-white), he doused himself in body make-up on opening night. As he made his dash past Ronnie, Don heard him singing a popular song under his breath. It was *Orange Coloured Sky*, except Ronnie changed it to *Orange Coloured Guy*.

One Saturday, between matinée and evening performance, there was a brisk squall lashing the Brighton pier. A glamorous older woman, prominent on the local theatre scene, was kind enough to invite him to tea. She lived near the theatre, and it seemed such a long way to Mrs. Bone's, no matter how creative she was with potatoes.

In no time, he was enjoying hot crumpets and jam in front of a cosy fire. She suggested that he would be much more comfortable without all those wet clothes on, and he began to see her point.

The next day was Sunday and Don went home to London as usual. When he arrived at Park West he hugged Gloria so hard that he was afraid he might have crushed their offspring, and tried not to look as guilty as he felt.

Never mind *his* feelings — *I* was the one caught in the middle! However, there would be ample opportunity to express myself after leaving the womb.

13

GRACIOUS HEROINES, A HECKLER AND HEROES

THANKS to the new National Health Service, the obstetrical aspect of things seemed pretty well taken care of, but Donald was worried about the responsibilities of fatherhood and a third mouth to feed. Also, he knew that *Spring Thaw '51* was gearing up, and hated to miss it. Perhaps it was time to head home.

But then a legend asked him to lunch. Britain's most beloved comedienne, Gracie Fields, who lived on the isle of Capri, was in London to do another twenty-six week series for Radio Luxembourg. In those days there was no commercial radio, only the BBC, but many popular programs reached British ears from the pirate station across the Channel. The programs were recorded, quite legally, in London.

"Our Gracie" needed a new continuity writer because her old one, Bernard Braden, was far too busy. *Breakfast with Braden* was such a hit that "the Beeb" was launching an evening show as well, with the appropriate title *Bedtime with Braden*. He suggested Gracie hire Don Harron as his replacement. She looked him over, and agreed.

The Gracie series was a very pleasant assignment, thanks to the gracious nature of its star, one of the sweetest, and in some ways saddest, people Don has ever met. He had the impression she would rather be at home in Capri with her ex-garage mechanic husband than in London gladdening the hearts of millions.

Gracie introduced him to the man who paid the salaries, Harry Alan Towers. His firm, Towers of London, had a few other syndicated series, including one narrated by Orson Welles which featured classic potboilers like *Dr. Jekyll and Mr. Hyde*, played by the likes of Laurence Olivier. Welles complained about the quality of the scripts, which Don suspects were the work of Harry Alan himself. Towers hired Don to re-write some of Orson's narrations.

Acting jobs in radio came his way too. Andrew Allan had arrived from Toronto in hot pursuit of Dianne Foster, whose charms Don had shielded with such chivalry in Morley Callaghan's *To Tell the Truth*. Dianne was appearing in an Agatha Christie thriller at the Fortune Theatre.

At the BBC, Andrew was treated with the reverence due to one of the best radio producers in the world. They persuaded him to do a drama series while he was in town, which would only be for as long as Dianne's whodunnit lasted in the West End. Fortunately for Canada, it wasn't *The Mousetrap*.

Andrew hired Don for one of these episodes starring Sir Ralph Richardson. Don was so excited just to be in the same room with him, let alone share a microphone, that he was afraid he might disgrace himself (verbally speaking). To his amazement, "Sir Rafe," as everyone called him, fluffed and fumbled his way through every line of the first reading.

Don assumed all this foolishness would cease when they got in front of a microphone, but it just got worse. His first experience of pre-recorded radio was spent waiting patiently while Sir Rafe's speeches were taped many times over. A couple of weeks later, he and Gogie went to the theatre and watched the same Ralph Richardson give a flawless performance. Don couldn't believe the transformation, but he understood that it had to do with live chemistry.

In uncanny repetition of his first day in London, Donald then landed two jobs at the same time: writing for BBC radio and acting in a West End play. The play was *The Seventh Veil*, a stage version of the successful film, and the radio series was *Bedtime with Braden*. Working with Eric Nicol, Dennis Norden and Frank Muir was exhilarating, but Don says the funniest part of all was watching Dennis and Frank, both six-foot-four, climb in and out of their tiny sports cars.

They were also blessed with one of those wonderfully deadpan BBC announcers to read their public service messages: "During these warm summer evenings, with one's windows open, a radio turned up too loud tends to annoy one's neighbours. . . . Another good way is to throw a dead cat on his lawn."

Don marvelled at the way they could create mayhem. They would write a sketch about Bernie visiting the dentist that was clinical in its accuracy, then repeat the same sketch from inside the patient's mouth with dive-bomber and pneumatic drill sound effects. As junior writer on the team, Don was expected to contribute five minutes' worth of material to each show.

Meanwhile, his agent Olive had sent him to audition for *The Seventh Veil*. It felt strange to be standing alone on the stage, reading a love scene with the stage manager. There was not another soul to be seen in the darkened theatre, but he could hear whispering in the back rows. A crisp "Thank you," and he was back on the street. By the time he got home, Gloria and I were bouncing up and down with the news that he had won the part.

Of the film's three stars, only James Mason was missing from the stage version. His replacement, Leo Genn, arrived at the first rehearsal by limousine, complete with liveried chauffeur. Next, Herbert Lom pulled up in a Czech sports car called a Tatra (imagine a 1934 Airflow Chrysler mating with a Buck Rogers spaceship), and a pair of three-inch Cuban heels.

The heroine of the piece, Ann Todd, accompanied by a secretary named Cookie, was delivered by her husband, film director David Lean. Don expected her to be all platinum and ice, but she was warm and sunny. He still thinks of her as the most beautiful woman he has ever seen.

Don played her first love, a brash young American trumpet player who coaxes her out of her shell and teaches her to dance. It was a waltz, which definitely involved feet, so director Michael MacOwan, "a very understanding soul," arranged for lessons. Three mornings a week, a hearty lady would hup-two-three him around her studio like a Lippizaner on a short rein.

They opened in Brighton, next door to the Dolphin at the Theatre Royal. David Lean came down, bringing with him the actor who had played the small part of Herbert Pocket in his brilliant film version of *Great Expectations*. Don had seen the movie many times and of course recognized Alec Guinness right away. He told him how much he'd admired that performance, and Guinness seemed genuinely surprised that anyone had noticed.

Next stop was the Manchester Opera House. Donald was given digs near the theatre, but there was no time to check them out before the show. The performance was given a warm reception, but nothing like the mob scene that greeted the stars at the stage door afterwards. This was his first encounter with British film fans, and even though they weren't looking for him, he was tossed to and fro like a lifeboat on a stormy sea. When Herbert Lom came out a few minutes later, a chilling cry went up from the crowd, and Don managed to scurry away.

Next morning, having gone to bed hungry the night before, he headed straight for the dining room. The table was set for eight but there wasn't a soul in sight, so he sat down and waited for something to happen. Suddenly, a voice by his elbow said, "Wotchya, Cock!", which isn't rude if you're a Cockney. A little man, no more than three feet high, clambered onto a chair beside him.

Don asked him the question uppermost in his mind: when would breakfast be served? The man pointed to the sideboard right in front of them, piled high with food. He told Don to help himself to a plateful, and he'd have the same: "Bring me a li''le of wot yew fancy, Guv, do me fine."

By the time Don had finished piling lukewarm Toad-in-the-hole, kedgeree, eggs, bangers, bacon and cold unbuttered toast onto both plates, there were two more men at the table. While he wolfed down his breakfast, other tired-looking men wandered in, until all the seats were filled. Don couldn't help noticing that he was the only person in the room whose chin was higher than the table.

Either he was hallucinating, or Manchester was a very unusual place. It was still early morning, but after breakfast he decided to head for the theatre. From the window of the tram a billboard caught his eye that explained everything: "NOW PLAYING AT THE HIPPO-DROME — *SNOW WHITE AND THE SEVEN DWARFS.*"

Opening night in London, the Prince's Theatre was packed to the rafters. When Ann Todd made her first entrance, after six years away from the West End stage, the rapturous cries of "Welcome back!" made it more like a dockside reunion when the troops came home than mere entertainment.

The critics' response was lukewarm. They liked Ann Todd, but most found Leo Genn lacked the sadistic magic James Mason had brought to the role. They all agreed that the transition from screen to stage was far from complete, as evidenced by the frequently descending curtain between scenes.

The Seventh Veil closed just as I was getting ready for my opening. My parents had a guest for dinner that evening: Andrew Allan was at loose ends while his beloved Dianne was being murdered at the Fortune Theatre. He and Don were talking in the living room when Gloria informed them that the cheese soufflé was in the oven and her water had burst.

Andrew ran down to the street to hail a cab while Gloria collected her things. Don recalls, "My wife, who was a skittish creature about most things, became an enormously calm Mother Earth when the great event was upon her. . . . She seemed so elementally in control, it was as if the gods had sent down one of their wisest goddesses to take over her body."

At the swing-doors leading to the obstetrical wing, her parting remark was, "The soufflé should be done by the time you get back to the flat." It was, perfectly, and he ate almost the whole thing. Andrew was too nervous — whether about Gloria's ordeal or his impending marriage to Dianne Foster, he didn't say.

A baby girl arrived about one a.m. Don showed up with a bunch of flowers shortly after daybreak, and was forced to cool his heels in a fish 'n chip shop until visiting hours. They let him see the child first. "It looked like a walnut with a sea urchin perched on top," he says, "purple in hue and covered with black hair." My mother says I was a radiant pale peach, with a bit of blond fuzz on top, so they must have shown him the wrong baby.

Gloria looked pale, but then she always did, between the freckles.

She said not a word about discomfort or fatigue, just thanked him for the flowers and told him to run along and enjoy himself until it was time to bring the baby home.

He went back to the flat, wondering what to do with his last few days of freedom. Lo and behold, an invitation had arrived from Toronto critic Herbert Whittaker. He was going up to Stratford-on-Avon to review a double-bill of Shakespeare's best, and had two tickets. By the time post-partum depression set in, Gloria's husband had left town.

Wending their way past tea shoppes with names like "Where the Kettle Sings," Don and Herbert arrived at the theatre, which reminded Don of Vaughan Road Collegiate. They went to their seats early and, as there was no curtain, were able to admire the stage. It looked like the Globe Theatre in Elizabeth I's day. Herbert explained that the design, by a woman named Tanya Moiseiwitsch ("Mow-ZAY-a-vitch"), was part of a return to the "bare boards and a passion" approach he had already experienced in Dora Mavor Moore's production of *King Lear*.

Don also received a full report on *Spring Thaw '51*, which had been a great success, "although not as good as last year." Among the highlights was a take-off on Toronto's three major drama critics. Peter Mews played Whittaker of the *Globe*, which amused the real Herbert no end, Connie Vernon was the *Telegram*'s Rose Macdonald, and Lou Jacobi did a devastatingly accurate Nathan Cohen of the *Star*.

Between *Henry IV, Part 1,* and *Henry IV, Part 2,* Herbert led Don backstage to meet Leo Ciceri, the Montrealer they had just seen playing Pistol, Prince Hal's low-life companion. Leo showed them the sights, including a set being prepared for *The Tempest*.

Designer Loudon Sainthill planned a full-scale shipwreck, with lots of actors doing push-ups under a huge green and blue cloth to make waves. "I suddenly got an overwhelming urge to be part of such a company," Don recalls. All that fitness, and in a 16th-century setting — who could resist?

Two days later, on the train back to London, all he could think about was Shakespeare. He didn't want to do contemporary plays any more. He wanted to wear tights (I mean hose), stand with one foot placed carefully in front of the other, and speak in iambic pentameter.

Gloria and I were still in hospital, so he went to see Lena Horne at the Palladium. She was everything he had hoped for, but the opening act on the bill made an even deeper impression on him. A man named Bernard Miles came out. Don recognised the actor who played Joe in Lean's *Great Expectations*. He was dressed like a farmer and pushing an enormous wagon wheel which appeared to be heavily encrusted with bird droppings. He stopped, looked at it, and said: "Oi found this. Oi'm gonna take 'ee 'ome an' mike a ladder outen it." The future Lord Miles's topics that night included the two schools of thought on killing fleas (cracking them or drowning them in spittle) and his feud with the town librarian. She accused him of drunkenness after seeing his bicycle parked outside the pub all afternoon, so he left it leaning against her cottage all night.

To Don, this looked like even more fun than Shakespeare. His head was swimming with both possibilities, and he didn't know which way to go. In the meantime, other opportunities presented themselves.

Don says it was his idea to name the baby Martha, after his mother-in-law, and both parents agreed on Ann without an "e" for the middle name, in honour of the gracious lady who had showered me with gifts and agreed to be my godmother. Ann Todd came to visit, and brought her husband with her.

David Lean seemed more interested in Don's features than the baby's: "You did jolly well in that play at the Prince's. Have you ever done any film?" Don confessed he hadn't. "Well, you look awfully like Ann, and I was wondering if you'd be interested in playing her younger brother in this film we're starting next week." It was called *The Sound Barrier*, and their father would be played by Sir Ralph Richardson.

There was a sharp intake of breath from Gloria, followed by a flat refusal from Don. He said his British accent just wasn't convincing enough. As soon as Ann and David left, his shy, adoring wife hit the roof: "You just turned down a major role in a film directed by David Lean! Are you out of your mind?!"

Don was surprised. He thought she only cared about his writing career. "Look, Gog, I can play an English accent in Canada, but I'd be a nervous wreck trying to sustain one in England."

"But this is a *film*, you idiot, and these people are friends! I'm sure he would do take after take until he was perfectly satisfied that you sounded authentic. And you *do* look like brother and sister."

At this point the baby began to howl. Don blamed it on colic, but I like to think my young self was trying to say, "You jerk! She's right! Pick up the phone! Call David Lean! Don't be a fool!" I kept it up for a week, but he wouldn't listen.

Actually, the crying didn't stop until August, when my personal physician, Dr. M.M. Fisher, arrived from Gravenhurst, Ontario. He weighed me, had Gloria breast-feed me, weighed me again, and pronounced his diagnosis: while his daughter sat and read Jane Austen, his grand-daughter was drinking four times as much milk as she ought to.

The dear man had dropped everything and taken his first trip overseas since 1924. Don and Gloria conspired to force him to have a real holiday for a change. Don started by buying him a ticket to *The Little Hut*, starring Robert Morley, which he liked so much he saw it three times in one week.

London's leading "little" theatre (equivalent to off-Broadway in New York) was The Arts Theatre Club, run by a wonderful actor named Alec Clunes. Clunes held a new play contest, with himself, Christopher Fry and Peter Ustinov as judges, and they whittled the 997 entries down to a three-way tie.

One of the winners was *Poor Judas*, written by Enid Bagnold, in between *National Velvet, The Chalk Garden* and other hits. Don was given the part of a young officer in the Royal Canadian Engineers, but he was very unhappy about his lines. They sounded like a mixture of Americanisms and English upper-crustisms.

The director, Roy Rich, was a kind, sensitive fellow, and couldn't help noticing Don was miserable. "I'll get Lady Jones up from the Brighton for the day, and you can have a proper natter with her. She told me the character's based on an actual person."

"Lady who?"

Lady Jones was Enid Bagnold's married name. She took Don to

lunch, and he found her to be a delightful combination of his favourite Ediths, Evans and Sitwell. "Now, what's the difficulty, young man?" she asked brightly. He said he was sorry, but the character didn't sound like any Canadian he'd ever met.

"Oh, but I knew the young man quite well!" she protested. "He was billeted with me during the war, one of the most articulate, fascinating creatures I ever met. Died after D-Day, unfortunately."

"Might I ask his name, Lady Jones?"

"His name was Sanderson, Captain Graham Sanderson."

Donald almost choked on his turbot. "I knew him! He was my commanding officer in the COTC!" He could hardly believe it — the charming medical officer, the one who had told them "It's possible to get VD from a toilet seat, but it's a hell of a place to take a woman."

"The C.O. what?"

"It doesn't matter. But you're absolutely right, Lady Jones, he was everything you say he was." (He was also one of Mavor Moore's closest friends.)

"Well, how splendid. We both have happy memories! And naturally, young man, if you find any of my constructions faulty, you must amend them to suit." What a Lady. Don did just that, the way *he* thought Graham would have said them, and was very pleased with himself.

The performance that stole the show was a brief one by the legendary Maire (pronounced "Mary") O'Neill, a founder and mainstay of the great Abbey Theatre in Dublin. "She shuffled in and, without even trying, wiped the stage with all of us," Donald recalls. "A less charitable person might say she knocked us out with the gin on her breath, but it never affected her artistry."

During the run of *Poor Judas* at the Arts, there was a disastrous fire at the Abbey Theatre. Even Don's Northern Irish Protestant blood ran cold at the news. To poor Maire it was more like the loss of a child. After the show, she and Don repaired to the pub next door to drink the night away.

Until 11 p.m., when English pubs shut, he knocked back ginger beer while Maire sipped something stronger. He let her do all the talking: it was music to his ears. She told him about the first-ever production of *Playboy of the Western World*, and how she'd learned her lines as Pegeen Mike: "Oi had a stoy in my oy, that toime, and Sean" (referring to the play's author, John Millington Synge) "Sean had to rade me me loines as I coodn't see the print on the page. And radin' those luvly loines to each uther, we fell in luv, shore there was no help for it." Don asked if she still remembered the words. "Acch, Oi doubt it," she said, "One or two, mebbe."

He recalled some for her, the Playboy talking to Pegeen Mike, from the New Play Society's very first production: ". . . and making mighty kisses with our wetted mouths, or gaming in a gap of sunshine, with yourself stretched back unto your necklace, in the flowers of the earth."

He would have stopped there, but Maire came back with Pegeen Mike's reply, softly: "I'd be nice so, is it?"

They may not have been word-perfect, but the scene flowed effortlessly between them right to the end. Then they laughed, cried and laughed some more, drinking toasts to the dear old Abbey Theatre, in loving memory of Sean Synge.

The night after *Poor Judas* closed, the Arts Theatre Club had a fire of its own. Quite a few actors, including Don, volunteered to salvage what was left of the stage. As they chipped, scrubbed and sanded away at the charred remains, he couldn't help comparing British "pluck" in action to the spoiled life of a radio actor he had led in Toronto.

In spite of himself, he ended up in *The Sound Barrier*. It was not the big part he'd turned down, but the small part of an Air Transport Command Officer, appearing in one short scene. David Lean assured him that the character could be an American or a Canadian, to forestall any attempt to chicken out on the grounds that he couldn't do a convincing American accent *either*.

He was given a dressing room in an old house on the lot at Shepperton Studios. While he waited for his call, Don was treated to the most hideous caterwauling from the dressing room next door. He learned later that it was created by the owner of the Harley Davidson motorcycle parked outside, who swooped in every morning dressed like a Hell's Angel. Sir Ralph Richardson had taken up the violin.

During wardrobe and make-up, Don was told that Lean had made his Dickens masterpieces there — "inside this very soundstage," the make-up man assured him, and he'd been with Lean since *Brief Encounter*.

"Well, not the *whole* thing inside," Don corrected him, having seen both films so many times he knew them by heart. "Not the graveyard scene in *Great Expectations* with the cows in the marsh, or the storm scene outside the orphanage in *Oliver Twist*!"

"All of it," the man replied. "In them days David never stirred a foot outside to get a shot. It weren't really 'til *Passionate Friends*, when him and Ann fell in love in Switzerland, that he took a breath of fresh air." He's certainly had lots of it since, with *Bridge on the River Kwai*, *Lawrence of Arabia* and *A Passage to India*.

When an assistant director ushered Don into the studio, he found himself alone with the director, a cameraman, a lighting man and Nigel Patrick (playing Ann's husband), the only other actor in the scene. He suddenly got very nervous.

"Hello, Donald old boy, know your lines yet?"

"Yes sir, Mr. Lean."

"It's David, dear heart. Feeling a bit chilly?"

"No." He was trembling like a leaf.

"Oh, a bit nervy perhaps. Look, just to relax ourselves, let's just say the lines once or twice. Old Nige here has got a bit of the wind up because he forgot today's matinée day, and he has to bugger off in about an hour. Just do the old lines the way you must have gone over them this morning in your bedroom."

Nigel grinned, "And if you forget the bloody words, just make 'em up. I always do." They ran through the scene, and to Don's surprise it felt very relaxed and easy.

"Now that was just splendid, Donald. I knew it would be," said Lean. "In fact, I had my cameraman turning all the time you were talking. I'm sure it's going to look just right in the dailies, dear boy, so there's no reason why you can't go home right now. I'm sure old Nige will give you a lift into town." And that was that — another lesson in non-acting from a master.

Back in London, the only work he had was writing for *Bedtime with Braden*, which made him feel like a failure even though it paid well and he loved doing it. He handled this by having a fight with his wife for wanting him to be a writer. I ended it by out-screaming the pair of them. When Donald returned from pushing my pram around the park, there was a message for him to call Christopher Fry.

Fry without an ''e'' was being hailed as a born-again Shakespeare for bringing imagery and verse drama back to commercial theatre. Don called, as fast as he could get to the phone. A mellifluous voice answered, "Hello, Mr. Harron, this is Kit Fry. Have you by any chance seen my play *A Sleep of Prisoners*?"

Don blushed to confess that he hadn't. It was playing in a bombed church somewhere off Regent Street, the high cultural event of the West End season. Fry said, "There'll be a ticket for you tonight. Do go along and have a peek, and tell me if you're interested in the part of Peter Able."

Fry's play was a kind of dramatic string quartet played by four soldiers, captured by the enemy in some war of the future. Locked up in a ruined church for the night, they dream fitful dreams drawn from Old Testament stories: Cain and Abel, Abraham and Isaac, David and Absalom, and good old Shadrach, Meschach and Abednego. It was an awesome assignment, much more demanding than the film role he'd fled from, but somehow he wasn't afraid of taking chances on stage, in front of a live audience.

Stanley Baker, Leonard White and Hugh Pryse gave splendid performances, and Denholm Elliott was "absolutely brilliant" as Peter Able. The part also called for him to play Abel, Isaac, Absalom and one of the three guys emerging from the fiery furnace in asbestos underwear. This was Don's idea of Heaven, and the part was his for the asking, no audition necessary. It was like a miracle, of Biblical proportions.

The next day he learned how this miracle had come about. Kit Fry had seen him in *Poor Judas*, when judging with Clunes and Ustinov, and was so impressed that he suggested him to *A Sleep of Prisoners'* director Michael MacOwan, who had already worked with Don in *The Seventh Veil*. These had both been small, undemanding roles, a fraction of what would be required of him as Able, but Fry and MacOwan agreed that young Harron was their man.

Don learned two other things that surprised him. He was not being hired for the West End, but for Broadway. The entire production was going to New York, minus Denholm Elliott, who was staying behind because he had just landed an important role in a major motion picture: playing the part Don had turned down in David Lean's *Sound Barrier*.

Years later, I didn't even recognise my own parent the first time I saw *The Sound Barrier*. The character who struck me most was Ann Todd's younger brother, played by Denholm Elliott. He was such a touching figure, even before he crashed to his death — a young man trying desperately to please his father by becoming a pilot, even though he gets airsick. I thought, "How sweet, just like my father."

Before leaving for New York, the Harrons indulged in an orgy of theatre-going with Dr. Fisher, who had decided to stay on to help with the packing and accompany his daughter and grand-daughter to Canada. (It was high time the other grandparents had a chance to adore me in person.) While they were out having a good time, I was left at home with my babysitter, Norman Jewison, who came whenever they asked him and didn't cost a shilling. I usually went to bed early, leaving Norman to get on with writing comedy sketches for BBC Radio's *Starlight Hour*.

One night, the lazy good-for-nothing watched the Sugar Ray Robinson-Randy Turpin fight on television instead. Mother never let me watch anything violent, but after the noise woke me up, I sat on Norman's knee for the closing rounds. In all the excitement he was only vaguely aware of a warm feeling flowing between us, that later turned impersonally cold. I had overflowed my diapers and peed all down his leg.

On our last night in London, my mother, father and grandfather went to opening night of the Old Vic's '51-'52 season. My parents had been to its grand re-opening the year before, and Gloria had had the thrill of a lifetime: A little man walked to his front row seat just before curtain up. It was Winston Churchill. Don says "my left-wing leaning, Labour Party loving spouse leapt up and cheered and cried like any bobby-soxer at a Frank Sinatra concert at the Brooklyn Paramount."

This time, it was Don's turn to flip, and for a man who looked like General de Gaulle. The production was Shakespeare's *Tamburlaine*, and it marked the triumphant return of director Tyrone Guthrie to the Old Vic. Don had heard a lot about Guthrie, and admired his daring from afar, but this was his first live experience.

Tamburlaine is a demanding role even by Elizabethan standards. He never leaves the stage during the play's three hours of butchery and mayhem. Thumbing his nose at the theatrical establishment, Guthrie had chosen the most unfashionable actor in England: Donald Wolfit, considered the epitome of ham.

At one point, an actor was shackled and strung high up in the flies of the theatre. On the other side of the stage, a row of archers drew their longbows and took aim. There was a woosh of sound, and instantly their high-flying victim was stuck full of arrows. Guessing they must have been hidden in the folds of his costume and pulled by wires made it no less spectacular.

In another scene the King of Persia, played by Leo McKern, bashed his own brains out against the bars of his cage. Tamburlaine's queen rolled in on a chariot composed of the writhing, near-naked bodies of her slaves. Through it all, after years in exile, with a ghostly, almost Kabuki-white face, Donald Wolfit roared and reigned.

Presiding over this evening of savagery, oriental splendour and special effects was Tyrone Guthrie, the true king as far as Donald Harron was concerned. He was delighted to be Broadway bound, but the minute *Sleep of Prisoners* was over, he wanted to come back to London and work for Guthrie.

14

THE SHOCK OF RECOGNITION

THE day Don got the part in *A Sleep of Prisoners*, he committed the unusual extravagance of phoning his parents in Toronto. The conversation lasted less than a minute. Lionel had to phone Canada Steamship Lines in Quebec City, to tell them to get his wife Delsia out of her cabin and off the ship before it sailed for England.

Poor Dutzie. She'd never been further afield than Atlantic city on her honeymoon, but she'd been persuaded to take the plunge. The night before she left, the neighbours gave her a splendid send-off. She caught the train to Quebec City with great expectations and mass quantities of essential items unavailable in England, like Lux soap, soft toilet paper and Wrigley's Doublemint Gum.

Somebody else was also in mid-ocean. Lou Jacobi had been so encouraged by Don's letters, and so inspired by the comic material Don had sent him, that he was steaming to his side. Poor Lou didn't know a soul in London, and was quite devastated to find his intended partner had flown the coop.

Donald knew nothing of this as he kissed his wife and child good-bye at the airport. He boarded a Pan Am flight for New York with his director, Michael MacOwan, while Gloria and Murray Fisher, with the baby in a carry-cot, flew by Trans-Canada Airlines to Toronto.

Don's plane stopped at Shannon Airport, where he loaded up on duty-free chocolate bars. When it took off again he tried to sleep, but the plane was buzzing with ongoing reports of the World Series game in progress. He began to feel very alone, and wondered when he would see his little family again.

They made an unscheduled stop in Gander, Newfoundland, probably to refuel. No reason was given, but there was no cause for alarm. In 1951, planes didn't get hijacked or blown up by terrorists. Don ambled out of the plane to stretch his legs, yawning from lack of sleep.

Suddenly, he felt wide awake. Sitting on the tarmac right in front of him was a Trans-Canada Airlines North Star. He rushed over and asked the stewardess to show him the passenger list (try that today without a warrant). He and Gloria and Grandpa spent the next fifteen minutes having a joyful family reunion. I slept through the whole thing.

Back on Pan Am, breakfast was served. It was very small by Harron standards, so he fortified himself with a couple of chocolate bars. High blood sugar sent him straight to the land of Nod, and MacOwan had trouble waking him up when they landed in New York.

In order to hit Broadway in style, Donald was wearing his favourite suit. Pale grey turned out to be an unfortunate choice. He had fallen asleep sitting on one of the chocolate bars, and it had melted all over the seat of his pants. He was nervous about his Broadway debut, but not *that* nervous. At that moment, he was very glad he wasn't famous — no photographers were waiting.

The next morning Don and Michael MacOwan went to St. James Episcopal Church at Madison Avenue and 71st Street, where they would be playing. The only thing it had in common with St. Thomas's, the London venue, was that they were both churches.

St. Thomas's was a charming, dusty little parish church. Apart from some bomb damage, it had stayed its Romanesque self while the big city grew around it. St. James, on the other hand, was a gaudy neo-Gothic palace, built by the filthy rich for their own use. Don said, "My God, Michael, they'd never leave prisoners of war in a snazzy dump like this!"

MacOwan did not respond immediately. He walked up to the

dais under the high vaulting nave and began to recite the play's
prologue, ending with:

> "We are plunged into an existence
> Fantastic to the point of nightmare
> And however hard we rationalise
>   Or however firm our religious faith
> However closely we dog the heels of science
> Or wheel among the stars of mysticism
> We cannot really make head or tail of it
>   Thank God
> We are no more than partly aware
>   Of a little at a time."

From his pew halfway back, Don could barely make out one word
in three. No wonder the pulpit had a microphone, and a canopy
to baffle the sound. Michael said he'd be damned if he'd have his
actors wired for vocal enhancement, and tripping over their own
power cords. After the elaborate fight sequences, they'd be trussed
up like turkeys.

At this point their new producers walked in, wreathed in smiles.
Lucille Lortel and Luther Greene were convinced they had a sure-
fire hit on their hands. MacOwan informed them gently but firmly
that there were serious problems, and asked to see the sound man
immediately.

"We don't have one, Mike," Luther announced cheerily, "I just
love the way my voice bounces off these walls!" Lucille seemed much
more concerned with the show as a social event, and explained that
they'd never get the carriage trade if they moved downtown to some
cosier church in Greenwich Village.

The rest of the cast arrived two days later and were visibly appalled
by what they found. As the tension mounted, grumblings about
America and Americans began to flow thick and fast between the
two Welshmen, Stanley Baker and Hugh Pryse, and the two
Englishmen, Leonard White and their understudy from the original
cast, Peter Vaughan. Then they would all glare at Don Harron.
Donald was treated not as a new member of the cast but as an alien

intruder. He felt like a Nashville fiddler joining the Orford String Quartet.

It seemed appropriate that his first task was to learn the fight sequences, and even more apt that he was the one getting slaughtered both times. First Leonard White playing Cain slew him as Abel, then Stanley Baker as David made mincemeat out of his Absalom. In the London production, staged by a master sergeant-at-arms, these unarmed combats had been authentic but boring. Michael called in a ballet choreographer, and the pas-de-deux of violence which resulted worked splendidly.

They were blessed with a brilliant lighting man, Abe Feder, who had worked with Clifford Odets in The Group Theater. He found them an expert Japanese acoustician from Upper Manhattan. The two of them worked feverishly overhead, trying to turn a mock-cathedral into a theatre.

Meanwhile, the cast shouted their way through rehearsals. The animal cries they were called upon to utter, especially in the fiery furnace, sounded great bouncing off the walls. The only thing missing was the subtle magic of Kit Fry's verse, lost in the Gothic rafters.

One day the celebrated photographer Eugene Smith showed up to take pictures for LIFE Magazine. The session lasted over eight hours, but they didn't mind. Don found out later his face almost made the cover but lost out at the last minute to Ginger Rogers in a red dress and a flop play. Still, it turned out to be a spectacular spread, with far-reaching results.

The two previews went amazingly well. Before they opened, their four faces appeared on the front page of the *Sunday New York Times* drama section, in an elegant Harry Hirschfeld cartoon. Most of Broadway's British contingent had already been backstage to congratulate them. Don ought to have been feeling better.

He remembers nothing of the opening night performance. What stands out in his mind is that the audience was full of old friends. To his surprise and delight, John and Claire Drainie, Lloyd and Ruth Bochner, Mavor and Dilly Moore had come down from Toronto; Anna Cameron, Toby Robins and John Atkinson had popped up from winter stock in Bermuda; Vincent Tovell from CBC at the UN

was there, and even Fletcher Markle had delayed his return to
Hollywood to be in the cheering section.

Everyone was there but Gloria, which seems very odd. She and
I were in Gravenhurst — I suppose because I was still hooked on
mother's milk. Everyone else went over to Sardi's to await the critics'
verdict.

Very few appreciated the play. Even Walter Kerr complained that
"It is couched in words that must be picked over in the library before
they can be made to yield much profit." Quite a few criticized the
venue, but all of the reviewers praised the four performers to the
skies. Baker, Pryse and White felt a sense of outraged loyalty to their
play and their playwright. When they saw that Don was just as
furious as they were, they began to think he might be an okay guy
— I mean a decent chap — after all.

A *Sleep of Prisoners* lasted five weeks in New York. By then,
thanks to Eugene Smith and *LIFE*, they had received offers from
churches all over the United States. They set off to tour the country, and take Fry's message to the people.

There were times when Don got tired of being in a play that had
to be explained to everybody afterwards. He found himself doing
this often, sometimes on Sunday from the pulpit of the church where
they played the rest of the week. One Saturday he delivered the
main address in a synagogue, Chicago's Temple Sholem.

They performed in theatres, churches, universities, the chapel of
the Pennsylvania College for Women, even a burlesque theatre in
Youngstown, Ohio. The further they got from Broadway, the better
audiences understood the play. By far the best places were the non-
conformist chapels. The little flat-roofed wooden structures had
perfect acoustics and wonderful audiences. To them it was a dramatic
experience, not a cultural must-see, and Biblical references required
no explanation.

Everybody in the cast was homesick. Hugh Pryse landed a part
in a movie and was replaced by Clarence Derwent, after whom are
named the Derwent Awards for promising Broadway newcomers.
Derwent's role called for him to occupy the top upstage bunk. From
there, his last line was supposed to be a rooster's crow awakening
mankind to a new dawn. Unfortunately, Clarence had a tendency

to eat a heavy lunch before matinées. More than once, Stanley Baker
on the bunk below had to wake him up with a good thump before
mankind could get going again.

Don's wife and child joined the tour in Washington, D.C., where
I immediately came down with the measles, forcing both parents
to conclude that touring was no way to raise a family. My career
as a backstage baby was ruined.

Mother took me back to Gravenhurst for safekeeping, and then
rejoined the tour. It lasted four months — any longer, and my father
would have been crippled for life. In those carefully orchestrated
stage fights, he'd slammed down on the same knee night after night,
plus matinées, for almost six months altogether. A wooden stage
would have been hard enough, but those cold stone church steps
gave him a permanent case of "water on the knee," a painful
reminder of his sacrifice at the altar.

After the play ended, Don and Gloria spent a week in New York,
in a hotel off Times Square. The room cost $85 for the week, cheap
in both ways and dirty to match, but they spent most of their time
going to the theatre.

From the fleabag hotel they went back to clean and tidy Toronto
for the spring, and *Spring Thaw '52*. Delsia Harron and Martha
Fisher presented them with a household of solid '30s furniture, collected from relatives, and Gloria found a duplex on St. Clair Avenue
to put it all in. Apart from requiring constant care, I had nothing
to do with it.

Don hadn't been home in two years, and there were many
changes. Canadian television would be starting in the fall, and a
lot of radio actors who hadn't bothered to do badly paid live theatre
were suddenly anxious to strut their stuff onstage.

A new company called the Jupiter Theatre was sharing the
Museum Theatre with the New Play Society. When Don arrived they
were in the midst of a wildly successful run of Lister Sinclair's play
Socrates, starring Frank Peddie. Hundreds of people were being
turned away each night for a Canadian play about an ancient Greek.
Could it happen today?

Don had been in the radio version, playing the witty, sophisticated
and inebriated playboy Alcibiades. In the Jupiter production a

newcomer had taken his place, and in Don's view was doing a much better job. His name was Christopher Plummer.

The New Play Society planned to do a production of Shaw's *Arms and the Man*, and Don was offered the best part, Bluntschli the realist. Hearing that Laurence Olivier had made quite a splash as the other male lead, Don insisted on playing Sergius the romantic instead. Robert Christie was recast as Bluntschli.

Reverting to his home town habits, Don cheated on his NPS rehearsals to do radio work on the side. He made it to a CBC rehearsal for *The Man of Mode*, a Restoration play by George Etheredge, just on time. Chris Plummer breezed in half an hour later, charmed his way out of a stiff fine, walked up to the microphone and effortlessly assumed the air of a 17th-century rake. Don felt sick with jealousy. The next thing he knew, Plummer had charmed him out of twenty-five bucks, "till next time."

The combination of rampant insecurity and self-miscasting made Harron go overboard in *Arms and the Man*. He suspects from the review that Herbert Whittaker knew about him switching roles with Bob Christie: "Seeing that he could not top Mr. Christie in robust romanticism, Harron has conceived the character of Sergius in the vein of high burlesque. Never such a snapping to attention, such deft flourishes, such facile embraces!"

He says the critics were far too kind, but he couldn't have been *that* bad because the Jupiter Theatre cast him opposite Lorne Greene and guest star Honor Blackman in their next production, Sartre's *Les Mains Sales*, translated into English as *Crime of Passion*.

Don spent his nights assassinating Lorne Greene for cuckolding him with Honor and his days writing sketches for *Spring Thaw '52*. Remember his solemn promise not to perform in his own work? He agreed to contribute five sketches that year, and cast himself in every one of them.

The final piece was aptly called *The Crowning Version*, a parody of *The Browning Version* by Terence Rattigan. Don's only comments in his memoirs were that he played Professor Tuck-Hamper, Norman Jewison played his pupil Pablum, and that Gloria "didn't think too much of my making fun of such a noble work". (My mother says, "This is a base calumny. I *loved* that sketch.")

Perhaps Father expected her to object because of the name given to Tuck-Hamper's "bitterly pretty young wife", played by Pegi Brown. The Mavor Moore archives yield the following exchange between Tuck-Hamper and another pupil, Wesley Stinks, played by Peter Mews:

STINKS: You and Gloria. It hasn't been much of a marriage, has it?
TUCK: No, it has not. You see, the trouble all started on our honeymoon.
STINKS: You mean . . . ?
TUCK: Yes; like a fool I took her with me.

In Don's scripts even the stage directions have puns, never heard by the audience:

GLORIA: *(coming out of Haydn and grabbing him passionately)* Oh Wesley, my little Bunsen Burner . . .
STINKS: Now, Gloria, please . . .
GLORIA: We cannot go on like this. It's bigger than both of us.
PABLUM: *(who has stopped to stare)* Oh, really?
STINKS: We mustn't say things like that with this student in the same room.
GLORIA   Why not? He's *older* than both of us. Come closer to me . . .

Stinks and Gloria repair to the Tuck-Hampers' bedroom offstage. At the end, Pablum promises the professor a little something to remember him by — he goes into the bedroom, closes the door and fires two shots:

TUCK: *(his back to the bedroom door)* Come in.
PABLUM: *(enters revolver in hand.)*
TUCK: Come, Pablum, the gift, the gift.
PABLUM: Oh sir, I get carried away.
TUCK: Good. . . . When?
PABLUM: You don't understand, sir. Look.

Very slowly Tuck-Hamper turns, looks into the bedroom, walks
to the far side of the stage and adjusts his spectacles:

TUCK: *(opening his arms and beaming)* Pablum, you shouldn't
         have done it.

(CURTAIN)

Don was in the middle of writing this when Mavor Moore dropped
by. He wanted Don to do a solo number in the show: "He knew
I couldn't sing or dance, but he wanted me to write myself a
monologue. The subject matter was up to me."

He remembered his dismal failure as a stand-up comedian in
Montreal. As Don Harron, without a mask, he had come off as a
young smart-ass, which wasn't funny. He thought about the way
everyone laughed when he tried to be serious with a rural accent
in Harry J. Boyle's *The Inheritance*, and about Bernard Miles cracking
fleas at the London Palladium. He would disguise himself as a
farmer!

For his setting he chose the Canadian National Exhibition, where
he'd seen many of those "red-faced, white-foreheaded fellows"
inspecting the back ends of quadrupeds in his old sleeping quarters,
the Horse Palace and the bull pen. "In the midst of all the hoopla
of the midway, and the commercial huckstering in the Pure Food
Building, these shy guys seemed to me what that big fair was really
about."

The accent was the one he'd been playing with for years, but it
had taken on a new meaning since meeting the Fisher family. Gloria
didn't sound like that, but her father did. So did her grandmother,
her Aunt Eleanor and her Uncle Allan, who all lived in Gravenhurst
but came from a farm in Huron County.

The first time her grandmother met Don she had looked him
over and asked him only one question, fiercely: "R'you a
Cawthlic?!" His mumbled answer that he was a prostitute had
seemed to satisfy her.

Dr. Murray Fisher was a wonderful storyteller, when coaxed, and
Don never tired of hearing his voice. He decided to make his

Don on bended knee to the great Katharine Cornell in Christopher Fry's *The Dark is Light Enough* (1955). (That's Tyrone Power at left, wondering why he didn't stick to movies.)

As Bassanio in Tyrone Guthrie's "anti-Gentile" *Merchant of Venice* at Stratford-on-Tario (1955). Portia was played by Frances Hyland, whom Don first met in London in 1950, while both Canadians were performing in the West End production of *A Streetcar Named Desire*.

Don tells Martha, "We mock the thing we are to become."

The first musical version of *Anne of Green Gables* was a 90-minute special on CBC-TV (1956). In the buggy are Toby Tarnow as Anne and John Drainie as Matthew, flanked by adaptor Don Harron (left) and composer Norman Campbell (right).

A portrait of the author as a spoiled brat—Martha Harron in Stratford, Connecticut (1956), while her father was performing at the "other" Shakespearean Festival for director John Houseman.

Friedman-Abeles. Reprinted with permission from CAVETT, by Dick Cavett and Christopher Porterfield, published by Harcourt Brace Jovanovich

Rehearsing with Katharine Hepburn and a bit player named Dick Cavett at Stratford, Connecticut in 1957.

One of Don's most treasured possessions—a self-portrait of Katharine Hepburn in *The Merchant of Venice* (1957) inscribed "To my Bassanio from his Portia".

In 1957 Don Harron went to Hollywood and signed a movie contract because Katharine Hepburn told him to. He is seen here with Gloria and daughters Mary (left) and Martha in their house on Summitridge Drive.

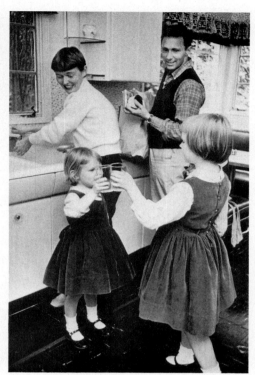

When *Look Back in Anger* opened in Cleveland on December 28, 1958, producer David Merrick phoned to say, "Mr. Harron, you saved all our asses last night." Pippa Scott played his long-suffering wife.

On location for *The Best of Everything* (1959) with author Rona Jaffe and co-star Martha Hyer. Few people know that Don Harron provided the inspiration for Ms. Jaffe's next novel, *Mr. Right is Dead*.

Don married Virginia Leith in 1960. She became a star overnight in Stanley Kubrick's first feature film, *Fear and Desire*, but is best remembered for her ninth movie, *The Brain that Wouldn't Die*, in which she played the title role.

Don in his "Ginger Rogers" wig, playing Christian in *Cyrano de Bergerac* on NBC's *Hallmark Hall of Fame* (1962).

Kate Reid, Eric House and Don Harron up to no good in the title role of Mavor Moore's *The Ottawa Man* at the Charlottetown Festival (1966).

George Wotton

Norman Campbell recalls: "When Alan Lund was mounting our musical *Turvey* at the Charlottetown Festival in 1966, I had to pursue Don to his dressing room to run down routines for the score. *Buy a Drink for Old Mother*, sung riotously by Kate Reid (above), was written a bar at a time with Don rushing out to deliver a scene from *The Ottawa Man*, then back to say 'Where were we?' then onto the stage for a few minutes, then back."

The cast and crew of *Spring Thaw '67*, including Peter Mews and Barbara Hamilton at the back, Doug Chamberlain on the left, Dinah Christie, Diane Nyland, Dean Regan, Ron Tanguay, and author Don Harron hiding unsuccessfully behind Catherine McKinnon's mini-skirt.

character from Parry Sound because he loved the way Murray said it, but the expression on his face came from the back end of a chicken, from his days on the Farm Service Force.

His farmer had no name, but talked about a friend of his named Charlie Farquharson: "He don't know the meaning of the word 'crooked.' Course there's a lot of other words Charlie don't know the meaning of either." Don had overheard Murray Fisher talking on the phone to the real Charlie Farquharson, the distinguished head of the Ontario Medical Association, and fell in love with the name.

For a costume, he went over to his parents' place and borrowed an old shiny blue serge suit of his father's, a bit short for him at the wrist and ankle. In the basement, he found a cardboard Indian head-dress with a few limp neon-coloured feathers still sticking out of it, and the letters "C.N.E." across the front. Perfect.

For props, he added a couple of shopping bags full of gew-gaws and samples from the "Poor Feed Buildin'." He says the image was really himself at age ten, coming back from the big fair with everything free that was offered and having spent, except for his car fare, the princely sum of thirty-five cents.

On opening night the little four-minute bit, simply entitled *Th' Ex,* was the last thing on his mind. There were far more complicated items on the *Spring Thaw* menu. Second on the bill was his *Spring Flaw*, about the annual opening-up-the-cottage and its attendant disasters. Don wrote it, but Jane Mallett contributed her real-life experiences and unerring eye for detail. Norman Jewison played her son, and Peter Mews her husband:

(HUSBAND BRINGS IN HIS MOTHER, DRESSED IN FUNERAL BLACK WITH MOURNING VEIL, THE CORPSE AT THE FEAST.)
HUBBY: I'm afraid Mother's not feeling too well, Verna. She must have eaten something that didn't agree with her.
WIFE: Don't be silly, Harold. It wouldn't dare.

"Mother," who did not speak but swigged Lydia Pinkham's and whined a lot, was Don Harron in drag. He wore the veil mostly so Jane wouldn't see him lip-synching her lines.

His next contribution was *Ad Finitum*, a pastiche of commercial slogans as written by hacks like Shakespeare, Wilde and Wagner. For a bakery, "Where is fancy bred?" At the drycleaners, "My Romeo vows to press his suit." Tristan and Isolde sang the praises of Alka-Seltzer to the tune of *Ride of the Valkeries:* "Mein stomach hertz!" etc.

As Don had hoped, his appearance as the farmer caused ripples of laughter. Then he opened his mouth. Every word he uttered through those pursed lips caused waves of hilarity for which he was totally unprepared. It was almost scary. They were laughing so hard at the way he was talking, it didn't seem to matter *what* he said. Was it ridicule, or could it be what critic Edmund Wilson called "the shock of recognition"?

There was no time to worry about it. In addition to everything else there were two full-scale musical parodies that year. Mavor Moore's RCMP horse opera à la Gilbert and Sullivan, *G. and S. on the G-G*, was the rousing closing number. Ending the first half, right after *Th' Ex*, was Don's *Guys and Squaws*:

The curtains open on an *Oklahoma*-like scene. Hero Curley Bonspiel sings:
>   Oh what a beautiful opening,
>   Oh what a musical play!
>   Welcome to old Manitoba,
>   Turn left when you reach Hudson's Bay. . . .

He leads the settlers in a rousing chorus of:
ALL: Ma-a-a-a-a-a-a-nitoba.
CURLEY: At the corner of Portage Street and Main.
>   Now let's shake a leg,
>   To build Winnipeg,
>   'Cause we need a place to store the grain!
ALL: Mani. . . toba Mani . . . toba Mani . . . toba
CURLEY: We know we belong to the East,
>   And the East treats us just like a beast!
>   We're shoutin'

ALL: Yi!
          I Yi Yi Yi Yi Yi Yi!!
CURLEY: We're stuck with you Manitoba.
ALL: Manitoba. . . . Yeah man!

After Curley's duet with Annie Oakville, called *Doin' What Comes Nationally*, the scene changes to an Indian encampment. Coureur-des-bois Emile Dufront and his Indian maiden Nellie Floorbrush sit by a campfire drinking liquor out of a jug and smoking pipes vigorously. They sing:

NELLIE: I love you a bushel and a quart
          A bushel and a quart and I'll have another snort.
EMILE: Have another snort, 'cause I'm sure it wouldn't hort.
NELLIE: Sure it wouldn't hort, if I have another snort. How 'bout you??
EMILE: How 'bout you??
NELLIE: Just a wee dram, I try to stick to Seagram!
EMILE: I love you, a tipple and a sniff,
NELLIE: (RISING) A tipple and a sniff. . .
          And I think I'm getting stiff.
          SHE SITS DOWN. THEY KISS. SHE SUDDENLY BREAKS AWAY.
NELLIE: Wait, white man. What was big frightening noise just now??
EMILE: That was you and me singing. (BACK TO CLINCH)
NELLIE: Wait, white man! We must not do this. You and I, we are not the same.
EMILE: Sure. You are woman. I am man. Is old-fashioned but I like it.

The first number after intermission was a song by Cliff Braggins called *THE R.M.C.*, lampooning the Canadian military establishment. It was so catchy the opening night audience clapped, cheered and demanded an instant replay. The four performers were so stunned they were unable to oblige.

This was followed by Donald's *TORONTOVIDEO*, purporting to give sneak previews of what Canadian television was going to be

like. In one segment, Don the announcer interviewed hockey star
Aubrey "Teeter" Totter, a Maple Leaf right-winger played by
Norman Jewison:

ANNOUNCER: You certainly are a perfect example of physical fit-
ness.
TEETER: (MODESTLY) I stink wit' healt'.
ANNOUNCER: You certainly do. . . . Well! I'm sure you must have
some health hints for the kids of today.
TEETER: Sure. Take my example kids. And don't drink nothin'
stronger than pop.
ANNOUNCER: Very sound advice too, gang!
TEETER: My Pop drinks nothin' but gin.

As the hugely successful run of *Spring Thaw '52* progressed, Don
became so addicted to Norman's infectious laugh that he would
ad lib shamelessly just to make him crack up. In *The Crowning Version*, Pablum would slowly crumple, giggling helplessly, until his
forehead hit the floor. These budding titans of Canadian culture
had come a long way since *The All-Varsity Revue* and football
sweaters reading "4" "Q" "2".

This was the last time *Spring Thaw* — or any other New Play
Society production for that matter — would be performed at the
Museum Theatre. In an ironic throw-back to the first *Thaw* theme
of *It'll Never Get Well if You Picket*, the Museum Theatre had
become a union-operated venue. Dora's dream was beset by
mercenary demands and commercial pressures on every side.

In the fall of 1952, the New Play Society School of the Drama
opened its doors, and Mrs. Moore carried on doing what she did
best: filling young hearts with a passion for the theatre, and all for
love. Her errant children, James Mavor and *Spring Thaw*, drew bigger
and bigger crowds in later years — at the Avenue Theatre, the Crest,
the Royal Alexandra, and finally across Canada. Errant co-star and
co-author Don Harron wasn't there.

15

THE TINY BOX AND KITCHEN
SINK DRAMA

ANOTHER Harron was in the works, conceived in that fleabag hotel off Times Square where the floor had been too dirty to walk on. The baby was due in January and this time it was going to Dr. Fisher, instead of the other way round. Gloria, foetus and I would go to Gravenhurst when the time drew nigh.

There was another birth that year, the birth of Canadian television. The first thing viewers saw on their screens opening day in Toronto was the CBC station's call letters upside down. The first human face to appear was not a talking head but a mug shot of the notorious bankrobber Edwin Alonzo Boyd. Canadian television was going to be different.

Boyd had escaped from the Don Jail, and one Toronto bank had already been robbed. A few days later, on the first edition of CBC's main variety show, *The Big Revue,* a farmer came on and talked about ''a bank gittin' robbed by outside parties — fer a change.'' He was wearing a suit that was too small for him and a cardboard Indian head-dress from the CNE.

The guest hosts of the show were Toby Robins and Don Harron, who had played the twins in Shaw's *You Never Can Tell*. On television his hair looked the same colour as hers even without lampblack. His co-star in the comedy sketches was Jane Mallett, doing old favourites from *Spring Thaw*.

He found the role of co-host much more difficult than the farmer. It was taped live, of course, and the switcher seemed to delight in

keeping the camera on him long after he had finished his announce-
ments. "Instead of looking poised and demure like Toby, I would
badger the camera to go away and leave me alone."

He was contracted to host *The Big Revue* once a month, but his
rural character was the big hit, and they wanted him to make regular
appearances too. The character's name had already chosen itself,
the one everybody remembered from the original monologue —
Charlie Farquharson. He couldn't go to the Ex forever, so Don settled
on the simplest of settings, something the CBC props department
could easily provide. It was a roadside mailbox, the classic signpost
of rural intercourse.

He needed a new costume, the kind of clothes Charlie would wear
on the farm, and he had a very clear picture of what he *didn't* want:
no straw hat, no corn-cob pipe, no bib overalls, no cliché object
of ridicule. He wanted to look like a real Canadian farmer.

Starting from the bottom up, he knew exactly the kind of footwear
he needed — a pair of Dr. Holt's, the boots all his older rural
customers used to ask for in Eaton's Annex. He found a pair in the
wardrobe department that fitted the bill, if not his feet. The pants
were his own, olive-drab, bought in New York, but the skinny
straight legs looked plenty comical sticking out of his Olive Oyl
specials.

He borrowed a couple of his father's old gardening shirts to wear
on alternate shows, lest folks think Charlie didn't wash. So far so
good, but more was needed to distinguish him from Don the host.
The image that kept coming to his mind was of his mother's cousin
Charles Hadden, in his peaked cap, buying a shawl-collar cardigan
in Sunderland on a Saturday night.

Charles Hadden only wore glasses for reading, but Don bought
a pair of wire-rimmed spectacle frames, without lenses, and Charlie
Farquharson wouldn't be Charlie without them. The floor manager
of *The Big Revue,* Norman Jewison, donated his father's old peaked
cap out of family feeling. His folks all talked like Charlie, including
his Aunt Valeeta Drain. He vouched for the cap's authenticity:
"Percy always wore it up Lefroy way when he pulled his cukes."

At the last minute Don found the sweater he was looking for —
on the back of the producer in the next studio, Norman Campbell.

Among other assignments, this Norman wrote and directed a kids' show starring a puppet, Uncle Chichimus, who bore a striking resemblance to CBC's chief television producer, Mavor Moore. Norman was hoping to add a puppet sidekick with antlers, named Mavor Moose.

Don asked if he could borrow the sweater, just to do his mailbox routine on *The Big Revue*. Charlie may not know the meaning of the word "crooked," but Don Harron sure does. He "forgot" to return the sweater that night, and he's forgotten ever since.

The first season of Canadian television was a workaholic's dream come true. With radio and theatre flourishing at the same time, it was almost like the life of an actor in London, doing a West End play at night, a film during the day and "telly" on weekends. Twenty-four-hour days were not uncommon. One Jupiter Theatre play had to hold rehearsals after 11 p.m.

Plenty of horrendous mistakes occurred on air, most often in the commercials, but Donald says he was personally responsible for the most intense two minutes of live television perhaps ever experienced.

Having scored a great success in Galsworthy's *Justice,* he had been cast as the younger son in Arthur Miller's *All My Sons.* He felt worn out after the dress rehearsal, and was nervous about the big confrontation scene with the father. Standing behind the canvas flats waiting for his cue, he closed his eyes and began going over the scene in his mind. Without realising it, he entered a trance-like state and when the cue came, he didn't hear it.

For what seemed like an eternity, nobody moved — not the cameraman, not the crew, not the two actresses waiting for him to interrupt them in mid-sentence, and certainly not Donald.

Until a stagehand was sent to fetch him, the camera stayed on a two-shot of the women. Not so much as one adlibbed cough passed between them. They just stared at one another with polite smiles on their lips and terror in their eyes. Afterwards, viewers objected not so much to the unbearable and interminable tension of the scene as to the fact that the unspoken conflict was never explained.

The Jupiter Theatre play with the midnight rehearsals was Christopher Fry's *The Lady's Not For Burning,* starring Christopher Plummer and Katherine Blake. Chris was back from Broadway, after a play that closed on opening night, and surprised Don by paying off his twenty-five-dollar debt without being asked.

"For once," Don had the pleasure of upstaging him. While Chris played a love scene with his leading lady, Don as the clerk washed the floor around them, reacting to their vows of love with innocent wistfulness. He says it was like any scene with a trained animal: "The pet always wins."

But the set designer managed to upstage everybody. Painter Harold Town had never done a set before, but he was more theatrical in person than most actors aspire to be onstage. He created a delightfully witty, gaudy, two-dimensional set that obstinately refused to stay in the background.

Don's second daughter made her debut on January 12, 1953, during the run of *The Lady's Not For Burning*. The tired father caught a midnight bus Saturday night to meet the new baby — not walnut-like, purple or covered in black hair, according to both parents.

It was Gloria's turn to choose a name, as Donald had chosen mine. Etiquette clearly indicated the other grandmother, who had three first names to choose from: Delsia, Ada and Maude. Gogie decided to call the baby Mary, after Don's sister. Martha and Mary, what a saintly combination.

Everybody made a tremendous fuss over her. I contained my rage, sort of, until we were back in the city. Gloria was cooing over the baby's filthy diapers, 'Oh you sweet, sweet little thing, your pooeys smell just like freshly baked bread!'' or some such drivel. Twenty-month-old Martha marched into the living room, defecated on the floor, and wiped it all over the television set. Lloyd Bochner, who happened to be visiting at the time, surveyed the scene and said brightly, "Oh, a critic!"

Against this background of domestic bliss, Donald continued to write and perform in a bewildering variety of shows. When he had time to add it all up, he was raking in a fortune of over $800 a week. With it he did selfish, extravagant things like buying his parents a new fridge and stove.

The acting community was buzzing with rumours of a Shakespearian festival in the works. Suddenly, Tyrone Guthrie

Himself appeared in Toronto. He stayed with Dora Mavor Moore, and spent his days interviewing actors in the rehearsal hall of the New Play Society, or holed up in the tiny office adjacent to it.

The mountain coming to Mohammed? It seemed too good to be true. When Donald was ushered into the office for his brief audience, "Tony," as everyone called him, seemed larger than the room. In fact, he was only about seven feet high.

"Understand you've had great success on the tiny box."

It took Don a few seconds to realise that Guthrie was referring to television, and nodded with what he hoped was a becoming modesty.

"Not really acting at all, is it?" the giant asked, rather sharply.

"No, I . . . uh . . . don't suppose it is," was Don's feeble reply.

"What sort of thing do you want to do at Stratters?"

"At what?"

"Stratford, Ontario."

Don blushed and stammered, "Oh, gosh, I don't know, I just want to be part of it. I'd be happy to sweep the stage."

Guthrie made a very brief scribble in his notes and said something like "Jolly dee. V grateful. Toodle-oo," and Don was out the door. He kicked himself all the way home for the way he'd behaved — fumbling, mumbling, gushing like a schoolboy! He probably *would* end up sweeping the stage after a performance like that. What a stupid thing to say. And him with four mouths to feed!

It wasn't long before the cast lists of both plays were announced, and Donald's name was on both. In *Richard III* he was to play Lovel, which he knew meant four lines at the most. "Oh well," he told himself, "it's still better than sweeping the stage."

He was not familiar with the comedy, *All's Well That Ends Well*, so he raced to the library to see what his Bertram character had to say. He gasped out loud. Bertram is *the* young man whose rejection of *the* young lady Helena forms the basis of the plot. Guthrie had made him the leading man, opposite Irene* Worth.

Several well-known actors were stunned to find their names omitted. Don later learned they had each told Guthrie that in view

* rhymes with Queenie

of the sacrifice involved in moving down to Stratford for the season, leaving all that lucrative radio and television work behind, they could only consider major roles.

Don was also surprised by the pay. He hadn't asked his New York or London agents to negotiate for him, because he was prepared to accept whatever pittance was offered. He would receive $400 a week, almost half what he'd been making in Toronto. He couldn't believe his good fortune.

He decided he needed more stage work, to prepare for the summer. A revival of *The Lady's Not For Burning* was already in the works, only four months after the first successful run. He persuaded Jupiter Theatre to do a quick production of *A Sleep of Prisoners* as well, just for a week at Easter.

Leonard White flew over from England, to raise Cain again with his Abel. For Stanley Baker's role, there was another future Avenger in town besides Honor Blackman: Patrick Macnee had dropped out of a tour in Toronto to do a television show, and stayed on for the rest of the season. To complete the quartet was W.H. Brodie, not an actor but a CBC executive who spent his days correcting announcers' pronunciation, but who turned in a wonderful performance.

They played in old St. Andrew's Presbyterian Church on King Street, a stone's throw from the Royal Alex. Patrick Macnee was a treat to work with, as of course was lion-maned Leonard White. Like any boom town, Toronto was attracting talented performers from all over, especially the U.K., and the invasion was beginning to cause some resentment. *Thaw* participant Gerry Sarracini remarked wistfully, "Oh to be in England, now that England's here!"

The day after *A Sleep of Prisoners* closed, the Harron family left for Stratford, or close to it. Because of the children, no accommodation was available in town. Perhaps my reputation as a television critic preceded me.

We were given lodgings on the farm of Ed and Phyllis Cardwell, a tolerant couple who incidentally provided a mine of future Farquharson material. Don commuted the three miles to and from town by bicycle every day.

The history of the Festival's precarious, monsoon-ridden beginnings has been so thoroughly documented, most recently by Tom Patterson, that it does not bear repeating here, not in the detail it deserves as one of Don's formative experiences. However, some of his most vivid memories may have escaped documentation elsewhere:

The cement had hardened during a rare dry spell, and rehearsals were being held on the actual stage. There was no tent to cover it yet, so Don sat on the brow of the hill to watch Alec Guinness rehearse his opening monologue as Richard III. A couple of local residents sat nearby.

They couldn't catch the words, because Guinness rehearsed in a whisper, but they could see him limping around and gesturing, with the peculiar spastic gait he had adopted for the cripple-who-would-be-king. "That'd be yer Alex Gwinnuss, yer movie man," said one old codger to the other.

"What's he doin' now?"

"He's practisin' on the platferm fer the concert they're gonna give."

"I can't hear a blame word he's sayin'."

"Oh, he's finished gittin' off all his words by heart. Now he's workin' up his gestures."

By the evening of the final technical rehearsal the tent was up and it was pouring buckets again, this time through the roof. Guthrie wandered about conducting operations in a huge yellow rain slicker, Jesus-type sandals and a pair of ancient woollen bathing trunks. When the string holding them up gave way, the shorts fell round his ankles. Without so much as a glance downward he stepped out of them, and carried on with the rehearsal like a dignified flasher.

Opening day dawned bright and clear, then turned hot and humid. There was one last run-through of the huge battle scene at the end of the play, orchestrated with blood-curdling zeal by the pacifist vegetarian, Douglas Campbell. The tent was like an oven. And they were wearing summer shirts and shorts. They wondered how it would be in their armour, velvets and brocades.

As usual, Don was the last to leave after the run-through. On his way out, he decided to take a final peak at the empty theatre.

To his surprise the stage was occupied by two incredibly tall, thin figures. Tony Guthrie and his wife Judy were sweeping the stage.

At intermission that evening, the Green Room backstage was rife with rumours. It was said that Brooks Atkinson had already left. In fact he hadn't arrived, but the seat next to his had been vacated by another New York critic, Walter Kerr. It was confirmed that several paying customers had already succumbed to heat prostration. The cast sweated in empathy.

Donald's upraised sword and battle cry would be the cue for the final free-for-all to begin. He rushed onstage but just before raising his arm, he paused and looked out into the audience. Something had caught his attention: it was a body, collapsed in the heat, being passed along a row to the St. John's Ambulance attendant waiting in the aisle. Even the patrons involved in passing the heavy, lifeless form had their eyes glued to the stage. "To hell with the critics," thought Don. "We're a hit!"

All's Well That Ends Well turned out to be an appropriate title. The second production was the bigger success, at least according to the New York critics. Don says Irene Worth was their guiding light, not only as an actress but as the only member of the cast who understood all of Shakespeare's jokes.

The Guthries left soon after the plays opened, ever onward and upward. Before leaving Tony Guthrie said something to Don that cut him to the quick: "I'm amazed you've come as far as you have with such a paucity of gesture!" He suggested Don go back to England and stretch his arms and legs in a first-rate repertory company. Needless to say, that's exactly what he did.

He kissed his family goodbye and headed for New York to catch the *Maasdam* back to England. Gloria and number one daughter would join him when he'd found a job in rep. Baby Mary would be left behind in Gravenhurst. Luckily for her she was too young to notice my insufferable gloating.

On his one-day stopover in New York Don met Chris Plummer for lunch at the Algonquin. Chris seemed hungry for news of Stratford, Ontario. "God, I would have given anything to be there!" He pounded the table for emphasis, sending escargot shells scattering in every direction. This young actor did not suffer from a paucity of gesture.

"Why the hell *weren't* you there?" asked Don from under the table, where he was hunting snails.

"For God's sake don't pick them up! What do you think waiters are for?" Plummer commanded in his most imperious, stentorian tones, adding peevishly, "Some cretinous eunuch in Montreal said I was a drunk, and I guess Guthrie believed him."

Don assumed he was referring to radio producer Rupert Kaplan. "Never mind, I'm going to see Tony in London. I'll tell him you're not a drunk . . . . Anyway, Plummer drunk is better than all the rest of us sober." He meant the last part sincerely.

Plummer cheerfully dismissed the offer: "Don't bother, dear heart, I'm talking to the Theater Guild about next summer in Stratford, Connecticut." Before they parted, Chris borrowed twenty-five dollars to pay for the lunch, "till next time".

When Don got to London the first thing he saw was *All's Well That Ends Well* at the Old Vic, with John Neville and Claire Bloom as Bertram and Helena. When the court jester Lavache began spouting his obscure Elizabethan witticisms, Don was glad Guthrie had eliminated the character in their production. Only one person in the whole theatre was laughing.

The solitary laughter was also a unique sound, "a sort of rich and rolling tinkle" that seemed strangely familiar. It was coming from the seat beside his. He turned and stared in amazement. He was sitting next to Irene Worth.

He took in Richard Burton's Hamlet at the Old Vic before taking tea with the Guthries. Their heads seemed higher than the low ceilings of their tiny rooms at Lincoln's Inn Fields. These were the same buildings referred to as the Inns of Court in *Henry IV,* and not much had changed.

In his Dickensian rabbit's warren lined with curling yellow pages, Tony searched for and somehow found the phone numbers and addresses for the Birmingham Repertory Theatre and the Bristol Old Vic. He explained that a London Old Vic contract would prevent Don from doing the next season at Stratford-on-Tario, so that was out of the question.

Guthrie sent his young protégé off to battle, armed with a letter of reference. Both companies said yes, and the pay was the same in both places, £10 a week to play and £5 to rehearse. Don chose Bristol because Douglas Campbell was in the company. They were friends, so Don wouldn't feel like a total outsider; moreover performing together presented a unique challenge. In *All's Well* at Stratford, Ontario, Campbell had played the braggart Parolles, and a couple of times had forgotten his lines. Not in the least perturbed, he would just throw in something from another play, usually *Macbeth*.

This would leave Don looking like the one who had forgotten his lines. He was determined that next time he would have the perfect comeback. After experimenting with all kinds of meaningless Bard-like phrases in iambic pentameter, he thought he had something that could deflect whatever Campbell might send his way.

He waited. Finally, one matinée in August, Dougie dried up completely. A second later, with a twinkle in his eye, he produced a line from *As You Like It*. This was it. Don made a sweeping bow, totally out of keeping with his modern-dress costume, and replied emphatically: "My dearest coz, an uséd car the government thereof!"

For a moment he thought he had Campbell by the short and curlies, but no such luck. Dougie just shrugged and left the stage, leaving Harron stranded once again. Don was looking forward to a rematch in Bristol.

Only when he arrived there and talked to the director did he discover that he had abandoned a flourishing career in Canada and crossed the Atlantic to play bit parts in the classics. He should have gone straight back to Toronto, but he stayed.

In *Antony and Cleopatra*, dangerous Dougie was Antony, while Don was the messenger Cleopatra beats up for telling her that Antony has gone and married another woman. "He deserved to be beaten for staying," says Gloria.

He roomed at the Bristol YMCA and, between rehearsals, looked for a flat to house his wife and child. On the edge of town he saw the famous Clifton suspension bridge built by Isambard Kingdom Brunel. Next to it stood the Royal Spa Hotel, followed by a row of 18th century rooming houses known collectively as Prince's Buildings. He went in.

The landlady showed him a ground floor flat overlooking the Avon

River, which had to be a good sign. It was not equipped with ev mod con, she admitted, but the lav-with-bath had a beautiful stained glass ceiling. Then she showed him her pride and joy: one of the panes in the front windows bore the letter "G". "Garrick," she said simply. Imagine, David Garrick living in a suburb of Bristol, and leaving his initial on the window! Don signed a six-month lease on the spot.

That wasn't nearly as dumb as his next move. He bought a book on Elizabethan hand gestures, representing every emotion of the human heart. He vowed to keep it by his bedside and memorize at least one emotional position a night. It was just like the old codger on the hillside had said, he'd finished "gittin' off all his words," and now he was "workin' up his gestures."

Fortunately it didn't take the rest of the cast long to talk him out of this fool's errand. They told him he looked like a Cub Scout practising semaphore with imaginary flags.

Don says the Bristol Old Vic's '53-'54 season is now thought of as an "amorphous interregnum" between the departure of John Neville and the arrival of Peter O'Toole. They were a cheerful, easy-going lot, and seemed to take the games of "shove ha-penny" backstage as seriously as the high drama out front. Nevertheless it was a very talented company, including Alan Dobie, Eric Porter, and a young singer from the West of England Light Opera Company who had never acted before, named Joan Plowright. The actor who seemed to have the most potential, in Don's view, was an intriguing young man named Patrick McGoohan, who later became known as television's *Secret Agent,* and *The Prisoner.*

Gloria and child arrived in due course, and the first thing we wanted was a hot bath. The landlady only permitted hot bath water once a week, so we waited for the lucky day. Unfortunately, the bathroom was four stories high; the beautiful skylight ceiling was right up on the roof. Body heat was sucked instantly up the giant flue, and the tepid water was cold before it hit the tub. We spent the next eight months taking turns bathing in the kitchen sink, which was fine by me.

Sitting in his neo-Dickensian rabbit's warren lined with curling yellow papers, an older and wiser Don Harron wrote:

"Looking back, I think a special medal should be struck for the wives of itinerant actors. Having stuck my wife *sans* car on a farm three miles outside of Stratford, I had now succeeded in banishing her to a suburb of Bristol where the nearest cultural institution was not the Old Vic but the Zoo."

My mother's comment on this is: "That whole eight-month expedition to the Bristol Old Vic, leaving our baby in Canada, was absolutely insane. Why did we do it? Just because Tony Guthrie said so?" (This is a rhetorical question.)

Be that as it may, the Clifton Zoo suited two-and-a-half-year old Martha just fine. I took my father there every week, rain or snow, and first stop was the choc-ice man. Mother's weekly treat was buying the latest *New Statesman* and *Nation* to read, but then she'd always been a cheap date.

16

PROGRESS BY PERVERSE PSYCHOLOGY

URING the run of *Comedy of Errors*, in which Don was playing yet another bit part, Pinch the Conjurer, a BBC friend happened to see the show. Ronnie Hill was in Bristol visiting his sick mother and recognised Don, in spite of the fake nose and beard. He went backstage afterwards, said he was preparing a comedy revue for a London theatre called The Watergate, and asked if Don would be interested in contributing some material.

Having quite a bit of time between Pinches, Don set to work and turned out three or four sketches in a couple of days. The results were enthusiastically received, first by Ronnie Hill and then by London audiences. Don says their success was due to the talented comedienne who starred in them, Beryl Reid, but he's just guessing. He never had a chance to see the show.

He was too busy in Bristol, performing in a new musical called *The Merry Gentleman*, starring Donald Harron the lightfooted Irish tenor. The Old Vic raised his salary from £10 to £14, although he still insists that he never could sing or dance. It must have been a pretty good musical because the authors, Julian Slade and Dorothy Reynolds, were hard at work on their next one, *Salad Days*, which was a smash hit. They asked Don's advice about the rocketship sequence, as if being North American automatically made him an expert in such matters.

Meanwhile, he and Tyrone Guthrie had exchanged progress reports during the season. While Don was having fun playing a villain in *The Shoemaker's Holiday*, he received another letter, telling him how things were shaping up for Stratford's second summer. Guthrie offered him two major "handsome young man" parts, and Don turned them both down.

He asked instead for "character" roles, and had the audacity to specify which ones he wanted. Guthrie agreed. Maybe he figured his devoted pupil had earned the right not to be a handsome young man if he didn't want to.

As the Bristol Old Vic season ended in April, Don says "there was time to get back to London and let my reclusive wife see some theatre" before going back to Canada. I wonder how he managed to convince himself that this meant putting his own desires on the back burner.

While they were at the London Old Vic, I had a wonderful time playing with the Campbell kids and their grandmother, Dame Sybil Thorndike. I have to congratulate my parents on going to no expense to provide me with first-rate babysitters.

Gloria's cousin was in Paris working for UNESCO, which meant more free babysitting. And they'd never seen Paris, in the spring or any other time. To Don it looked like a golden opportunity to let his reclusive wife see some French theatre.

In Paris we stayed at the Hotel Moderne. The plumbing wasn't, so we washed at Cousin Mary Winston's apartment, where the bathtub was in the kitchen, with a lid that doubled as a sink. It almost made us homesick for Bristol.

On the first day, Father walked for miles and miles admiring the most beautiful city he had ever seen and buying theatre tickets for every night of the week. Mother took me to the Parc Monceau, where I was astounded to meet people my own age who had already mastered a foreign language.

We got back to England in time to catch the ship home. Just before it was to sail I broke out in chicken pox, all over. The authorities refused to let me on board, so Mother kept me company in quarantine and Father went on alone.

Actually, he wasn't alone. Douglas Campbell was on board with his whole family. After the Festival, they planned to stay on, and were hoping to take world-class theatre to remote communities that had never seen a play.

The children — Dirk, Theresa and future Stratford star baby Ben — were of course vegetarians like their parents. At breakfast, they primly tapped on the shells of their eggs while Don tucked into his bacon. Dirk, the eldest, watched him with evident distaste: "Why do you eat flesh?" he asked.

It was a simple question, but God help anyone who attempts to stand between Donald and his breakfast, even an innocent child. "I don't know," he replied crossly. "Why do you eat unborn baby chickens?"

Theresa swallowed hard and looked him straight in the eye. "Why haven't you brought Muffin with you?"

"Because she got the pox in Paris," he said ominously, and left it at that.

Back at Stratford-on-Tario, it seemed as though everything had changed. The year before, they had been "on a crackpot trip to the moon"; the atmosphere had been charged with the daring born of having everything to gain and nothing to lose. Now that they had triumphed, cautiousness was taking over. Only Guthrie hadn't changed. He carried on in the same pioneer spirit, as if the first season had never happened. Don was reminded of Kenneth Tynan's observation: "Guthrie's weakness is that he has never learned from his failures. His strength is that he has never learned from his successes."

He always arrived at the first rehearsal knowing every face by name, cast and crew. He would call a halt in mid-scene to ask the advice of the lowliest walk-on; he never picked on underlings. But he could also be absolutely ruthless.

He had decided on a Wild West version of *The Taming of the Shrew*, with Mavor Moore as Petruchio. To play the role, Mavor had resigned his post as production chief of the two-year-old CBC television network, giving it all up for art in the grand old Moore tradition. Don was glad to see him starring at Stratford. "Mavor excelled at many things," he writes in his memoirs, "but to me he was best as an actor, resourceful and imaginative under the most difficult circumstances."

More difficult circumstances than Donald could have imagined were on the way. At the first rehearsal, Mavor broke two ribs. Guthrie summoned Donald to his office and came right to the point: "I want you to take over Petruchio."

Don was appalled. Knowing the Moores, a couple of cracked ribs would if anything improve Mavor's performance. He pointed this out, but Guthrie was adamant. He said that in any case, Mavor's traditional interpretation of the role was totally at variance with his own.

At that Don exploded: "Well, what the hell *is* your interpretation of the part? You haven't told any of us, including Mavor!" When Guthrie finished explaining how he saw Petruchio, Don whistled in disbelief. "Jesus Christ, Tony, you want a Harold Lloyd!"

"Exactly," was the reply. It would have been nice if Guthrie had thought of saying so before Mavor, a father with two children to support, quit his big well-paying job at the CBC. But Guthrie didn't worry about that: Moore was out, and Harron was in.

Don refused to take over his friend's part. "You don't want me, you've got Harold Lloyd standing right in front of you on the stage, glasses and all."

For once Guthrie was slow on the uptake. "Who?"

"Bill Needles."

"Done!" said Guthrie. He made the cast change right after lunch, without apologies.

Mavor was disappointed, as who wouldn't be, but he did not leave Stratford. "I was under contract!" says he.

Rehearsals for *The Taming of the Shrew* carried on, with Don playing Tranio, the servant who tells his master what to do. He claims it was Guthrie who made him go to the dentist to be fitted with a set of false buck teeth, to give the character an added dimension, no doubt.

Measure for Measure, starring James Mason, opened first. Even Shakespeare got bad press from the New York critics the next day, but the most violent reaction came backstage on the first night. Mason's wife, Pamela Kellino, marched into his dressing room at intermission and said that she, for one, had no intention of sticking around to watch the second half. Don learned this from Mason's dresser, who had witnessed the scene, and says if the cast had known it at the time they might have burned the witch at the stake.

The person who impressed him most that night was in a minor role. Mavor Moore was playing the one part he had left, Escalus the wise counsellor. Mavor says with two broken ribs, he *had* to be philosophical.

The following night was the opening of *The Taming of the Shrew*. It was a riotous success, although with his beaver teeth in place Don made a fine spray whenever he pronounced certain consonants. Afterwards he met the wife of one cast member, who returned his greetings with distinct coolness. He wasn't wearing his buck teeth at the time but she was, for hers were permanently attached. He felt terrible. Later Guthrie agreed to let him try Tranio without the extra teeth, and he managed to get almost as many laughs without dampening the rest of the cast. He hasn't worn buck teeth since — though mind you, Eaton's haven't yet asked him back to play Bugs Bunny.

The crowning artistic achievement of the season was *Oedipus Rex*, featuring a bold return to the masks and high platform shoes which the actors of ancient Greece wore to give themselves more godlike proportions. Opening night for *Oedipus* began with coughing fits in the audience, but not because they were bored. Guthrie had conceived his tragic figures as emerging from the primeval mists and the smoke machine worked just fine, but the body heat of the spectators drew the mists in their direction, leaving the stage prosaically bare.

Don's former landlord and lady, Ed and Phyllis Cardwell, were there. Ed didn't want to be, but Phyllis had heard *Odius Rex* was about a sexy family. Ed only asked one question, right near the end: "Now just a minute — is this girl his wife or his mother?"

Phyllis pointed to Creon and said, "I'm not too darned sure, but I know this one is her brother."

By the end of the Festival's second season, Don had been offered two starring roles on Broadway. A few days before the Festival went into hibernation, a producer flew up from New York in his private plane to see if he would play the lead in a revival of Sean O'Casey's *Red Roses for Me*. Don thinks O'Casey's *Juno and the Paycock* is one of the greatest plays ever written, but not this one, so he turned it down.

He had already agreed to join Dougie Campbell, who had done just what he said he was going to do: formed an off-shoot of the Festival which would stretch its tendrils all the way to James Bay. Called the Canadian Players, their first production would be Shaw's *St. Joan*.

Dougie's wife, Ann Casson, would be starring in the title role, which her mother Dame Sybil had played in Shaw's original production. Don had been offered a peach of a part, the Dauphin of France, whom Joan calls "Charlie."

A feature article by Jock Carroll appeared in the *Telegram Weekend Magazine* about Don Harron, the actor "who would rather learn than earn . . . someone who gave up $2,000 dollars a month in television to work for $28 a week in an English rep company." It was true, and he had the empty savings account to prove it.

Just as he was about to sign his Canadian Players contract, he received an urgent message from the Theater Guild in New York. They had a play trying out in Westport, Connecticut, due to open at the Booth Theatre on Broadway, and needed to replace the juvenile lead.

The play was called *Home is the Hero*, and the part was so fantastic that Don says he couldn't resist it, "unfortunately." He thinks he should have gone to James Bay. Certainly Douglas Campbell thought so, and never forgave him.

He had to get to Connecticut right away. By a stroke of luck the first producer, whose *Red Roses* he had rejected, was flying back to New York that day. He offered Don a lift in his private plane, which was very gallant of him under the circumstances.

The very next time that plane took off, the producer disappeared into the waters of Lake Ontario. But first, he deposited Donald safely in New York. Hurricane Hazel struck the next day, and threw Don against a wall in Shubert Alley. By the time he made it to Westport, it was sitting in three feet of water.

Home Is the Hero is an Irish play, about a man who comes home after five years in jail for killing his friend in a brawl. The author, Walter Macken, had had a great success in Dublin, acting in the title role, and hoped to repeat it on Broadway. Don would play the "hero's" son, permanently lame since infancy, thanks to an over-enthusiastic toss in the air from his drunken father. With orders from the Theater Guild to stay in hiding until they were ready to make the switch, Don put a stone in his shoe and limped around his hotel room learning the lines.

The actor he was replacing was Richard Lupino, Ida's nephew, a thoroughly pleasant sort who didn't seem to bear any personal grudge against his usurper, and decided to stay on as Donald's understudy. All the same, Don felt terribly awkward in his presence.

When he was introduced to the rest of the cast, he was amazed to find Christopher Plummer in a minor role. The first thing Chris did was pay Don back the twenty-five bucks he had borrowed the last time. This was very flattering, as rumours of unpaid tailors' bills, etc. had spread far and wide. A couple of weeks later, he borrowed it again, till next time.

Don had ten days of rehearsal before opening on Broadway. The only interference was from Theater Guild minions attempting neurotic minor adjustments. They persuaded Peggy Anne Garner to dye her naturally blonde hair black, imagining this to be more Irish, and succeeded only in making her look depressed.

Very late the night before the opening, the phone rang in his hotel room. "Donald," said the sweet voice of a Theater Guildian, "We've decided that you should have curly hair."

"Dick," replied Don just as sweetly, "I've decided to tell you to piss off." He slammed the phone down and instructed the switchboard to hold all calls. He hadn't spent two seasons under Tony Guthrie for nothing.

When the reviews came in, it seemed the critics liked everything except the play and the author's performance. Don says the look in Walter Macken's eyes for the rest of the run was more painful than a stone in the shoe. His own notices were amazing. One critic described him as "one of the three best young actors in North America."

He was tempted to ask who the other two were, until he remembered what happened when Shaw said Sir Cedric Hardwicke was one of the five best actors in the world. Overjoyed, Hardwicke cabled asking the names of the other four and Shaw replied with a postcard that read: "THE MARX BROTHERS".

M.G.M. called, and Don went to Dore Schary's New York office. After a ten-minute interview, he was offered a seven-year movie contract. He said no. He had a note from Tyrone Guthrie in his pocket, asking him to save himself for Stratford.

Between the closing of *Home is the Hero* and the end of May, when he would go home to Stratford, Don agreed to go on tour in yet another Christopher Fry play, *The Dark is Light Enough*, starring Katharine Cornell and Tyrone Power, with Don and Chris Plummer in secondary roles.

They shared a dressing room. Chris was always late, and never bought a scrap of make-up, preferring to borrow Don's for a few quick dabs, seconds before curtain time. For Christmas, Don gave his friend an empty cigar box with the bottom carved out. Chris asked what it was for, and was treated to a demonstration: Don slipped it neatly over his own full box and slid it over to Chris's side of the dressing table.

He received another letter from Guthrie, announcing the plays for the third season. *Oedipus Rex* would be repeated, with Dougie Campbell filling James Mason's platform shoes, and he wanted Don back in the Chorus. He also offered him Lorenzo in *The Merchant of Venice* and Octavius Caesar in *Julius Caesar*, which would be directed by Michael Langham.

In addition to the acting assignments, Guthrie wanted him to spend three weeks directing some of the junior players in scenes of his choice. Perhaps he wanted his protégé to become his apprentice, although he didn't put it that way.

Don wrote back immediately, rejecting everything the Doctor had prescribed, except the part of Octavius Caesar. He flatly refused to have anything to do with directing. As for *The Merchant of Venice*, he didn't want Lorenzo, but would like the leading role of Bassanio instead. Finally, he added a caustic comment about the wisdom of putting on an anti-Semitic play just ten years after the discovery of the Holocaust.

Guthrie wrote back immediately, full of good humour, and let the boy have what he wanted. He said that on the contrary he regarded *The Merchant of Venice* as an anti-Gentile play, adding ''Wait and see.''

The Dark Is Light Enough closed just in time for Harron and Plummer to head off to their separate Stratfords. The rival Shakespearian Festival in Connecticut was in its fledgling year, while the Ontario version was already behaving like a comfortable, established institution. So was the Harron family, who had rented a house in town.

First rehearsals with Guthrie were always thrilling, straight to work, no read-through. He would whisper suggestions in your ear that would throw the character into a new and sharper focus, never quite recaptured in the more mundane business of nightly performance. At the first rehearsal for *The Merchant of Venice*, Don learned he was to play Bassanio as a bisexual who had been living in sin with Antonio but was anxious to raise his status by becoming a heterosexual fortune hunter. He and Antonio were part of the Venetian country club set, dabbling in the stock market and with each other, while Shylock had to earn his living honestly, in the only way the law allowed him.

This interpretation was not spelled out for the audience; the only hint was a trifle-too-long embrace as Bassanio departed for Belmont to win Portia's hand. The observant might have caught some smouldering looks, but no fondling and definitely no mincing.

The true star of the Festival was, as always, costume designer Tanya Moiseiwitch. In *The Merchant of Venice* she invoked the spirit of Botticelli, and the effect was truly spectacular. In the casket scene, Bassanio would have won Portia's heart even if he'd chosen the wrong box.

His doublet and hose were a pale champagne colour, accented in gold, with sleeves that flowed almost to the ground. Add to that a great pair of legs, an olive complexion (summer tan plus a little Leichner), a crown of soft black curls (not his own) and a smouldering pair of eyes (thanks to Guthrie's direction), and he looked like Elizabeth Taylor's twin brother.

On the day of *The Merchant*'s opening Don read the notices for *Julius Caesar*, which had opened the night before. They were fairly negative, so he had an argument with Gloria about her wanting him to be a writer, his usual way of blowing off steam whenever he had doubts about his acting career.

This pastime was interrupted by the telephone. The voice said, "Hello, this is Walter Kerr."

It couldn't be *the* Walter Kerr, the New York critic, so Don said, "Oh screw off! Who is it really? Is that you, Bill?" He thought it was William Shatner, playing one of his practical jokes.

"No, Donald, it really is Walter Kerr. . . . Hello? You still there? Look, I know you've got a lot on your mind with tonight's opening. I just wanted to say that we'd like to have you co-star with Donald Cook in Jean's play as soon as we get a theatre in London."

He was talking about *King of Hearts*, Jean Kerr's first play. It had already been a hit on Broadway with Cook as the cartoonist with an insufferable ego. That meant they were offering him Jackie Cooper's part, the klutz with the heart of gold who gets the girl. Perfect.

"Could you just keep us in mind, and let us know if some other offer comes in the way?" Could he? He cancelled all his plans for the fall.

At the time Don couldn't understand how they could possibly have pegged him as a comedian after seeing him as Octavius Caesar. Looking back many years later, he realized that his career had been progressing according to a pattern of reverse psychology.

The summer before, he had turned down handsome-young-hero parts in favour of character roles, and was offered two handsome-young-hero parts on Broadway. This summer he had gone for the handsome-young-hero parts, and now he was offered a starring role in a comedy. Even Robertson Davies, the Festival's official biographer, had this comment in his annual round-up: "Donald Harron could charm the birds out of the trees, but he is a light comedian not a romantic hero."

What was the message? If you want to do something, try the opposite? This happened to suit his own perverse psyche just fine, although he probably didn't realise it. He had something much more important on his mind: right after the triumphant opening of his *Merchant of Venice*, Tyrone Guthrie disappeared from the Festival, leaving his crown and sceptre to *Caesar*'s director Michael Langham.

No one knew where he had gone. Some said he was off to rescue the floundering Festival in Stratford, Connecticut. Others thought he might be starting a new one, either at the North Pole or the South Pole. Wherever he was, he was hard at work breaking new ground. At first Don felt like a fatherless child, but he comforted himself with the knowledge that some day, from somewhere, another precious note might arrive in the mail.

17

FINE FRENZY ON THE HOUSATONIC

WAITING for *King of Hearts*, Don decided the most pleasant way to pass the time was to go to Toronto and do a revue with Jane Mallett. Robert Christie was looking for a change of pace after getting stabbed in the back every night as Julius Caesar, so the three of them formed a company called Jane Mallett Associates and put on a show.

It seems shocking that Dora and Mavor Moore were not asked to have a hand in this, as it was essentially a fall version of *Spring Thaw*. In fact, Don was going to call it *Fall Freeze*, like the reaction he was getting from the New Play Society, until he found a catchy phrase by Shakespeare, "the poet's eye in a fine frenzy rolling."

Because of his treachery, no copy of *Fine Frenzy* lies carefully preserved in the Moore archives, which is a kind of poetic justice. The script was thrown together and rehearsed with unseemly haste for a short run at the Avenue Theatre, as Don expected to be called away to London at any moment.

The cast included current *Thaw* regulars like Dave Broadfoot, Araby Lockhart and Eric House, who appeared as country singer "Merle Hives, the Fey Wearing Stranger." Charlie Farquharson was there, and they did another *Oklahoma*-type musical parody, set in Saskatchewan during the Depression, with hits like "Gang! Gang! The Hail's All Here!"

Before *Fine Frenzy* ended, Walter Kerr phoned to say that Donald Cook had died of a heart attack and there were no plans to mount *King of Hearts* without him.

A few nights later, Norman Campbell from the CBC came backstage to visit his sweater, and asked if Don would like to collaborate on a ninety-minute television special, a musical. Norman would write the music and Don would write the words. He said it could be an adaptation, so Don suggested the book he happened to be reading to his kids at the time. It was a great story, and incidentally one hundred per cent Canadian content: *Anne of Green Gables* by Lucy Maud Montgomery.

We had been staying with Don's parents at Pinewood, but moved in with Gloria's while he worked on the musical. Gravenhurst was much more like Green Gables country, beautiful and simple and quiet. The outline was accepted and he planned to stay there till the script was finished.

In the midst of this tranquillity, a letter arrived which sent him careening off on another track. It was a short, impersonal note from Guthrie's successor, Michael Langham, offering him Fenton in *The Merry Wives of Windsor* and Lord Scroop in *Henry V* at Stratford the following summer.

On the last night of the Festival, Langham had said he was planning to cast Chris Plummer as his Henry V, and asked Don which part he wanted. Without hesitation, Don had asked for the Chorus, and Langham had agreed. Or so Don thought.

Fenton was a boring, handsome young man in his unfavourite Shakespeare play, and Lord Scroop was taken away to have his head chopped off almost as soon as he appeared. Don was in such a rage he fired off a telegram that said "SCROOP YOU LANGHAM!" Then he phoned his New York agent and told him he wanted a summer job in Stratford, Connecticut. In the meantime, he'd take any television work that was going.

The Americans were tightening up on Canadian actors, so he had to hire an immigration lawyer. In New York, while doing shows on the tiny box with Robert Perston, Joanne Woodward, Katharine Cornell, gracious as ever, and a very cranky Helen Hayes, he tried to keep working on *Anne of Green Gables*. The CBC New York staff co-operated by relaying what he had written via U.N. teletype to Norman Campbell in Toronto.

Two weeks later, Campbell was still waiting. Don claims that the

F.B.I. had become suspicious of all the talk about red hair and red roads, and were intercepting his transmissions. They failed to crack the code, and eventually the missing pieces of script arrived. Norman suspects this is an unusually elaborate version of "The dog ate my homework," but Don swears it is true.

Harron's green card finally came through, making him an official American resident, and he came back to Canada just long enough to see the taping of *Anne of Green Gables*. John Drainie was unforgettable as tender-hearted Matthew Cuthbert, in fine contrast to Margot Christie, almost Ibsen-like as his stern sister Marilla. Starring as the red-headed orphan who wins their hearts was brunette Toby Tarnow, "a nice Jewish city girl with delicious freckles." She was running a high fever and could barely speak in the dress rehearsal, but rose to the occasion and sparkled all the way through.

We moved into a ground floor apartment in Greenwich Village with a family of mice who lived there already. Mary and I attended the Bank Street School, nursery and junior kindergarten respectively, the only time I ever went to a private school. Mother would not allow us to play with the kids in the neighbourhood, so I watched enviously out the window as they roller-skated in and out of traffic, shouting obscenities at the passing cars.

Fortunately, she had no qualms about letting us visit the nice lesbian couple who lived in the next building. Having no one else to play with, we made them adoptive aunts whether they liked it or not, and they gave us a copy of *Harold and the Purple Crayon* which I still treasure.

Don was accorded observer's status at Lee Strasberg's Actor's Studio, where the weekly sessions were full of blacklisted actors trying to eke out a living off-Broadway. Marilyn Monroe would sit in the corner, without make-up, looking pale and frightened, never saying a word. Don thought Strasberg was brilliant at taking things apart, but never saw him put anything back together.

He decided to take classes from Sanford Meisner instead. Sandy had a great sense of humour, unlike Strasberg, and was always chiding him good-humouredly for writing instead of acting in the improvisations. He felt very comfortable working with Farley Granger, in exile from Hollywood, and a brilliant actor named Peter Falk who couldn't make it in movies because he had a glass eye.

The good news about Stratford, Connecticut, was that the Theater Guilders, who had tried to give him a permanent wave in *Home Is the Hero*, were out of the picture. Don was very impressed by the new director, John Houseman, but disappointed to learn that two of the three productions would be *Measure for Measure* and *Taming of the Shrew*, which he had already done at Stratford, Ontario.

However, he had Scrooped his bridges in Stratford, Ont. so off we went to Stratford, Conn., almost as pretty as the Stratford we were used to. We rented a white frame house on a tree-lined thoroughfare, prompting me to compose a song of celebration entitled *Dreams Come True on Main Street*, our new address.

Donald had three good parts, even if they were handsome young men: the Dauphin in *King John*, Claudio in *Measure for Measure*, and in *Taming of the Shrew* the role he had rejected two years earlier, Tranio's master Lucentio.

They began with *King John*. Donald missed Tanya Moiseiwitch, her stage and her costumes, especially her light fibreglass armour that lets your skin breathe. The designer had been asked to give the characters epic proportions and had settled for gigantic, studiously avoiding porous materials.

Halfway through the first dressed confrontation between the forces of England and France, the director called a two-hour dinner break. Twelve bodies littered the stage, in varying stages of dehydration. The designer told Houseman they were "a bunch of amateurs." When Don came to, Morris Karnovsky was still out cold beside him, and had to be cut free from his costume.

During the break, Don sat and read the papers, especially the glowing reviews of *Henry V* in Ontario. Not for the first time, he regretted his decision. Then he had a cup of tea and changed his mind: better to be on another crackpot trip to the moon. Others might panic and run, but Houseman was acting like a true leader, so he would be a brave lieutenant.

They came back from dinner to find their costumes punctured, gouged, slashed and gutted, with tons of cotton padding ripped out by a director who cared more for performances than appearances. The designer cried sabotage, but the cast cried "Hurray!" By the time they opened a week later, the fighting men had added quite a few cuts and punctures of their own. Houseman decided the effect was even more epic and medieval than before.

Luckily *Measure for Measure* was in almost-modern dress. When Don made his first entrance in costume, Houseman bounded onto the stage and practically ripped the shirt off his back. "What the hell is he doing with this modern collar? He looks like Tony Curtis!" Don was flattered.

Although Connecticut was a lot closer to New York than Ontario, Houseman had adopted the same strategy of back-to-back openings, which was very hard on the cast but spared the critics an extra trip. The exhausted performers were able to read the dreadful *King John* reviews in the morning, before facing the same bunch again that night.

It was sink or swim time. If *Measure for Measure* got the same bad press, there was little hope of surviving the season. Don couldn't help thinking of the Broadway offers that had come his way since moving to Main Street, but was actually feeling quite cheerful. The critics had been kind to him personally; Brooks Atkinson of the *New York Times* had complimented him on his Dauphin, and his biggest nightmare was behind him: he had managed to say "What lusty trumpet thus hath summoned us?" without tripping over his tongue. If you think that's easy, try it a few times.

They had a technical run-through in the morning, before the dress rehearsal in the afternoon. While the discouraged cast members were down in the dressing rooms putting on their costumes, they heard a resounding thud over the intercom. An electrician had fallen from the top of a thirty-two foot ladder onto the stage. The crew stood around their fallen comrade, waiting for the ambulance, and said they weren't going back to work until they had a full report from the hospital.

Any delay and the opening would be postponed, the critics would head back to New York to review something else, and they wouldn't have a hope. Suddenly, the head electrician climbed up the ladder, and called to the rest of the crew to come and steady it for him. They did, and went on with the show. Their comrade miraculously survived and was back at work in a week.

In his theatre memoirs, *Final Dress*, John Houseman says that this dress rehearsal was "tense, slow and labored" but when evening came, all the pent-up frustration and accumulated adrenalin were "suddenly released into a performance that went far beyond anything that had been seen in rehearsal."

This *Measure for Measure*'s first exposure to a real live audience, obviously delighted by what it was seeing, spurred the performers to new heights. As they took their final bows to prolonged, ecstatic applause, the critics scurried away with blank expressions on their faces, and retreated to a separate building, equipped with typewriters and phone lines, where each would compose his verdict.

At the cast party, the mood was one of exhilaration. They knew the critics could still put them out of business, as word-of-mouth alone would not spread quickly enough to fill all the seats and rescue them from bankruptcy, but they knew they had participated in something magical.

Just after midnight, their press agent rushed in with a vital piece of evidence. After helping all the critics make their telephone connections to dictate what they had written, and the last one had driven away, he had gone back to lock up the building. In the wastepaper basket next to where Brooks Atkinson had been sitting, he had found a crumpled sheet of used carbon paper.

Houseman grabbed it and ran to his office. Jack Landau grabbed a secretary and followed in hot pursuit. It took quite a long time, but by holding it up to the light, Houseman and Landau managed to decipher what Atkinson had written, and they dictated it to the secretary, who typed it. They raced back to the party, a hushed silence descended and Houseman read the page out loud. It ended: "Shakespeare's bitterest comedy has never seemed so delightful and the acting on the Stratford stage has never seemed so accomplished. I urge you to hurry . . ." That was all there was, but it was enough.

They had a matinée the following day, but stayed up past dawn to hear the rest of that and all the other raves read by friends over the phone as soon as the New York papers came out. Houseman relates that Atkinson admired "the perfection of Donald Harron's Claudio," but Norman Lloyd got even bigger raves in his old comic role of Lucio, and that is what Don remembers.

They were able to go ahead with *The Taming of the Shrew*,

directed by Norman Lloyd, and it was another comic triumph. Apprentices were sent outside each night to capture the big moths which would flutter out when Gremio opened his book of ledgers to calculate Bianca's dowry. The *Times'* Arthur Gelb called it ''inspired madness,'' which pretty well sums up the whole summer.

Job offers are never more plentiful than when an actor is tied to the run of a hit play, or plays as in this case. An offer even came in from Canada. Don flew up to Montreal on a Sunday morning, recorded a narration for the National Film Board, and was back before curtain up Monday night.

A few days before *Shrew* opened, he received a call from Canadian producer Robert Whitehead, who was planning a big season on Broadway, six shows in all, including Terence Rattigan's *Separate Tables*, which had been a smash hit in London. Whitehead said he was importing the British production, all the stars minus a few support cast, and invited Don to audition. No member of the company could be spared so close to opening, but Houseman agreed to give him the afternoon off.

Don says he desperately wanted the part because *Separate Tables* was assured of a long run, which meant the family could spend fall, winter and possibly spring snug as bugs (I mean mice) in our apartment at 120 Perry Street, ''and perhaps my wife would stop trying to turn me into a writer.'' Of course if Gloria hadn't been such a nag, he wouldn't have been interested in appearing in a sure-fire hit on Broadway with Margaret Leighton.

In order to complete his return trip on the New Haven & Hartford Railway before the evening performance at Stratford, Don was obliged to explain to Whitehead and his stage manager that he could only spare them a few minutes of his time. They would probably have given him the part anyway, but no doubt all this dashing was good for his image.

Articles kept appearing about the turn-around on the Housatonic and by the end of August it was standing room only on weekends. *LIFE* magazine sent a photographer up (not Eugene Smith, but who's complaining), and did a five-page spread, especially of *Measure's* ''trollops, petty crooks, woeful lovers and corrupt officials'' in their gaudy gowns, celluloid collars and derby hats.

Don was having a marvellous time, even as the Dauphin in *King*

John. As Claudio in *Measure for Measure*, condemned to death for getting his girlfriend pregnant, the Bard compensated by giving him some of his most vivid verse about death, an Elizabethan specialty. As his sister Isabella, Nina Foch (''Foash'') gave her all to save his life every time.

As the Shrew, Nina was always rowdy and funny, affectionate and touching. The same could not be said of her Petruchio, however. Pernell Roberts was magnificent until he'd collected his clippings, but couldn't be bothered to give his all just for the folks who bought tickets.* He was the most blatant example of the American focus on getting ahead, instead of enjoying where you are.

The British cast of *Separate Tables* were quite the opposite, tucking into their plates of simulated chicken (apple) and little dishes of Jello eight times a week with the same relish (I mean enthusiasm) as they had done for two whole years in the West End. Don got the Jello, and says his finger and toe nails were never healthier.

Director Peter Glenville had a marvellous eye for detail, and gave Don some of the best notes he's ever had. Most of the cast already knew the play backwards, so on the pre-Broadway tour there was nothing to do except eight shows a week, no rehearsals or family to distract him.

On his last visit to Canada Don had come away with a paperback in his pocket, a touch of home called *The Adventures of Private Turvey*. It was a novel by Earle Birney, best known as a poet. Don decided this picaresque tale of a mousey Canadian soldier in World War I would make a great play, and the pre-Broadway tour was the time to do it. He banged away at his typewriter in the hotel, ordering room service, letting each page fall to the floor as he began the next.

After two and a half weeks, he came back to New York with two acts down and one to go. Gloria was so delighted that she kept us in the playground at Washington Square until our fingers turned blue, so as not to disturb the artist at work. As soon as he had finished he phoned Mavor Moore, who had taken over the Avenue Theatre, former home of *Fine Frenzy*, for a season of new Canadian plays. His musical adaptation of Voltaire's *Candide*, more humorous and

---

*Houseman blamed it on Robert's marital problems, but that's no excuse for an actor: it's an occupational hazard.

tuneful in Don's opinion than the subsequent version by Lillian Hellman and Leonard Bernstein, was in the middle of a successful run.

Mavor told Don to send him the script right away, optioned it less than two weeks later, and just two months after that, on January 11, 1957, had *Turvey* playing to audiences nightly. Four months earlier, it had been but a twinkle in my father's eye.

The reviews were quite friendly, and most of the cast members were old friends, including Alfie Scopp from *Thaw* and *Frenzy*, and Larry Mann from Grade Thirteen typing class. Turvey was played by Stratford star Douglas Rain. The director was Bob Christie, who'd pulled Don through directing *Riel* in one piece.

Don was dying to see it, but Robert Whitehead's office wouldn't give him a day off, despite his protests that he was not in a starring role and had a very capable understudy. Eventually he got through to Whitehead on the phone and told him what a rotten Canadian he was to prevent a home-grown playwright from seeing his own work performed. The biggest producer on Broadway (four hits out of six) burst out laughing, and told his irate actor/author to go to Toronto, and let him know whether this *Turvey* was worth a shot in New York.

It wasn't. The production was wonderful, but there were serious flaws in the script, mainly due to slavish devotion by the adaptor to Birney's original. The more he thought about it, the more he felt a musical was the answer, and set to work on rewrites.

He tried to keep going, but ran out of steam. He became very listless, and after a while had to conserve his energy all day just to make it through the performance at night. Wednesdays and Saturdays, with matinée and evening performances, were killers. The doctor couldn't find anything wrong and referred him to another doctor who said he had incipient mononucleosis, and gave him a series of injections. It went away in a few days. By then, *Turvey* had begun to collect dust (not literally — Gloria was always a terror with the vacuum cleaner) and he couldn't get started again.

Even before opening on Broadway the British cast of *Separate Tables* had learned that, after two years on two continents in the same dreary seaside hotel, their parts in the film version had been given to Laurence Olivier, Vivien Leigh, David Niven . . . none of the original cast. To their credit, this disappointment never affected their performance.

David Niven came to see the play, although he did not come backstage to say hello. He must have studied Eric Portman awfully carefully, because when Don saw *Separate Tables* the movie, Niven's excellent Major was a carbon copy of Portman's, in word and gesture.

One night Katharine Hepburn knocked at Don's dressing room. He opened the door, and there she was, "all the bones exactly in place." Her skin was dappled with pale, blotchy freckles that disappeared when she smiled. She said she had come to the play expressly to see him, I assume at John Houseman's suggestion, and wanted to know if he would play her beau at Stratford, Connecticut. It was a part he knew well, Bassanio in *The Merchant of Venice*, but the interpretation would have to be different this time: with such a Portia, a bisexual fortune hunter wouldn't last five seconds.

Just a few days earlier, he had received another offer from Michael Langham to come back to Stratford, Ontario, this time as Laertes to Chris Plummer's Hamlet. I presume this was Plummer's idea, and not because he was trying to save on make-up. Don had turned it down, still in high dudgeon about his precious Chorus.

There was no question of turning down this new offer: "To say no while looking directly into the eyes of Katharine Hepburn would be like shaking your head from side to side as Winston Churchill offered you nothing but blood, sweat and fighting on the beaches. I gulped and said I would."

Now all he had to do was figure out how to perform in one state while rehearsing in another, because the Stratford, Connecticut rehearsals and *Separate Tables* in New York overlapped by three weeks — not to mention the state he was in at the thought of playing opposite Katharine the Great. This situation was further complicated by the suicide of Robert Young, the head of the New Haven & Hartford Railway, who must have cracked under the pressure of holding it all together, because the formerly efficient service became a nightmare web of breakdowns and delays.

One day, Don was marooned in Darien, New York, where the only available taxi had already been commandeered by Judy Holliday, who was playing across the street from him in *The Bells Are Ringing*. Don threw himself across the hood and pleaded for mercy. She let him in.

Another day, trying to run from Grand Central Station to 45th Street in record time, he had to stop for a red light. The elegant woman standing next to him said to her companion, "Darling, we've got to hurry or we'll be awfully late!" Don looked at the tickets the man was holding; they were for *Separate Tables*. There was no time for make-up, but he made it into his costume and onto the stage just as the curtain was rising. The understudy, who had his lines and make-up ready, never forgave him.

It wasn't until after the performance that he noticed a telegram marked "Urgent" sitting in his cubbyhole. It was from Michael Langham, asking him to reconsider Laertes. Don admits he was tempted. Sword-fighting with Chris Plummer to their mutual deaths would have been such fun. But there was no turning back.

He wrote to Langham suggesting Michael Kane instead, Kane the Canadian that is, not Caine the Cockney. He insists he was just trying to be helpful, and anyway it was Gloria's suggestion. She had seen him off-Broadway in James Joyce's *Exiles*, and said he was "terribly good." Yeah, Don knew Kane could be brilliant, but he was also completely wacko and a prankster of epic proportions, personally responsible for halting construction of Toronto's first subway line by impersonating an architect and moving construction three feet to the left.

Meanwhile, back on the Housatonic, *The Merchant of Venice* was being directed officially by Jack Landau but in fact by Kate Hepburn, who had even managed to wrap the designer, Reuben Ter-Arutunian the Intractable, around her little finger. The only thing that bothered Don was Portia's tendency to shed copious tears. Guthrie had taught him that this was the audience's job, not the actor's.

In *Final Dress*, Houseman says that Spencer Tracy tried but failed to visit his leading lady in Stratford that summer, but Donald is convinced that he did manage a secret weekend. Kate had told him her *real* beau was coming (she rarely mentioned him by name) and he must have, because from that time on she never shed another tear. Evidently there was one man from whom Miss Hepburn would take direction.

Don tried to conceal his anxiety over the difference in their ages, but she could see right through him and said sweetly, "Donald, don't you worry. When you choose that casket and turn to kiss me, I shall be five years old." She looked radiant in her costume and sure enough, when he turned to "claim her with a loving kiss" she was hopping about with girlish glee.

First-string theatre critics, demi-gods in those days, liked nothing better than ripping film stars to shreds every time they dared to tread the boards. She bore it much more cheerfully than most. Walter Kerr complained that "Miss Hepburn jiggles up and down with the impatient ecstasy of a woman of six." He was only a year off.

John Houseman directed the next production, *Much Ado About Nothing*. He had not intended to come back, having four years to go on his contract as a director at M.G.M. However, his greatest ally had been ousted as head of production, and with him any hope of producing quality work, so Houseman had kissed Culver City goodbye. That ally was Dore Schary, who had also offered Don a seven-year contract.

Much Ado was set in Spanish California instead of Renaissance Sicily, with sombreros and mantillas. Don says Houseman's concept worked beautifully, and Houseman says it was Katharine Hepburn's idea. She was a natural for feisty, charming Beatrice. The crying jags and tantrums came out in this one, but the audience lapped it up with delight.

Don was given a character part in *Much Ado About Nothing*, and had a wonderful time doing it. He played the ancient "headborough" Verges, assistant to Constable Dogberry, which in old California terms meant Deputy Sheriff, and was dressed like a Pony Express rider much the worse for wear.

Thanks to Lionel Harron's clipping service, Don learned that Michael Kane had been hired as Plummer's Laertes, fired before opening night for lack of discipline, and had hired a lawyer to sue the Stratford, Ontario Festival for character assassination. The next week Don received a short telegram from Michael Langham saying that he was coming down to Connecticut to see him in person. He didn't say when.

Oh God. Langham didn't look like the type to come all the way to Connecticut to punch him in the nose. Actually, he looked just like a young George VI. Maybe he wanted to slap his face with a writ instead. Whatever it was, Don rehearsed the conversation over and over in his mind.

One August afternoon, he came out of the theatre into the sunshine and saw one of the most exquisite sights he has ever seen in his life. It was a living portrait of Gladys Cooper and Cathleen Nesbitt, two of the great beauties of all time. Then in their early seventies, they were standing together, in ice-blue summer dresses, gazing out at the waters of Long Island Sound.

As they gazed, he gazed, until a clipped British voice spoke his name. He whipped round and there was Langham, who had been waiting for him outside instead of coming backstage. He had a thick sheaf of papers with him, awfully hefty for a habeus corpus.

He said not a work about Scroops, Danes, Kanes or anything else in the spilt milk department. He had heard about *Turvey* and wanted to know if Don would be interested in adapting Heinrich von Kleist's one-act comedy *Der Zerbröchene Krug* ("The Broken Jug") for the Stratford company. If so, it would be performed with Shakespeare's *Two Gentlemen of Verona* on a tour which would end up at the Phoenix Theatre in New York.

Don didn't say anything, he just stood and stared in amazement. Langham placed the script in his hands, an English translation by the renowned Goethe scholar Barker Fairley, and said, "Read it over. Remember it's just a literal translation, and you can do anything you want with it, but I should like it to have a Canadian setting."

Without waiting for a reply, Langham turned and walked noiselessly away, a habit no doubt acquired during his years as a prisoner of war. Don didn't even see him leave. He was reading *The Broken Jug*.

18

THE WHOLE SUCCESS KIT

THE first time I remember getting spanked by my father was during *Separate Tables*, for chasing my little sister round and round the tiny apartment until she bashed her head on a chest of drawers. The next time was for wrecking our first record player when it was brand new. Parents are so cranky.

My first vivid memories of my father are of him coming home from *Separate Tables*, always in his glamorous, voluminous Burberry trenchcoat, usually soaked with rain; and the air would become suffused with the delicate scent of Pro-Ker hair lotion. Mary and I would dive for the pockets, and there were many, trying to find whatever treat he had brought home. He always managed some novelty, like shells that grew flowers in a glass of water, or ice cubes with flies in them.

Trying to raise a family while constantly on the move was hard on Don, and especially Gloria, who did the actual packing up while he flew on ahead. They kept worrying about how hard it was on us, forgetting that to a child everything is normal except parents, who are weird.

Unless they are prepared to live out of a suitcase, or can afford to maintain a permanent residence they may not see for months at a time, itinerant actors are forced to find someone who will pay the rent, utilities and phone bill, water the plants, feed the pets and clear out on short notice if the show folds in Poughkeepsie and they have to come home. This is almost as hard as landing the part in the first place.

I'm sure all these considerations were on my father's mind when Katharine Hepburn told him to go to Hollywood before he got too old. He was thirty-four, which suddenly did sound old for a handsome young man. This time she had looked in his eyes and ordered nothing but fame, fortune and tanning on the beaches. Needless to say, he did as he was told.

By now I've done all the usual things to give a parent failure: smoked marijuana, thrown an expensive university education in the garbage, borne children out of wedlock . . . nothing has fazed him. However, when I read in his memoirs that Katharine Hepburn had invited him to dinner, alone in her salt spray-soaked shack on the Housatonic to discuss his career while nibbling on nuts and berries, I said something that really shocked him.

All he provided by way of graphic detail was that he wolfed down a burger, fries and a jumbo malt on the way home. I said, "So, come on F.B., you can tell me."

Father Bear bristled. "What do you mean?"

"I mean, you went on and on about how amazing she was, and I know you weren't faithful to Mother, so . . . didn't you even *try* anything?!"

He looked completely, utterly, totally horrified and said "Martha! How could I? She belonged to *Him*."

Him was Spencer Tracy, of course, who gave Don a huge bearhug the first time he walked into the 20th Century Fox production office in L.A. This impressed the director and producer far more than his curriculum vitae. As he and Him had never met before, Spence must have been coached by Connecticut Kate.

The day after the Stratford, Conn. season ended, Don left Gloria to somehow dispose of the Perry Street apartment and its worldly goods, and caught a plane to L.A. His agent, Lillian Small, had made appointments at all the major studios except M.G.M. where her brother Dore Schary used to work. Her son, Edgar Small, met Don at the airport and drove him to the Montecito, where the "fun bunch" stayed — New York actors who couldn't afford the Château Marmont. He ended up in Lou Jacobi's old room, two doors down from Lorne Greene.

On the way, as they drove along Hollywood Boulevard, Edgar

explained that Hollywood the geographical location, as opposed to Hollywood the Land of Dreams, was a tacky district of Los Angeles nobody visited except to eat at the Musso Frank's and/or pick up their unemployment cheques. He said the Fun Bunch spent the rest of the time sitting around the pool, waiting for their agents to call with an offer for a New York play. Don thought he was joking.

He was to meet Lillian and Edgar for dinner that night in a fashionable Beverly Hills restaurant and took a cab, as he had no idea where it was. The cab driver was a New York actor and he didn't know either. They paused at a drugstore where a phonebook revealed he was already in the right place, on the Sunset Strip, so he told the cabby to buy a map with the tip.

Over dinner, they chatted with the couple at the next table, a distinguished gentleman and beautiful wife forty years his junior — Mr. and Mrs. Edward G. Robinson. He had just finished a Broadway run of Paddy Chayefsky's *Middle of the Night*, about a man who wins a beautiful younger woman away from her young husband. There was no trace of dese, dem and dose in his speech like in de movies. He said he only made those to pay for the pictures he cared about — his collection of paintings.

It didn't take Don long to realise that a Hollywood actor needs a hobby. Fortunately he had *The Broken Jug* to write, when he wasn't hanging around the Montecito pool with the other hopefuls, testing one another on their lines. Fellow tenant Lee Meriwether, bright as well as beautiful, phoned his room one night to say that the gang was going over to Grauman's Chinese Theatre to see a movie. Would he like to come along?

He said he couldn't, he had a play to write. She said, "Oh my gosh, how wonderful. You do that, sorry to bother you!" and hung up before he could change his mind.

He thought, "Some day I'm going to tell my grandchildren I turned down Miss America!"

As always when they were apart, Don wrote to Gloria frequently. Because we were in Gravenhurst at the time, this series of letters joined the pre-marital ones in the little green trunk. All were addressed to "Gogie darling," and the first contains the following description:

The town? Well, it just isn't true. It's a bad set really. Stucco and tiles and real live palm trees that look like elephantiasis at the bottom and a fan dancer's trunk at the top. . . . Everything looks like a 1935 Exposition that they never took down. I did see copies of the *Listener* and *Encounter* at a newsstand though. . . .''

Hollywood is really a kind of corny place, the people have the worst taste in clothes, the women all dress like salesgirls in Kresge's on their day off, but the weather is glorious and you go to bed early and get up early and see a lot of your family, and you can buy books and records. Maybe it'll be all right. I know I wouldn't mind it. Give my girls big hugs and a couple of wides and tell them they're irreplaceable. And so are you and don't forget it.

He went to Sunday dinner at Fletcher and Mercedes ''McMarkles'', and reported that ''they have the whole Success Kit, house high on a hill,'' etc. Mercedes loaned him a book on Zen Buddhism, ''it's amazing the way every line of it applies to acting,'' and Fletcher played him an amazing Dylan Thomas record. Together they introduced him to an exciting new kind of sharp, political stand-up comedian: ''We went to see Mort Sahl, America's only working philosopher, and like the Dylan Thomas recording I cried aloud for you to be with me.''

Auditioning for movie moguls was totally different from anything he had ever experienced, and he hated it. Instead of meeting the enemy head on, you had to make a screen test with another actor, usually somebody of the opposite sex who was already under contract. You would repeat a scene, often from an existing blockbuster by the same studio, in medium range and close-up, over and over, taking turns with your back to and facing the camera. The most important thing was not to begin speaking until your co-star had completely finished, as it would interfere with splicing each person's best bits of on-camera dialogue into a stirring conversation.

The results would be thrown up on a wall across town, where your image would be dissected by people you would probably never meet. It was most unnerving, and the worst part was that Don knew the essence of film star quality was to be yourself — or, at least, be the yourself they were looking for, which in Don's case seemed to mean an endless succession of young, sensitive, slightly-but-not-too-intellectual parts.

Columbia Pictures had paid his return flight from New York, but he couldn't stand the drama coach — "very theatrical and snobbish about theatuh actors" — and could see there was no hope for comic roles. Their contract offer was low, and he turned it down.

Finally he got to meet director George Seaton at Paramount, who had just finished *Teacher's Pet* with Doris Day and Clark Gable. Seaton had never heard of Harron, but Don asked him about when he wrote for the Marx Brothers and they got along like a house on fire. George said working with the Marx Brothers was extremely difficult because they thought of themselves as writers first and performers second. Don tried to look as though he'd never seen a typewriter. Seaton agreed to give him a test.

Don decided to clear out afterwards, rather than hang around the pool to await the results. There was television work waiting for him in Toronto, where it seemed producers much preferred long distance to local calls. The family reunited at Pinewood while Don did two television specials. The first was in the title role of a heart-breaking drama called *The Prizewinner*, about an office innocent who gets duped by his fellow employees into believing that he has won a huge lottery prize. He is shattered by the experience. Badly in debt, too.

Seven-year-old Martha, watching the program, was shattered by what those terrible people were doing to her father, and could not be consoled. A week later Charlie Farquharson appeared on *The Big Revue*. My younger sister Mary curled up under a chair and cried for an hour.

Father, his Kleist play and his typewriter came to Gravenhurst with us. The Harron girls were enrolled in Kindergarten and Grade 2 respectively, and Don enrolled himself in the local library where Gloria had misspent her youth. "My wife was at home with the father she adored and the mother she loved to fight with. Everybody was happy."

The Broken Jug was a short, sweet and simple folk comedy, full of dalliance and chicanery. Don chose as his Canadian setting a tiny

almost-border town during the War of 1812. The more he read about
it, the more he realised that, to the inhabitants, the conflict between
their British overlords and the Americans was a colossal nuisance.
As well as trampling your crop with their troops, conscripting your
sons and slaughtering your livestock, they'd tax the life out of you
to pay for it.

Michael Langham was very helpful with the construction of
Adam's Fall, the more Biblical sub-title Don had chosen for his adaptation. It pretty well sums up what happens when the main character
finds himself the judge in criminal proceedings where he himself
was the culprit. Under his wig he bears the mark of an heirloom
jug, cracked by the heroine in an attempt to fend off his amorous
advances.

Don already knew who the cast would be — the Stratford crew
from *Two Gents of Verona*, which would be touring with *Adam's
Fall*. Douglas Campbell would be Master Adam, Douglas Rain his
wily clerk, and the owner of the broken jug would be Helen Burns.
Plus Bruno Gerussi, Anne Morrish, Millie Hall, Powys Thomas . . . a
dependable bunch of comedians.

While Don was typing out the second draft in Gravenhurst, the
news came that on George Seaton's recommendation Paramount
was offering him a seven-year contract at $750 a week, fifty-two weeks
a year, even if he sat on his butt the whole time. ''My wife whooped
for joy because she knew if I did that I would be sitting on my butt
in front of a typewriter.'' He said yes, and Gloria started packing
up for California.

So there we were with the whole Success Kit, house high on a
hill etc. The road below us, which led to the Beverly Hills Hotel,
was called Summitridge Drive — which Don was drawn to as the
name of a tune by Artie Shaw — and our driveway would have made
a great ski slope if it ever snowed. He claims that what really sold
him was discovering that the owner of the house next door, Johnny
Mathis's manager Helen Noga, had a six-year-old granddaughter
who lived there too.

The first time I ever remember my sister getting spanked was for
saying she hated that little girl. Funny, it's okay for grown-ups to
hate people they've only read about in the paper. Anyway, I was

the culprit, making Mary turn the skipping rope while Sheryl and
I skipped, and so forth. I got spanked that year for marking a deck
of cards. I admit purple crayon wasn't the subtlest choice but as
my sister so wisely observed, "Wiv and wearn."

Don rented a station wagon and Gloria spent her time chauffeuring the children to and from Warner Avenue School in
Westwood, many miles away. Mary and I complained about the
quality of education ("Oh Daddy, it feels like recess all the time!"),
and before we knew it, we were enrolled in after-school tuition with
Mummy. Not that there was much else to do. The freedom to roam
the streets and visit schoolmates had been left behind in Gravenhurst.

Until Donald learned to drive, Gloria had to chauffeur him too.
He discovered that the only difference between being under contract and before was the $750 a week. He spent his time doing screen
tests with young hopefuls, including a handsome young Texan named Ty Hungerford, changed to Hardin by the studio. They did a
scene together from *The Philadelphia Story*, with Don in Jimmy
Stewart's role and Ty in Cary Grant's. Afterwards, Ty slapped him
on the back and said, "Ah thought yew played it more comical,
while ah jist played it more swave!"

He was taken to the publicity department, where he found a really
nice bunch of unpretentious people. The hype-makers showed him
the first fruit of their efforts, a mention in Hedda Hopper's column: "Paramount has succeeded in signing legit actor Donald Harron. They say he is a combination of Leslie Howard and Montgomery
Clift. Wow!"

The Broken Jug, or Adam's Fall, opened in London, Ontario,
not far from where the story takes place. Michael Langham pronounced it a success but said rewrites were needed to tighten the
action, so Don flew up to Toronto and straight into a blizzard. He
suddenly felt like a Californian. To himself he said, "No more snow
shovelling, just acting in a studio and playwriting outside on a
terrace!"

He was treated like a visiting celebrity. One columnist quoted
him as saying, "Hollywood is just Scarborough with millionaires,"
and he meant it apart from the snow shovelling, which he told
another journalist was "just like playwriting — you do it in your

spare time." Easy for him to say. The Toronto opening went very well; Rose Macdonald of the *Telegram* called *The Broken Jug* a "lively lampoon" and Whittaker of the *Globe* "a fascinating comedy, making the period more lively and far more human than the schoolbooks have done."

The next morning Don was sitting in a CBC studio with interviewer June Dennis, listening to the on-air broadcast from a nearby studio while awaiting their cue. It was the wheezy voice of Nathan Cohen, who began his theatre round-up by saying "Donald Harron's little play has two weaknesses. It has no plot and no characters," then went on to speak of other things.

June suggested they ignore the remark, but Don said no one else would, so he'd rather deal with it. He racked his brain for a comeback, and June seemed almost as nervous as he was. "Well, Don, what do you think of what Mr. Cohen just said about your play?" Then it came to him.

"Oh, I don't care what everybody else says, June — I like Nathan Cohen. And I admire him. I admire him because he has what I haven't got. Character. And plot. What about that little plot he concocted this morning to assassinate me?"

While Don and Gloria were in New York for *The Broken Jug*'s début at the Phoenix Theatre, my sister and I were undergoing a trauma in California. It was the first time we had ever been in the care of a person who didn't think the sun rose and set on our shiny twin haircuts. It was chilling. I will not name the perpetrator. Suffice it to say she wrote scripts for *Lassie* and lived in Laurel Canyon with a dozen cats. Anyway, we didn't "tell" on her, and at the airport in L.A. we greeted our parents with brave smiles.

Don arrived home to a phone call from producer Joe Hyman, commissioning the adaptation of a Canadian novel for Broadway. How could he resist? It was *Leaven of Malice* by Robertson Davies. He went straight to the typewriter.

He worked at it for months, but the harder he tried, the more convinced he became that *Leaven of Malice* was too gentle and literary for a Broadway play. On the other hand, it would be perfect as a movie, like an Ealing comedy, if you could find a Canadian Alec Guinness to play Solly Bridgewater. He wrote to the producer and told him just that. Hyman wrote back that he was handing the project over to the original author, Robertson Davies.

Meanwhile, as soon as he signed the writing contract for *Leaven of Malice*, things started to get busy on the acting front. Not at Paramount, though. They were making two movies, a Jerry Lewis picture and *I Married a Monster from Outer Space*. Don was considered too dignified. Instead, he was lent to Desilu Studios to play John Wilkes Booth in a television drama, not being too dignified-looking to assassinate Lincoln.

The only live TV drama left in Hollywood was NBC's *Matinée Theatre*, which borrowed Don to play an English lord who chain-smokes cigars in a farce called *On Approval*. The cigars almost killed him, but he was a great hit as the asthmatic aristocrat.

He tried out for a comedy at RKO, but again his reputation as a classical actor preceded him. In Hollywood, "classical" meant "serious," unless it was British comedy which didn't count. One of RKO's producers admitted that he had seen Don's father perform comedy on television up in Canada. Don tried to convince him that *he* was Charlie Farquharson, but the producer clearly thought he was lying.

Until the studio came up with some work for his well-paid butt, gardening was his only escape from the typewriter. Gardening is a serene pastime for some, but in Don's case consisted of bending over, never kneeling, and yanking unwelcome vegetation out of the ground with fierce concentration. By the end of the summer he was brown on the front, black on the back and white with rage inside.

During this time he finally acquired a driver's license and second-hand convertible, but without mastering the emergency brake. One day he parked at the top of the driveway and announced that he was taking Mary and me to Disneyland. We ran for the car — Disneyland with Don Harron is any child's dream come true; his childish glee makes it twice as much fun. Fortunately we didn't reach the car before it rolled down the steep hill and smashed into a pine tree. My father says this is not true — it was a eucalyptus.

The principal occupation in Hollywood seemed to be dinner, so the Harrons gave dinner parties. Unlike most Hollywood couples, they not only allowed their children to eat with the guests, they would gaze adoringly at us, admiring our precocious behaviour no matter how deplorable. At least they had the good sense not to subject Mort Sahl to our ballet routine.

I have committed far worse deeds in my life, but the act of gratuitous malice that will haunt me to my grave was committed the night Nina Foch came to dinner. She was elegant, she was sophisticated and right in the middle of the main course I asked her, "Why do you eat like a pig?" Nobody said *anything*. I was horrified, as I'm sure was everyone else at the table except Mary, who was used to it; she'd practically given up eating altogether.

I don't know where it came from, it just popped out. I probably looked brazen, but inside I was writhing. Miss Foch's table manners were impeccable, unlike mine, but I couldn't think of a graceful way to say, "I'm sorry. You *don't* eat like a pig." She came to dinner again some months later and I still didn't have the guts to apologise. I have thought about this for thirty years. Please, parents — be like Marilla Cuthbert — send the kid to her room until she's ready to eat humble pie.

Desilu Studios borrowed Don from Paramount again, this time to play opposite Ernie Kovacs in a Desilu Playhouse comedy. It was about a guy who spends his lunch hours in a hospital wandering the halls with a stethoscope around his neck, making patients feel better. Kovacs was wonderful to work with, and talk with, but Don hated playing the straight-man jerk rival with the perpetual sneer. He was afraid of getting typecast, like Lloyd Bochner who had described his own series of Hollywood roles as "the snob with the moustache who beats his wife."

Just before Christmas, and before Don had had even one chance to earn his $750 a week actually on the premises, Paramount Studios confirmed the rumours by dropping all twenty-five of their contract players. Nice seasonal touch.

At 6 a.m. on Christmas Eve, just as he was leaving for his last day at Desilu, the phone rang. It was his agent, Marty Baum, in New York. "Can you fly to Washington tonight?"

What would make such a devoted family man leave his home on Christmas Eve? The starring role in the American tour of *Look Back in Anger*, that's what. Don had seen Kenneth Haig play Jimmy

Porter on Broadway, and thought it was the best part for a young actor written in this century. It was also one of the most demanding, and he would have only three days in which to learn it and rehearse with the cast before opening in Cleveland.

The producer, David Merrick, had hired John Barrymore Jr., who fled in terror after the first rehearsal, and telephoned from the airport in Rome to say that he could not cope with the role, which had more lines than Hamlet. They were up the creek, and offered Harron twice what he had been making at Paramount. Harron shouted, 'Yes, by Christ, yes!!'' and Marty told him the plane ticket would be waiting for him by the time he got back from the studio. Gogie would have to do his packing, and handle Santa alone.

When he told them the news at Desilu, Ann Carroll drove all the way home to Beverly Hills and back again to lend him her copy of John Osborne's play, and she and Michael Landon helped him learn his lines. Ernie Kovacs sent him home with a case of champagne.

The four of us wept and wailed as we hugged him and kissed him goodbye. Another Christmas without snow was bad enough, but without our king, our court jester, our master of ceremonies? Who would screw up the bedtime stories? Who would play the giant in the apple orchard, pretending to be asleep while Mary and I snuck up on him? Who would make us laugh?

Imagine how we would have carried on if we'd known that the Donald Harron who left us on Christmas Eve, 1958, would never come home again. Directors and drama schools devote so much energy to helping the actor *become* the character. If they could teach the actor how to get *out* of it again, they would be doing performers and their families a big favour.

19

MR. RIGHT IS DEAD

THE plane landed in Washington very early Christmas morning, and the entire cast of *Look Back in Anger* was waiting for their new Jimmy Porter onstage. Don hadn't played a part like this since Edmund in *King Lear*, and decided that a modern Bastard with a Midland accent would have to see him through for the present, while he concentrated on learning all those lines.

They rehearsed until it was time for the rest of the cast to do their final matinée with Donald Madden, the current Jimmy Porter, who was leaving to play Hamlet at the Phoenix in New York. As Don studied the later parts of the play, he realised that the character expressed more anguish than he had ever felt, or been called upon to produce. He decided to imagine that he was an actor far from home on Christmas Day, caught up in a situation that was too much for him to handle.

When he came to the part where Jimmy learns of his mother's death, he tried to picture what would have happened if Mary and I had been in that convertible when it rolled down the hill. "There is nothing a desperate actor will not do, in thought at any rate." This turned out to be a dangerous mental exercise. Without realising it, he began to recreate events at Summitridge Drive as if Jimmy Porter, not Donald Harron, had been there. He literally looked back in anger, and rewrote his own history.

Reading his memoirs many years later, I thought I had blocked these events from my memory, but I have now conferred with my mother and sister, and it's three against one: he accuses himself of all kinds of beastly words and deeds he never committed. He claims, for instance, that he and Gloria had a huge fight several days before Christmas, were still not speaking by the time he left for Washington, and that to spite her he set up a new trampoline in the living room as a parting gift to the children. *It never happened*. Oh, he gave us a trampoline all right, but that was outside, the following summer.

After a Christmas dinner consisting of a cold corned beef sandwich and a cup of tea, he went to see Madden give his final performance as Jimmy Porter. When Jimmy described his mother-in-law as "rougher than a night in a Bombay brothel," five people went storming up the aisle muttering about filth and desecration. Don sank down in his seat — this never happened to Edmund.

The scariest part was that he had to sing, solo, *a capella*, to an improvised blues tune. He decided to try to imitate his fave rave Joe Turner, and hope for the best. Before he went onstage in Cleveland that fateful opening night, he did something he hadn't done in a long time. He got down on his knees and begged God, if He was up there, to see him through *Look Back in Anger* in one piece. The answer, if He was up there, was yes and no.

The next thing he remembers is the phone ringing early the next morning. It was the producer, David Merrick: "Congratulations, Mr. Harron. You saved all our asses last night. If you don't mind I'd like to extend the tour beyond its present limits, to end in May instead of March. Okay?"

Don said that was okay with him, and ran for the morning papers to read the reviews. He thought *The Plain Dealer*'s comment on his performance could be taken several ways: "His reading of the piece's most compelling speeches is something most theatre-goers won't forget for some time."

Reading?! Don says, "I memorized the whole damned thing in three days!"

The Cleveland News praised Don's "artful way with the conscienceless hero heel" adding, "If Mr. Harron hasn't spent his life to here flouting the moralities, railing against the social order, and sleeping in any bed with any partner, then in the persuasiveness of his performance, we must concede that he is an actor — a gifted actor!"

By the end of the run, the answer to this was "All of the above."
It is possible to become another person eight times a week and walk
away from it the rest of the time, but hard to do with no family
life, with descriptions like "brilliant" and "dazzling" greeting you
at every stop along the road. Just about the only dissenter was Nathan
Cohen. *Look Back in Anger* didn't play Toronto, so Nathan went
all the way to Montreal to give him a good panning. Don kept a
copy of it in his wallet and peeked at it whenever he thought he
was getting too conceited.

He began to swagger a bit, to talk back to head waiters and talk
show hosts. The *Chicago Sun-Times* reported: "Don Harron, the
Look Back in Anger star, looked back in anger at WBKB's Marty
Faye the other night. Harron was devastating." Society belles began
to throw themselves at more than his feet. He describes his reaction this way: "It was as if the Greek theory of acting was in force,
that some God descended from Olympus and took possession of
the actor's body, while his spirit sat the whole thing out in the dressing room." (This is the thespian version of the Devil made me do it.)

By the time they got to Denver in April he was in a state of
collapse, totally drained by his experiences offstage and on. He never
even saw the theatre in Denver, but stayed in bed with B-12 while
his understudy went on in his place. Lo and behold, Murray and
Martha Fisher were in the audience opening night, in town for a
medical convention. Heaven knows what they thought of the play,
but they showered their son-in-law with tender concern. Boy did
he feel like a heel.

They put him on a plane for Los Angeles, the next date on the
tour anyway, for a few days' rest with his family. Bedtime stories
had always been such a riot, with Father playing all the parts in
different voices and punning up the text to wails of "Oh, Daddy,
read it straight!" although we clearly didn't mean it. But this time
was different. He just didn't have the old pep.

Neither did Mother. His letters home must have spelled a distinct
change in their relationship, no crying aloud to be together. Without
that, the months of smog and sole parenting had begun to take
their toll — especially the chauffeuring: *three* return trips a day to
Westwood. She never once asked us to brown-bag it in the

schoolyard, and we never thought to offer. What else have mothers got to do?

There was Don, flat on his back with exhaustion, and Gloria ''seemed peevish.'' This was not the cheerful and adoring woman he had married. ''Physically weak though I was, I responded by playing Jimmy Porter, and treating my long-suffering wife with the contempt I had grown accustomed to meting out to my long-suffering wife on stage every night.'' She responded by saying she wished she worked in a bookshop, it would be so much easier than looking after him.

Everybody else seemed to appreciate him. Thanks to his creative press agent Ronnie Cowan, a constant stream of false rumours kept appearing in the local tabloids, the *Hollywood Reporter* and *Daily Variety*. Articles linked him with a variety of leading ladies he'd never met, in film projects he'd never heard of, with all the attendant innuendos.

Opening night at the Biltmore was his first day out of bed, but the notices were as ecstatic as usual. Even Hedda Hopper went, and wrote: ''Donald Harron who gives a brilliant performance in *Look Back in Anger* (and how I loathed that play) was here a year under contract to Paramount Pictures and never made a picture. I don't think it will be long before he gets a picture.''

It wasn't long before he got a picture. It all happened at a huge cocktail party his press agent threw in his honour. She told him it was an essential career move, well worth the $2,000 it was going to cost him. It was a glittering affair, the food and the guests were in excellent taste, and everyone had a wonderful time. Pity neither Donald nor Gloria could make it.

Gloria was at home looking after the girls, who had chickenpox. That's right, I got it twice. Anyway, she hated parties and was thoroughly sick of the whole Hollywood scene. Don was called away to a rehearsal just as the first guests were arriving. Cast member Al Muscari had broken his leg in a motorcycle accident, and the understudy had never played his part before. By the time they'd finished rehearsing, Donald had missed his own do.

This experience taught him two very valuable lessons about Hollywood: everything important happens when you're not there, and cocktail parties are far more crucial than appointments in producers' offices. He was given a firm offer by 20th Century Fox to appear in one of those all-star big-budget blockbusters. They didn't know which part they wanted him for, they just wanted him. It was called *The Best of Everything*.

There was no script to be had yet, but in the meantime there was the bestselling novel of the same name by Rona Jaffe. He took a copy with him to San Francisco, where the tour of *Look Back in Anger* would wind up with a three-week run. The book was about hard-bitten ambition in a big New York publishing house. There were lots of good conscienceless heel parts — the message seemed to be that nine men out of ten are up to no good.

As soon as we were over the chickenpox, Gloria took Mary and me to San Francisco, paradise on earth after Los Angeles, to see our father spout filth and desecration. When asked what I thought of seeing my Daddy behave that way, I replied casually, "Oh, he's worse than that at home." This was untrue — not *worse*. It was a cheap shot.

Don had been sending a steady stream of wildly enthusiastic *Look Back in Anger* reviews to his New York agents, hoping for a Broadway play. They in turn had been spreading copies around. One morning Abe Newborn phoned to say that Paddy Chayefsky had actually read the clippings they had sent him, and was seriously considering him for the title role in his new play, *The Tenth Man*. The director would be Tyrone Guthrie.

Guthrie! Don had given up waiting for a little note in the mail. Instead, a return ticket arrived from Paddy Chayefsky. He caught a flight after the second show that Saturday, changed planes in Dallas and was in New York in time for a late Sunday breakfast with his agent. Abe Newborn met him at the airport, and gave him the lowdown before taking him to the producer's office on Fifth Avenue, where Chayefsky and Guthrie were waiting.

The Tenth Man is about this neurotic Jewish intellectual, deep in analysis, who wanders into a Long Island synagogue after an all-night drunk and is asked to participate in an exorcism ceremony for a beautiful young girl possessed by an evil spirit. Don said, "Sounds great, Abe, but New York is crawling with *real* Jewish actors deep in analysis. Why me?"

"Don't ask. Paddy was knocked out with your reviews, and he's knocked out with Guthrie. If the Big Guy gives you the nod, you're in."

When Don walked in, the tall Irishman and the short New York Jew stood up. The Jewish one was named Paddy. They shook hands, talked for two minutes, and shook hands again. It was a deal. There was just one condition: would Don please read the play before flying back to San Francisco, and see if he liked it?

He didn't just like it, he loved it. He phoned the agency the next morning to thank them before catching his plane. Abe wasn't there, but Marty Baum was and told him to forget about the whole thing — a much bigger offer had just come in. Lerner and Loewe had written a new musical based on T.H. White's *The Once and Future King*, and were looking for a Lancelot. Don said it was one of his favourite books, but what did this have to do with him?

Marty said, "You don't understand, it's all together. It's called *Camelot* and they've already got Richard Burton and Julie Andrews as Arthur and Guinevere. They auditioned Laurence Harvey and Chris Plummer for Lancelot, but now they're interested in *you*."

"Marty, are you crazy? I've just landed a part I love in a play I love, with a director I love!"

"Yes, but Donald, musicals pay a lot better than plays, and you get to do this great number called *If Ever I Should Leave You*."

"I can't even sing!"

"What do you mean you can't sing?! Everybody's raving about that blues number you did in *Anger*!"

"Marty! Forget it!! I can't sing to save my life, be happy with what you've got. And if they're looking for a Lancelot, tell them to phone CBC in Toronto and ask for a guy named Robert Goulet."

Marty Baum was an agent, not a referral service, so he tracked Goulet down in Bermuda and brought him to New York. When Bob got the part, Marty split the commission with Goulet's agent, who hadn't bothered to propose his unknown client for such a starring role. And so it goes in showbiz.

When he got back to San Francisco Don phoned Gloria in L.A. to tell her that we were moving back to New York in September, but there would be time for a stopover in Canada first. "She seemed cheerful for the first time in months." Then she told him her news.

The studio had decided to cast him as Sidney in *The Best of Everything*! He answered with a derisive raspberry.

Just his luck. All those cads, and he gets stuck playing boring old Mr. Nice Guy, the only one who ends up doing the decent thing by his office affair. "Sidney was one of those 'sensitive' men who bore you to death with their proper manners and passivity." (Speak for yourself, Donald, there's a long waiting list for guys like that.)

He wanted to be the drunk or the rapist or the one who runs out on the girl just before her abortion. Louis Jourdan got to drive Suzy Parker to suicide, and he was stuck with making an honest woman out of drippy old Martha Hyer.

At the first set up, in the garden behind the Museum of Modern Art in New York, he was introduced to Rona Jaffe. Straight out, he asked the author of *The Best of Everything* why Sidney was such a wimp. Her eyes opened wide with shock. She said that Sidney was "Mr. Right," the true hero of the novel. She had personally chosen Don for the part because of the sensitivity she had seen in his face when they screened his old Paramount tests. Ah, but that was before he became Jimmy Porter. . . .

Ms. Jaffe's next novel was entitled *Mr. Right is Dead*.

Back in Hollywood he learned that there were four whole weeks to spend with his family before shooting resumed in the studio. "I was really feeling withdrawal symptoms from *Look Back in Anger* and the first chance I got to do the play again, I took it." The call was from Bob Gibson, who was doing a summer season at Laguna Beach. He was intending to do Shaw's *Man and Superman*, and naturally thought of Don for the title role: they were doing the shorter platform version, *Don Juan in Hell*.

"Hmmm. How about *Look Back in Anger* instead?"

Bob had worked with Don in Canada enough to laugh and reply, "How about *Look Back in Anger* as *well*?"

"Done!" said Harron, and off we went to Laguna Beach. Mary and Martha had a great time collecting abalone shells but Gloria, that dreadful hag, thought it was a shame to be wasting a $1,000-a-month house back in Beverly Hills, using up money we would be sure to need in New York.

Any lack of enthusiasm on her part might have had something

to do with the fact that Don was having affairs with not one but both of his leading ladies. This didn't leave much time for abalone shells, but he couldn't help it. For years his wife had held him back with this ridiculous business about being a writer, and never appreciated his true self, emerging at last. Leslie Howard? Montgomery Clift? Ha! None of that sensitive stuff. He was Don Harron, the irresistible Angry Young Superstud.

Don Juan in Hell was hard work of a different kind, and he loved it. He says Shaw requires more passion than Shakespeare, albeit an intellectual passion, because the speeches are constructed like operatic arias. Playing his father-in-law was Patrick Macnee, their first appearance together since *A Sleep of Prisoners* in Toronto. Pat was involved with three women too, but as they all lived in the same beach house in Malibu, Don thought Pat had his sleep easy.

Back in Los Angeles, during his first day on the set of *The Best of Everything*, Don was sent for by the big, BIG star of the picture, Joan Crawford. She wanted to meet the "classical theatre actor." She offered him a bottle of Pepsi, and asked him to sit down. She then launched into a long one-sided conversation about her brother, whom she described as a hopeless drunk. Don couldn't help noticing that her shoes didn't match, and one was a particularly ugly plastic.

He didn't have any scenes with her, let alone screen kisses thank heaven, and they didn't meet again until the day he took Mary and me along with him to the studio to view some rushes. She had brought her daughters, who looked like twins, to do the same. Watching the daily rushes can be extremely tedious. We saw the same scene dozens of times from every conceivable angle, including under the table. It was a restaurant scene with a bit of footsy work.

Mary and I didn't mind because we were new to it, but for Crawford's daughters it must have been a familiar form of torture. They sat quiet as mice through the whole thing, to a constant barrage of criticism from their mother: "Why can't you behave like Mr. Harron's daughters? They know how to sit properly. Mr. Harron's daughters behave like young ladies, not like you, blah blah blah." Anyone who could call Martha Harron a proper young lady had to be a very sick person. Ask Nina Foch.

As soon as the filming was over, we (Gloria) packed up and took the Superchief train back to Canada. When we were delayed by flash floods in Colorado, I swear there were flowers the next morning. It was wonderful to spend August in Gravenhurst instead of L.A. Don taught us to ride bicycles, which meant we could spin over to Gull Lake for a swim and back again. When it was time to move back to New York, it was decided to leave the little girls behind.

In New York, rehearsals for *The Tenth Man* began in the top floor roof garden of the abandoned Amsterdam Theater on seedy 42nd St. Guthrie and Chayefsky had assembled a stellar cast of Jewish actors, including Lou Jacobi. Czech comedian George Voskovec and Donald Harron were the only Gentiles, apart from their Irish director of course.

Guthrie began by stating in his usual Oxford undergrad manner that he was "hopelessly Goy and V grateful for help from Orthodox sources." He wondered if it was perhaps by some oversight that the first out-of-town preview was planned for Yom Kippur. Two dignified Jewish gentlemen, the producers, made a frantic dash for the phones.

As usual Tony went straight to staging, no read-through. Don's character, Arthur Landau, did not appear right away, so he was able to sit back and thrill to the sight of the master at work once again. As for the author, the play was a real departure for Chayefsky. This time the King of kitchen sink drama had spun a Yiddish folk tale in a contemporary urban setting, based on Ansky's *The Dybbuk* (named after the evil spirit to be exorcised). The only problem was that, in the transfer to spoken word from printed page, the prose sounded too literary, with three adjectives for every noun.

Master and pupil conferred briefly at the first break, and Don asked Tony if he could do anything about Paddy's "adjectivitis." Tony said he would try. As rehearsals progressed, Chayefsky seemed to love everything Guthrie did, even though he slashed left and right with fiendish glee until the roof garden was knee-deep in excised epithets.

The only member of the cast who dropped out was Jack Pearl, radio's Baron Munchausen in the '30s, who was wonderful in rehearsal but comfortably retired. He phoned after a few days to say that it was too hard on his nerves. The next morning, a Sunday, Don was sitting on a bench in one of those little concrete quadrangles that passes for a park in New York, brooding all by himself in a tortured, neurotic, intellectual way, when comedian Jack Gilford came walking by. Don asked if he was working, and Jack said no, the blacklist you know . . .

By Monday morning, Gilford was a member of the cast, replacing Jack Pearl. His dialogue with Lou Jacobi on the complexities of the New York subway system became the most hilarious scene in the play.

The cast was so marvellous, Don didn't mind playing the straight man this once. He spent his evening reading weighty books about psychoanalysis, and somehow the more he read, the more repressed and withdrawn Gloria seemed. He spent some social evenings with a group of psychiatrists, bursting with questions about his new obsession. He decided that their immature, alcoholic behaviour must be the result of solving other people's problems all day long.

Don's character was by far the most neurotic, but the most dramatic figure in the play was the young girl possessed by the dybbuk. The same day Risa Schwartz landed the best part in the play, the only female role, she also enrolled in Hunter College. All her spare time was spent sitting quietly in a corner studying mathematics. Boy, was she repressed and withdrawn.

Don found the scene where he and the girl are alone in the Rabbi's office very hard to do. It was intensely emotional yet very delicate, and he turned to Guthrie for guidance. Tony told him to keep moving restlessly round and round the desk, never stopping for a moment. Don remembered Elia Kazan's crack about Guthrie substituting locomotion for emotion, swallowed hard and said nothing.

On Yom Kippur they did not open in Philadelphia, but went to schul to celebrate the Day of Atonement. When they did open, the reviews were pretty dreadful. As Philadelphia was the only pre-Broadway stop, this meant bad vibes in *Variety* and no nice quotations for the marquee, but Chayefsky and Guthrie stuck to their guns. There would be no major changes.

Next stop was the Booth Theatre, where Don had won all hearts in *Home Is the Hero*. The first preview was sparsely attended, and the second packed to the rafters for a benefit performance at fifty dollars a crack. The spectators sat on their hands, stared at one another instead of the stage and laughed in all the wrong places, including the dramatic climax of the play.

Opening night audiences could be even worse. By then not only was Donald tortured and neurotic, he was a nervous wreck. The worst part was that the *Toronto Star* had sent a cub reporter down. His assignment was to follow Harron's every move during the twenty-four hours prior to curtain up on opening night, and Maurice Duff fulfilled this mission with grim determination.

Jimmy Porter would have given Duff a swift kick where it counts, but Arthur Landau let him sit in his Perry St. apartment until 4:30 in the morning. Gloria retreated into some Proust while Don and his friend Peter Baldwin made stilted conversation in the living room, waiting for Maurice and his notepad to go away. Peter had been Don's bosom friend during their paid vacation as contract players at Paramount, so I'm sure much was left unsaid. Peter promised to try to make it to the performance that night, or at least to Sardi's afterwards to join in the wait/wake for the reviews, and have a *real* talk.

When Don and Gloria awoke the next morning, Maurice Duff was standing at the door. When Donald actually let him *in*, Gloria went pale. Duff probably didn't notice, or care, but Don could see between the freckles and decided to go shopping for opening night gifts, with Duff in tow.

While prowling the joke stores for spring-loaded chocolates and squirting flowers, Don grumbled that he wished he could skip the first night, and go straight to the second, to an audience with no axe to grind. Duff said, "Maybe there won't be a second night, did you ever think of that?"

Duff followed Don home to Greenwich Village to watch him eat a dozen oysters and go over his lines. Suddenly Don sprang to the phone, called Tyrone Guthrie and said he needed a line changed. Tony replied in a weary but calm voice that there would be plenty of time for that the second night, without throwing the rest of the cast at the last minute.

Duff breathed down his neck all the way to the stage door, where Don politely told him where to go: to his seat, to review the play like everybody else. Don doesn't remember the performance itself, just that Gloria looked particularly repressed and withdrawn as they walked over to Sardi's afterwards.

Cast and friends gathered upstairs with a funereal air. Even the Guthries and Chayefskys were very quiet. Tony talked about his plans to establish a repertory company in Minneapolis. Don said he had played there in *Anger*, and found a real thirst for theatre. Tony asked if he would be interested in joining him there and Don replied, "Whither thou goest, I will go."*

Tony smiled and asked if that would include following him to the theatre right next door, to play Solly Bridgewater in his next production, Robertson Davies' *Leaven of Malice*. Don laughed, explained that he'd spent six months working on it, and told him to try Richard Easton instead. No hard feelings — he just wasn't right for the part.

Just then their press agent walked in with sweat on his brow and a damp piece of paper in his hand. It was the *Times* review, which began, "Being a genuine writer, Paddy Chayefsky can make the impossible happen. He has written an enchanting play. . . ." A few minutes later the *Herald Tribune* added, "it is a work of the creative imagination. Let me try to explain what a rare thing a work of the creative imagination is on Broadway. . . ."

The funeral party turned into Mardi Gras. A few minutes later, Don's friend Peter Baldwin walked in with an extraordinarily beautiful woman. Her name was Virginia Leith, and Don recognised her face from the movies. She didn't want to talk about that, she was deep in analysis. She was quiet, but you could tell she didn't have a repressed bone in her body.

The Tenth Man was a huge, huge hit and was still going strong when Don left fifteen months later. *Leaven of Malice*, without Don Harron or Richard Easton, opened and closed within a week at the theatre next door. At the Booth, tensions developed almost immediately between the veteran actors, accusing one another of upstaging.

*Ruth 1.16, but she was talking to her mother-in-law.

David Vardi from Israel's Habimah Theatre was branded "Vardi the Gonef" (thief) for inventing bits of comic business during other people's speeches.

Comedy is no laughing matter to its participants, and backstage screaming matches were frequent. As the young outsider, Don was appointed to referee these multilingual free-for-alls. He felt like Dag Hammarskjøld at the U.N. Meanwhile, his own home life was falling apart.

The way my father remembers it, he had been outvoted by Gloria and her parents, who felt it was better for the little girls to spend the year in Gravenhurst rather than in dirty, crowded New York City. When she read the manuscript of this book, my mother wrote in the margin: "In fact, I'd just finished painting and furnishing your room, but this is so well written I think you'd better leave it as it is." Either way, I can't help wishing Mary and I had been there all along, to provide the sticky hands and faces that keep couples together through trying times.

Murray and Martha Fisher brought us to New York at Christmas — Don thinks it was just for the holidays — and certain details are branded on my memory. We went to see *The Tenth Man*, of course, and I was particularly delighted to see "Uncle Lou" Jacobi on the stage. Father looked dark and haggard and terribly dashing.

The dramatic climax of the play is the exorcism performed by the minyan of ten men — that's a quorum in a synagogue. To everyone's surprise, the dybbuk, the evil spirit, emerged not from the girl in the centre but from my father, The Tenth Man. After all the sound and the fury had left him, he collapsed lifelessly onto the stage. He had been doing this eight times a week for months. Even Nathan Cohen liked it.

The only dissenting critic I know of was Maurice Duff of the *Toronto Star*, who wrote: "The play opens on a note of comedy but the lines are too Jewish for a general audience. Toronto's Lou Jacobi however has some funny lines. Don Harron has a somewhat less rewarding part. In the first act, his is a 'nothing role'. In the second he appears to be hampered by bad editing and the play's worst lines. But through it all he builds to a triumphant conclusion." That's one way of putting it.

The cast of *Hee Haw* first assembled in Nashville in 1969, including Don Harron (seated, left). Producer Frank Peppiatt recalls: "Admittedly Charlie Farquharson had never appeared in the U.S., but John Aylesworth and I knew that he had been making Canadians laugh for years. We also knew that making Canadians laugh for years was not easy unless you were a politician."

Seen here in 1973 with third wife Catherine McKinnon and their three-year-old daughter Kelley. When Don proposed to Catherine he also wrote to her manager, Paul Simmons, asking for the 85 percent of her that wasn't already spoken for.

Interviewing "The Chief", John Diefenbaker. Don Harron was host of CBC Radio's *Morningside* from 1977 to 1982. He called it "the most stimulating thing I've ever done. My producer had more faith in me than I had in myself. I took the job on and it changed my whole life."

Charlie in his "All Farces" uniform.

Don captured in a rare moment of repose during a pool-side interview for CBC's *Radio Guide* (November 7–20, 1981) which concludes thusly: "'The trick really is to know your limitations,' he says. 'What you have to do is try to be in public what you are in private.' He steps onto the diving board, and with a bounce, disappears beneath a quiet splash."

Portrait of a tired man who can't say no. As Mavor Moore says, "Seldom has one of our natural resources been so richly mined and generously handed out."

Don in drag as Valerie Rosedale, the society matron who believes that equality for women is a terrible step down. "Give a man an inch, and he thinks he's a ruler!"

Ray McFadden

As mascot and cheerleader for the Easter Seals Society's handicapped children, Don has participated in skate-a-thons, walk-a-thons, bike-a-thons and even snowmobile-a-thons. (A driver for the snowmobile is now wisely supplied.)

Hamming it up with 1982–83 Easter Seals Timmy Brian Kupferschmidt. Charlie is having an unmistakeable influence on the next generation.

Don-in-a-dog-collar hamming it up in *Mass Appeal*, P.E.I. 1986.

On the steps of his Alma Mater, Victoria College (now Victoria University) with its Chancellor, Dr. Northrop Frye, and fellow alumnus the Hon. Pauline McGibbon.

Literary agent Matie Molinaro says, "Only in Canada, I believe, is it possible for a writer to outsell his compatriots, sell tens of thousands of copies of his book—seven of them in fifteen years—and not make it to the bestseller list. Only in Canada, you say?...Pity!"

The Doctor of Personal Experience giving Catherine McKinnon his honorary degree from Mount Allison University for putting up with him all these years. They will be celebrating their twentieth wedding anniversary on March 12, 1989.

Charlie Farquharson, D.O.P.E., standing on the porch of the old Hunter homestead in Dunbarton. The self-proclaimed leader of the "F.U." Party ("Farmers Unite!") declares, "It's time we had a reel common man in yer Common House."

According to long-time friend and colleague Mavor Moore, "Harn contains several opposites: scholar and clown, nationalist and internationalist, sophisticate and sentimentalist, puritan and hedonist, poet and punster, old fart and eternal youth. What saves him from utter derangement is a genius for transmuting the lot into laughter."

Dr. Fisher left right after Christmas to get back to his patients. As soon as his father-in-law was gone, Don told his wife that their relationship was not fulfilling, and gave her an ultimatum: "I'm giving you until September to start having orgasms, and then I'm leaving." This was a threat guaranteed to set any girl's pants on fire, but Gloria took several hours to react.

That night, a Sunday, Don took his family to a cosy, elegant French restaurant. Suddenly my mother stood up and started shrieking at my father. All he remembers is her slapping him across the face with a force that left him speechless.

Out on the street, my sister and I tried to hold on to both parents at once. I didn't understand what was happening until we got back to the apartment, where my grandmother, dressed all in black and ashen-faced, threw her handbag on the floor and declared, "I will *not* have a divorce in this family!"

Donald and Martha Sr. retired to my parents' bedroom to have a talk. I got down on my hands and knees and kept busy retrieving Grandma's bits and pieces; then I knocked on the door and handed her the purse. Mary and I were put to bed — "Sweet dreams!" — but I refused to go to sleep until my mother and my father came in and promised to stay together. We held hands, and they promised.

When I woke up in the morning, he was gone.

20

PSYCHODRAMA

DONALD recalls, "I literally fled from the restaurant. Nor did I go back to our apartment that night. I phoned Virginia and asked if I could stay with her." He told his new love that she had saved his life, and I believe that he meant it with every fibre of his tortured, neurotic being. He lost fifteen pounds and spent a fortune in analysis. Finally, he wrote to Guthrie and asked him what to do. Tony wrote back, "Accept yourself."

While his lawyer was negotiating the divorce, Don flew up to Toronto to spend a Sunday afternoon with his daughters at Pinewood. After several months apart, it was a relief to fly back to New York secure in the knowledge that we were healthy and happy, pre-occupied with the joys of childhood. I had put on twenty pounds, and Mary thought she was a cat.

I know because I gave her the idea. But really, she was better off. It never ceases to amaze me how the most well-meaning adults can make comments like, "You know, if it wasn't for the children, she'd *kill* herself," when the children are well within earshot. There was a lot of talk about a "scarlet woman," and when Donald wrote about a friend of his who had a pussycat, I knew what he meant.

That constant trickle of funny postcards from our father was a godsend. By the age of eight or nine, as Mary and I were, children have long since given up expecting their parents to be perfect. They'll settle for unswerving devotion, even if you can't spare them your presence in person.

Gloria settled for what he offered her, a third of his gross income,

226

and got a job at the CBC answering audience mail. She worked late into the night, and lived in a rooming house nearby. Her parents gave her a car so that she could drive up to Gravenhurst every Friday afternoon and leave at dawn Monday morning. Her mother would wave from the kitchen window.

I saw one of those viewer's letters once, when Mary and I were taken to inspect the desk where Mother spent her time.* Her reply began something like this: "Dear Jimmy, I wish I could come to your birthday party, but I'm so busy saving lives in the Q Outback." It was signed, "The Flying Doctor."

For The Flying Dybbuk, 1960 began with Virginia Leith at Lee Strasberg's New Year's Eve party. Everyone that glittered was there. Don made the mistake of greeting Peter O'Toole, who replied, "Oh fuck off, you idiot!" When Chris Plummer told him he'd just snarled at The Tenth Man, O'Toole threw his arms around Don and said, "Forgive a drunken old fool. I saw you in the play this afternoon and you were ab-so-lutely bloody *mahvelous*!" He forgave.

As usual, *The Tenth Man* reviews were followed by a flood of offers Don couldn't accept, mostly bad ideas for television series, including one about an ex-king who becomes a private eye. One offer he couldn't resist was from David Susskind, to repeat his old role as the homicidal cuckold in *Crime of Passion* for the Play of the Week series.

Killing his wife's lover on television, on top of leaving his family and getting exorcised all the time, proved too much of a strain. B-12 shots didn't seem to help, so a friend in the *Crime of Passion* cast gave him a bottle of pick-me-up pills which did the trick. He floated through some heavy twenty-four-hour workdays and when the Play of the Week was over, felt well enough to do without them. He soon discovered that methadrine is highly addictive, and swore off the stuff. He had enough problems.

CBS made him host of a series about the meaning of Chanukah, although he told them he wasn't Jewish. He also agreed to speak at a B'nai Brith luncheon about the trials and tribulations of bringing

*I probably remember the letter because it was from someone my age, and addressed to one of my television heroes.

The Tenth Man to Broadway. He asked Lou Jacobi to give him a nice phrase in Hebrew to round off the speech. Repeating what Lou had written for him phonetically, he said "Le Shalom Habor Bei Yerushaleim," and was surprised to get a standing ovation. When he got back to the Booth, Lou told him it meant "Next year in Jerusalem!", the cry of hope since the Babylonian exile.

Life was full. After the wife-murderer he played another psychotic for David Susskind in Moss Hart's *Climate of Eden*, and then starred in a drama for NBC, but that was as a thoroughly wasted alcoholic. He can't even remember the name of it. His tortured image became so familiar on the American tiny box that an anonymous fan sent him a poem. I'm a fan of hers (his?). If you can supply the other twenty lines, please contact my publisher:

LINES TO AN ACTOR WHO IS TOO CONVINCING

Between the quiz and the western
And the suds that depress the soul
Comes a flash in the TV darkness
That is known as a Harron role.
It is less a light than a lightning
The neuroses fall like rain.
Our Don is extremely charming
But he isn't the least bit sane.

* * *

A gun is his best companion
A razor his dearest friend,
And girls who are chased by Donald
May come to a grisly end.
"Nobody loves me," he mutters
And the blade of his knife is keen;
His viewers watch from the safety
Of the other side of the screen

* * *

Not so Virginia, who had the privilege of watching Donald perform psychodrama in her tiny apartment. She vividly recalls the first time her mother-in-law came to visit. Don and Virginia spent half the night on the bedroom floor trying to strangle one another. This was nothing new, but they were saying "I'm going to kill you, you (son of a) bitch!!" to each other *in whispers*, so as not to disturb Dutzie who was sleeping in the next room.

Virginia Leith became a star overnight in Stanley Kubrick's first movie, *Fear and Desire* (typecasting), but is best known for her ninth picture, the one that was so bad she didn't want to talk about it. It was called *The Brain that Wouldn't Die* (typecasting), with Virginia in the title role. I don't know why they call it that, when it's clearly not just a brain but Virginia's whole head sitting in that pan of bubbling red liquid. She told Don that Rilke's poetry saved her life, and I believe that she meant it with every fibre of her tortured, neurotic being.

The Tenth Man had met his match. The only time his understudy got to fill in for him was when he flew to Mexico to get his divorce. He sent Gloria a postcard from Juarez, telling her it was official. In his last Broadway run, *Separate Tables*, he had also missed just one performance but that was to see *Turvey*. It was the same understudy, just a different wife.

Don and Virginia were married under a bower of white roses in the apartment of Broadway photographer Joe Abeles, a dear friend who had photographed the former Harron family on many occasions. Chris Plummer was best man, which was particularly apt as Don had introduced him to his wife Tammy Grimes.

The ceremony was performed by Reverend Bill Glenesk, the pastor of the showbiz church where Don performed on Sundays, giving readings from *The Book of Job* and other bits he identified with. A psychology book had revealed how similar his torment was to Christ's own, at the same age. His pastor's marriage sermon contained extracts not from the Bible, but from Shaw, T.S. Eliot and *The Skin of Our Teeth*. The 1960s had arrived, with a vengeance.

Don missed most of his wedding reception because he had to go to the theatre — only divorces rate understudies, apparently. Before he left, one of his psychiatrist-guests told him that there was nothing between the newlyweds but sex and it wouldn't last more than six or seven years. Don remembers thinking that sounded pretty good.

Back home, near dawn, he and his bride were engaged in a friendly game of Canasta when the phone rang. It was Virginia's matron of honour, a beautiful *Vogue* model, informing them that she had just spent the night in her bathtub with Don's best man, who insisted on singing loudly and wearing her best hat.

Chris Plummer was in the throws of divorce from Tammy Grimes. Don felt responsible and suggested his friend join him in a few rounds of therapy. Chris said, "What do you mean, psychoanalysis? That sort of thing gets rid of your neuroses!"

"That's right!" said Don, hopefully.

"Are you crazy? If I get rid of my kinks, what will I do for talent?!"

Finally, to Don's relief and delight, someone approached him to do a comedy series. It was two guys from Toronto named Frank Peppiatt and John Aylesworth. Peppiatt had played the office ringleader who shattered my psyche in *The Prizewinner* on CBC-TV. They wanted Charlie Farquharson, who shattered my sister's psyche in *The Big Revue*, to play Dennis Weaver's country cousin in a pilot for a hick version of *The Perry Como Show*, a shattering thought in itself.

Don could only shave lightly on Wednesday and Saturday nights because of *The Tenth Man*, but that suited Charlie just fine. Jewison's cap and Campbell's sweater were in storage at Pinewood Ave., so Frank and John dressed him up in a tight tweed suit with a bow tie. Then they painted freckles on his face and parted his hair in the middle with a cowlick. He looked just like Alfalfa on *Spanky and Our Gang*.

He was bitterly disappointed when the series didn't sell, which gives you some idea of his mental condition. He looked great, though. I know because he brought his new bride up to Toronto the Sunday before Christmas. We were dolled up in our best matching dresses (God how I hated that; it made me look a year younger than my age) and taken out to the airport by Lionel and Dutzie. We were encouraged to practise our Shirley Temple curtsey while we waited, in fear and loathing.

I can still remember the sick feeling in the pit of my stomach as we stared through the glass at the back of their heads coming up the escalator. They had the same colour of hair. When I saw the scarlet woman's face I did not forgive my father, but I understood him. He couldn't help it. She had beauty, she had mystery, you could tell she didn't have a repressed bone in her body.

With her dark gleaming hair, in her dark gleaming fur coat and sunglasses, she represented everything forbidden and fascinating — sex, glamour, danger . . . I fell hopelessly in love. When Mary and I curtsied simultaneously in our twin haircuts and party dresses, Virginia got this sick feeling in the pit of her stomach, but she repressed it for the moment.

They arrived with matching suitcases, which were monogrammed "M.A.H." and "M.M.H.", and filled with presents for Mary and me. We knew we were being bought off, but why make a scene. Don announced that he was leaving *The Tenth Man* in January, and flying to Hollywood to play the handsome prince in Hans Christian Anderson's *The Little Mermaid*. The little mermaid would be played by — guess who? Shirley Temple!

Don recalls, "For the first time in a long time I was a hero in the eyes of my children." Hero is putting it a little strongly, but I have to admit we were impressed. It was also a relief to know he hadn't signed to tour as Hitler or something.

This trip to Los Angeles was to be their official honeymoon, marking the end of fifteen months as The Tenth Man. After over 500 exorcisms on stage, and all those psychos on the tiny box, he was really looking forward to a little sun and relaxation. A few days later, he sliced his arm open with a butcher knife.

This event was triggered by the hideous spectacle of his new bride and her mother playing a continuous rerun of *Whatever Happened to Baby Jane?*, with Virginia as the *real* Joan Crawford. How could this elegant, sensitive woman of 34, so wise about other people's problems, be locked in a life-and-death battle of recrimination with a lurid old manicurist who belonged to the "Mothers of Hollywood Stars Club"? Suddenly, it all came crashing down on him.

His dreadful new mother-in-law had sent her only child to a series of convent boarding schools, so her almost-as-dreadful father wouldn't find her. Virginia had repaid this unkindness by giving her mother the down-payment on a house on the edge of Beverly Hills, the better to hate her at close quarters. Don pleaded with her to, in Guthrie's oft-repeated phrase, "Rise above and get on with it." Virginia recoiled in horror, as if he were trying to rob her of her birthright.

So, one night, with *Baby Jane* hot and heavy in the living room, he ran to the kitchen and grabbed the butcher knife. To his surprise, real blood gushed out in torrents, and he was rushed to the UCLA emergency department. He had almost killed himself, like Alfalfa from *Spanky and Our Gang*.

Fortunately he failed, and showed up on the set of *The Little Mermaid* next morning with his right arm swathed in bandages. When people asked him what happened, he just smiled and said, "Oh, you know, tried to kill myself!" and they'd smile back. The first thing Shirley Temple did was curl his hair. He had told the Theater Guild to piss off for trying the same thing, but he was in no mood to argue about anything.

The best things about the show were the contraptions called Kirby's flying harnesses. As most of the scenes were underwater, the Prince had to learn to swim and float in the air. He felt free, like Peter Pan. He loved it so much he spent all his breaks and lunch hours practising loops and spins, holding a sandwich with his good arm.

When we saw the show on TV, Mary and I were very disappointed to discover that Shirley Temple had grown up and lost her charm. Moreover, as producer-star-script supervisor-unofficial director, and evidently also film editor, Mrs. Shirley Temple Black had left every possible trace of other people's close-ups on the cutting room floor. We saw a lot of the back of Donald's head, and much of the mermaid herself. So much for NBC's Fairy Tale Theatre — Miss Shirley starred in every episode. Don wonders what she did to whole countries as U.S. ambassador.

You'd think his next move would be to get the hell out of Tinseltown and away from Baby Jane, but no. "The plan for us was to stay on in California and do television." By this he means that he would do television, with Virginia acting as his adviser. From the moment he moved in with her, it never occurred to either of them that she should earn a living. In the dark days before female equality, this was not unusual.

Thank God, he got an invitation to go back to Stratford-on-the-Housatonic, which he had the good sense to accept. They moved into a cottage in Lordship, Connecticut, near the theatre and the beach, and bought a 1948 Mercury for fifty dollars. It was grey with a bright blue roof and dubbed Natasha, in honour of Virginia's vocal coach at 20th Century Fox, Natasha Litess, a grey Slav with a blue rinse.

Don was cast as Orlando, the handsome young hero in *As You Like It*, opposite Kim Hunter as Rosalind. She had an Oscar, but couldn't handle the soaring verse, so director Word Baker conceived of the lovebirds tossing a soaring rubber ball back and forth while lobbing lumps of poetry. One night Don missed the ball and it landed in the audience. He said to the man closest to it on the aisle, "I prithee, Sire, the sphere of Vulcan!" and got his ball back. To his surprise, this modern dress production was a big hit with the New York critics.

Dear Grandma Harron and her bad legs brought Mary and me down to Connecticut on the train. Virginia threw a fit because Gloria had sent us with a chaperone, as if she couldn't be trusted. Don recalls, "I thought it was a tempest in a teapot if dear Mum wanted to sleep on the sofa, but Virginia was adamant and it all ended in a huge fight with the chief victim, Farley the cat, being thrown out of doors by me for yowling at the wrong time."

Now Farley was a very intelligent cat, and even he would have told you that it was much harder on Dutzie to be thrown out of her son's house than it was on him. However, to Virginia the inner truth was the only truth, and it was absolutely pointless to be nice to people if you didn't really mean it. Sadly, this precluded any hope of a sane family life.

I responded to all this by throwing myself at Virginia's feet and pouring out my soul to her. (Well, most of it. No child is *that* dumb.) Even my father had noticed that I had put on weight (he says forty pounds, which is a bit thick). Not so my dreadfully blonde sister, who thanks to me had kept her feline figure. Don was convinced that we must be well adjusted because, thanks to Gloria's tutoring, not her chauffeuring, we had both skipped a grade at Gravenhurst Public School. In his memoirs, he proudly records the fact that the principal marched me up to the grade eight class, to show them how reading aloud should be done. That wasn't me, that was Mary. Prrrrrr.

There was, we discovered, a beneficial side to all this inner truth business. I told V, as we called her, that I wished I could live with my mother in Toronto. Virginia told Don, who phoned Gloria, and when we got back from two action-packed weeks in Connecticut, Mary and I found ourselves living in our mother's apartment in Rosedale — much to the stoic dismay of her cheerful flatmates, both of whom eventually moved out. It had never occurred to Gloria that any member of her family might want to live with her. We did!

While the theatre took a back seat in his mind to the drama at home, Don was in all three productions of the American Shakespeare Festival's 1961 summer season, and we went to see them. *Macbeth* featured the unlikely pairing of the divine Jessica Tandy as Lady Macbeth and earth-bound Pat Hingle playing her hen-pecked husband as if he was the third murderer. Mind you, it was hard to see much of anything in the murky mists. Witches injured themselves regularly trying to find their way off the blasted heath, cursing the lighting director, a butch lady everyone referred to as "The Prince of Darkness." Donald played Banquo, and one of the few things you could see clearly was the bloody, ashen face of Banquo's ghost at the banquet, rising to the occasion on a hidden platform.

This time I didn't say "He's worse than that at home," but we couldn't help noticing the big scar across the inside of his forearm. He admitted what he'd done — he didn't say why, but we didn't think we needed to ask — and warned us never to try it, because the pain is unbelievable. This is one parental command I have found easy to keep.

"But," he said bitterly, "if I'd really been trying to kill myself, I would have done it there!" and pointed to the wrist, two inches from the slash mark. In other words, what really bothered him was not that he'd almost thrown his life away, or broken so many hearts, but that he hadn't been *sincere* about it! Psychoanalysis said the inner man was all that mattered, and he was taking it literally.

After two years as Jimmy Porter and Arthur Landau, two of the most gruelling roles written in this century, poor Don didn't know which Id was up, where his inner man ended and Jimmy's or Arthur's began. His memoirs are a clear indication that he has yet to recover: he discusses John Houseman's direction of *Troilus and Cressida* at Stratford, Conn. in detail, quotes several conversations they had on various topics, yet dismisses his "phony" wrist slitting in a paragraph. You can still see the scar clear as day — and Houseman wasn't even in Connecticut that summer.

However, many can attest to the fact that Donald "Three Faces of Yves" Harron was there, and being a bit unhinged certainly didn't do him any harm as an actor. *As You Like It* was the biggest hit of the season, with Donald in a denim jacket he "forgot" to return to wardrobe. The poor fellow thinks he stole it from John Houseman. . . .

But his greatest personal triumph, and satisfaction, was as Thersites* in *Troilus and Cressida*. Although he complained about the American Civil War setting ("The war between the states was fought over the issue of slavery, not some blonde bimbo called Helen!") it enabled him to combine two of his favourite things: Shakespeare and Charlie Farquharson. Why not? The first time Guthrie heard one of Don's farmer monologues, he said Charlie's speech patterns were much closer to the original Elizabethan than current Oxford English.

From this Rhett 'n Scarlett *Troilus and Cressida*, with Greek soldiers in Union blue and Trojans in Confederate grey, I remember two big showstoppers — first Jessica Tandy, all in black, as Cassandra the prophetess, who enters raving and tells the Trojans they're done for: "Cry, Trojans, cry! Practise your eyes with tears!" The second was Thersites Farquharson, tellin' them Greek fellers the same blame thing.

Thersites is described as "a deformed and scurrilous Grecian" and Don thought, "That's the part for me!" In this version he was the Yankee camp cook, and arrived onstage pulling a chuck wagon for a canteen. It wasn't Charlie, but the black sheep of the Farquharson family, chewing tobacco (licorice) and spittooning the juice, telling everybody off left, right and centre. He hadn't shaved, and

*rhymes with "nighties"

was wearing a ragged, dirty pair of red longjohns — the Hick from Vic, a little the worse for wear, but magnificent.

He combined Thersites' two soliloquies into one long monologue, and it brought the house down every time. The only objection amongst the raves was from *The New York Times* critic, who thought he went too far when he picked his nose. Don says, "Oh dear, fell off the tightrope of taste again," but after all, it was in character. The soliloquy begins, "How now, Thersites! what, lost in the labyrinth of the fury!" Yes, indeed.

Thersites is a freelancer, not a team player, and survives the final battle as an unconscientious objector:

MARGARELON: Turn, slave, and fight.
THERSITES: What art thou?
MARGARELON: A bastard son of Priam's.
THERSITES: I'm a bastard too; I love bastards. . . .

Don was sorry to see the season end. Classical repertory is what most dedicated actors love best. People like Charles Laughton, Tony Randall, Charlton Heston, George Segal and Joanne Woodward would come backstage to tell him how much they envied his lot. But the only offer out of all those good reviews was a new comedy by John Patrick called *Everybody Loves Opal*. He turned it down. They upped the offer. He turned it down again. It was about three swindlers trying to kill a harmless old bag lady for the insurance policy they had just sold her, and he didn't think that was funny.

They upped the offer again, and before he could refuse, he received a whopping great bill from his children's dentist. He took the job. The cast was first-rate, with Eileen Heckart as Opal, and Stubby Kaye and Brenda Vaccaro as Don's sidekicks, but he kept wondering how he was going to douse the old lady with kerosene and make the audience laugh at the same time.

On opening night in Wilmington, Delaware, he accidentally hooked the fringe of Opal's shawl with one of his cuff buttons, and it followed him wherever he went for the rest of the hectic scene, including the tango with Stubby Kaye. It was uproariously funny, and in the morning along with raves in the newspapers came a dozen long-stemmed roses from the director, Cyril Ritchard, best known as Captain Hook in *Peter Pan*.

Unfortunately, the roses did not come with instructions on how to catch the shawl on his cuff every night, and the reviews encouraged the powers-that-be to take off in their Jags and Rolls for the weekend, instead of holding rehearsals to make the show better. They opened at the Longacre in New York and to his surprise, the reviews were excellent in the press, on television and over the wire services. There were just two exceptions, the *Times* and the *Trib*, the *sine qua non* of success. Walter Kerr echoed Don's own sentiments exactly, saying that *Everybody Loves Opal* was just "three seedy people being absolutely beastly to Eileen Heckart all evening." He noted, "Because Mr. Harron is a very good actor, he tries to find something to act in the role." *Opal* lasted a month.

Supporting two households was no joke, especially with my rotten teeth. Before Christmas, he found himself lining up for an unemployment cheque for the first time in his life. Practically his last dime was spent on a visit to Toronto with Virginia, their suitcases full of presents. She really loved us, especially when we weren't there, and worked hard to make holidays fun-filled occasions. They were always memorable.

Poor or not, Father had the good sense not to stay at Pinewood. While in town, they lodged at the Waldorf-Astoria, not like the one in New York but Toronto's version of the Montecito, where the "fun bunch" stay. It was also walking distance from the top of Sherbourne St., where Mary and I lived with Mother, who by then had been promoted to editor of CBC-Radio's *Trans-Canada Matinée*. She worked late, and a kind friend of Dutzie's, Sadie Wilson, came from Pinewood Ave. every day to feed us and try to teach us some manners.

Don agreed to participate in a Variety Club telethon with Monty Hall but when he got to the TV studio, he bent over to pick up a 25¢ piece and the seat of his pants ripped wide open. It was the fabric, not the seam, and he fled without a word to anyone, although I'm sure the wardrobe department would gladly have come up with a pair of trousers for the visiting celebrity. He hadn't made room in his suitcase for a second pair, nor did he have the money to buy any. He slunk back to New York with his jacket pulled low over his hips.

To make ends meet, Virginia went out and did a Palmolive beauty soap commercial, something her face could do any time she wanted. I can still remember it—she was coming up an escalator. Her husband felt terrible. When she'd met him, he was the toast of Broadway, and now she had to degrade herself to support him. His only steady work came from non-sponsored Sunday shows on CBS and NBC like *Lamp Unto My Feet* and *Camera Three*, where he played the likes of Thomas Merton and Aaron Burr with fellow failures Ed Asner and Larry Hagman.

He was thrilled when the CBC brought him back to Toronto for a ninety-minute version of *The Lady's Not For Burning*, not to sweep the floor this time, but to swap love poetry with Zoe Caldwell. Virginia kept telling him to assert himself, so he grew a beard and dyed his eyebrows raven black. He says Zoe was magical, but he wasn't: "I was still blinded by the memory of Chris Plummer."

It wasn't Plummer's shadow that haunted him so much as the voice of his first wife, shrieking "Why don't you face it, you'll never be as good an actor as Chris Plummer!" in that cosy French restaurant. She doesn't remember saying any such thing. She admits that she did shriek, and she did say she regretted the time she had wasted on him and his superficial infatuation with his own image on stage, on film and in the mirror, but she never said he wasn't good at it.

She may have made that remark about Plummer — some women get a bit testy when their husbands leave them. However, Donald is so adept at inventing his own worst nightmares that I'm inclined to believe she didn't. In any case, he condemned himself to playing it over and over in one ear, leaving the other free for his second wife telling him to be more aggressive — nagging in stereo.

While agonizing his way through *The Lady's Not For Burning*, he was asked to participate in a CBC-TV panel discussion with Pierre Berton, asking Michael Langham questions about the Stratford Festival. It was an amiable interview, which was not what the producer had in mind, and he cued Berton to liven things up by pitting Harron against Langham. Don fell right into the trap, and regretted it immediately afterwards. "I felt terrible that I had been so rude to the man who had helped me so much with my playwriting. That beard was making me act a character part that I couldn't really handle.'' Imagine, and look how far Hitler got on just a teensy weensy moustache.

You see, by 1962 Angry Jimmy and Tortured Arthur had pretty well worn off, except for the scar on his arm and tattered bits of psyche flapping in the breeze. What remained was his attachment to Virginia, and he didn't want her to find out that in fact he was Nice Sidney, ''one of those 'sensitive' men who bore you to death with their proper manners and passivity'' — the kind of Mr. Right who'd do the decent thing by his office affair.

One of Virginia's friends was later to remark, ''You know, many men in New York were in love with Virginia. Your father was the only one naïve enough to marry her.''

I call her ''The Mouth that Wouldn't Quit.'' and she laughs.

21

TO BE OR NOT TO BE

DON decided that he had reached a crisis point in his career: "I was beginning to think that I would never make the transition from juvenile to leading man. I would either become a good second-lead character actor, or I would end up as the dean emeritus of Canadian juveniles, and that way lay madness."

Which way lay madness? He had already *made* the transition to leading man. What else would you call the starring roles in *Look Back in Anger* and *The Tenth Man*? He had always avoided typecasting, and here he was doing it to himself. He was determined to be aggressive, yet he'd done so well turning down golden opportunities like *The Sound Barrier* with mystifying regularity. He'd risen to the top ranks as a stage actor on nothing more than talent, hard work and a knack for charming the birds out of the trees.

In case I left you with the impression that his performance in *The Lady's Not for Burning* was so appalling his career lay in ruins, I should mention that Don and his beard were invited straight back to Toronto to co-star with Barbara Chilcott in Ugo Betti's *The Queen and the Rebels*. Again, he says he wasn't very good, "a bit like Tony Randall playing John Wayne".

He can't imagine why, but Don sans beard was invited straight back a second time to star in a third television drama called *The Town that Didn't Care*, in which he played the one man in town who did. He probably would have convinced himself that he wasn't very good in that either, but the show scored such a huge success when it was released in the U.S. that it prompted him to pluck up his courage and ask director Joe Papp for a job.

The *New York Times* had reported that *King Lear* would be part of the upcoming "Shakespeare in Central Park" season, and he desperately wanted to play Edmund again. He could still remember the thrill of the role in Dora Mavor Moore's production at the New Play Society. He didn't even call an agent, he just got Papp on the phone and asked him straight out.

The reply was "Okay, Donald, I'll put your name down, but I'll have to have you read." A few hours later, Papp phoned back to say, "I've just been checking your credentials in Shakespeare, and I don't think I'll bother to have you read. You've got the part."

Don replied, "That's too bad, Joe, because I was planning to come over there and knock you on your ass with my reading." Ah, already the Bastard's blood was beginning to course in his veins. Virginia offered to coach him, as usual, and he cut her dead: "Don't tell me how to play Shakespeare!" he commanded, his eyes glittering darkly.

The only problem was how to support two families through the summer on $175 a week, the paltry fee for Shakespeare in the Park. To stock up on cash, he accepted an invitation from Kim Hunter, his Rosalind on the Housatonic, to come to Chicago and co-star with her in a production of *Write Me a Murder*, even though it seemed to have been written by Frederick *"Dial M for Murder"* Knott when he was a little short on ideas.

Kim Hunter was great to work with but the neophyte producer, a local businessman, alternated between showering his stars with generosity (he even let Don drive his Lincoln Continental) and throwing tantrums about the stage carpenter wanting an extra pound of nails.

Don asked a local priest about this guy, and he said, "Oh, is that what he's doing now? I haven't heard of him since the horsemeat scandal!" The priest, who must have seen Spencer Tracy in *Boys' Town* too many times, was giving Don a scenic tour of Chicago in his personal police cruiser, going through red lights with the siren at full blast.

Edmund was all Don cared about, or could think about; it is still his all-time favourite role. When they opened in New York, the headline in *The Times* of London read "Spirited Edmund in an American Production of *King Lear*." The *New York Times* called

Donald "a director's dream," and *Variety* compared him to Olivier.
When Edmund made his first entrance, Virginia didn't even
recognize him. She said to Joe Abeles, sitting next to her, "*Who
is that man? He's a star!*"

After the second night, Joe Papp saw him and called out, "So
what do you want to play next, Harron?" Don shouted back,
"Harron's Hamlet!" and Papp gave him the thumbs-up signal.

Admission to the open-air theatre was free, and by the third night
people were lining up at lunchtime for the 8 p.m. performance.
Don would be upset if I left you with the impression that he was
the only attraction. One of his closest friends, Roscoe Lee Browne,
was a fantastic Fool. The innovative hook Papp had devised for this
production was casting black actors as the foolish King and his wise
jester. Frank Silvera as Lear paled a bit by comparison with Roscoe,
in performance as well as complexion.

Of course Mary and I had pull, so we didn't have to line up when
Virginia took us to our seats. This was the best visit we ever had
together, that summer of '62. As long as Donald was playing
Edmund the Bastard, he and she were of equal strength and the
result was almost unturbulent. Like the little girl with a curl in the
middle of her forehead, when Virginia's good she's fantastic.

He was fantastic, too. I will never forget his Edmund. Norman
Campbell managed to find some of the old CBC dramas like *The
Queen and the Rebels* to refresh my memory recently, and Don
Harron was good, he was just trying a bit too hard, striding around
looking assertive with his beard and beetle brows. But there, on
stage in Central Park, he was just plain magnificent. *Then*, he was
my hero. Forget the handsome prince with the curly hair, "stand
up for bastards!" as Edmund says.

Don landed two big jobs right after *King Lear*, and both turned
out to be disasters in his opinion: one was the role of Christian in
Cyrano de Bergerac in *The Hallmark Hall of Fame*; and the second
was co-starring with Maggie Smith in the West End production of
Jean Kerr's smash comedy *Mary, Mary*. He had almost played Mary
Mary's husband on Broadway, but it had been decided that he was
too young for Barbara Bel Geddes, who now lives in *Dallas*.

A few days after he was offered *Mary, Mary*, a handwritten note arrived in the mail from Mrs. Kerr: "I want you to know how really delighted I am to learn the negotiations are really in progress for you to play the part in London. It is a relief to me in many ways. I was beginning to think that by the time we found a leading lady young enough for you, *you* would be too old. Walter and I were out of the country when you were playing in the Park, but I am still hearing how marvellous you were. Faithfully and fondly, Jean".

Mary, Mary would open in the New Year, and he could hardly wait. Starring in a Kerr comedy at last, with Maggie Smith, and in London! Before tackling the problem of subletting their apartment on West 75th St., especially what to do about Farley the cat, there was Christian to play. Don had a problem with that too, although he would never admit it. The last time *Cyrano de Bergerac* had been done on television, Chris Plummer had played Christian to José Ferrer's Cyrano. This time, Don would be Christian and Plummer would be Cyrano.

The problem wasn't Plummer — he's one of Don's favourite people, as well as one of his favourite actors, in the whole world, and he'd been dying to lend him his make-up again. The problem was Gloria's spectre, shrieking, "Why don't you face it, you'll never be as good an actor as Chris Plummer . . !" A quarter of a century later he said to me with a haunted look in his eyes, "You don't understand, Martha. She was so *mean* to me." I had to read his memoirs to understand what he was talking about.

Mary and I watched this *Cyrano de Bergerac* on the tiny box, and I thought the pain in his eyes came from that ridiculous blonde page-boy wig they made him wear. Don referred to it as his "Ginger Rogers look" and I can see it now, shoulder-length with bangs, and all the ends curled under. Any sensible Roxanne would have turned and run. *He* says the look was panic, because the taping took place during the Cuban missile crisis.

Don managed to acquire palatial digs in London for *Mary, Mary*, thanks to a friend, director David Greene, who was just moving out. The rent was twenty-five guineas a week, which would be the hourly rate these days. Never mind a "G" on the windowpane, this one had a bona fide blue and white plaque on the front, stating that Joseph William Mallord Turner lived and died in that elegant townhouse on the Thames, 119 Cheyne Walk. Presumably he painted many of his immortal sunsets from the same window where the Harrons took tea and stared at the tourists who were staring back at us, or at least our plaque.

Practical considerations had never entered into Don's concept of house hunting, as his first wife well knew on a fraction of the income. Virginia is many wonderful things, but not a trooper; no grin and bear it, no stiff upper lip, certainly not in the amounts required to cope with the deafening roar of the lorries that thundered all night between the river and their bedroom window, bearing goods to the City and Covent Garden Market.

And then, at 10 p.m. on their first night in Turner's house, the heat went off. It always does if you're British in January. Even Gloria had insisted on forsaking Georgian grandeur for central heating on the Edgware Road, and V's a California girl. She and Don spent the rest of the night screaming at each other and trying to get the North Thames Gas Board on the phone.

One torrid reconciliation later, with the traffic going strong and the heating system doing its British best, they went to the theatre next door to where *Mary, Mary* would be playing, to see the hit Maggie Smith had just left. It was Peter Shaffer's *The Private Ear/The Public Eye*, which still had her co-star, the fabulously bitchy Kenneth Williams.

They were a few minutes late getting to their seats, and found themselves sitting behind a tall man with a narrow head and a short woman in a mink that needed Hollanderizing. Don complained to Virginia that the man's head was obstructing his view and she replied laconically, "Well ask his wife to remove it, because she's the Queen."

Rehearsals began for *Mary, Mary* with a Brit, a Canadian and an Australian, Ron Randell, all playing Yanks. Don noticed right from the very first reading that Maggie Smith was making no attempt to sound American, although she was perfectly capable of doing so. She was playing it with the same high-pitched nasal inflection she must have acquired from Kenneth Williams, and which has since become one of her trademarks.

Instead of verbal swordplay between divorcing husband and wife à la Tracy/Hepburn, as in the Broadway production, Maggie Smith's Mary would be the shy, awkward English rose with the razor-sharp wit, making fools of the American men in her life. The British audience was going to lap it up; he could see there was no hope for it but to play the chump.

The only pre-West End run was at the lovely Theatre Royal in Brighton, where he'd played in *Seventh Veil*. The weather was very mild for mid-February, and he resigned himself to the good life. V was happy prowling the bookstores and antique shops, and they dined every night in Don's favourite seafood restaurant, where he consumed vast quantities of fresh mussels.

Opening night in Brighton went very well. Laurence Olivier came down and spent a long time talking to Maggie Smith in her dressing room afterwards, wooing her for the National Theatre. She conveyed his congratulations to Don on an enjoyable performance and the review in *The Brighton and Hove Herald* said "Donald Harron is a magnificent complex of bewildered emotions as Bob McKellaway."

Back at Cheyne Walk the following week, he was a much more ghastly complex of bewildered emotions. Everything was going beautifully, yet he wished he was dead. By opening night he was impossible to live with, but being an actress Virginia knew better than to quarrel with him until after the show. Binkie Beaumont, his old boss from *A Streetcar Named Desire*, popped by before curtain up to thank him for Brighton and wish him good luck. He can't remember what he replied, just that he ran to the toilet and his pee was pink.

Don doesn't remember a thing about what went on in front of the audience that night, just that most of his off-stage moments were spent vomiting. Afterwards Virginia was very gentle with him, which was a bad sign, and neither she nor anyone else at the opening night party so much as hinted at what he suspected — that it was the biggest disaster of his career.

Lionel's voluminous scrapbook of clippings is singularly silent on the subject of *Mary, Mary*. However, the worst of the critics' remarks were faithfully recorded by Don in a letter to his parents: "a pop-eyed parody of Ian Carmichael" was advised that "it is not necessary to act the very furniture off the stage." He didn't blame the critics for that. What he couldn't understand was why they didn't appreciate the play. However, Maggie Smith was a smash hit so there was no escape from a long run.

He still did not go to a doctor, even though his urine was now a robust Beaujolais. On the second night he not only threw up between scenes, he actually had to exit between lines, chunder into the stage manager's wastebasket, and bound back on for the next sentence. This totally mystified his fellow actors and everybody in the audience except one person, Dr. M.M. Fisher from Gravenhurst, Ontario. Dr. M.M. Fisher Jr. that is, Gloria's little brother, the redheaded freckled kid called "Butterball" whose baby talk had created the name Gogie.

"Woody" Fisher was all grown up now, skinny as a rail and a liver specialist, thank God. Divorce or no divorce, saving Don's life was a Fisher tradition. He and his wife Beverly came straight backstage afterwards to find out what was wrong, and it took him about two seconds to reach a diagnosis — infectious hepatitis. Don wailed, "How could I get a thing like that?"

Woody replied, "Three ways: anal sex, excessive drinking or contaminated seafood. I know you don't drink, so unless you have a love life I don't know about, it has to be seafood." Don told him about how mussel-bound he'd been in Brighton, and Woody said, "The Swiss resort of Zermatt got closed down yesterday because of mussels." Great.

His ex-brother-in-law drove him home and sent him straight to bed. The next morning a Harley St. specialist appeared in black morning coat and striped trousers to confirm the verdict and pronounce sentence: "No more performances for you for three months, laddie."

"Can't you just give me something for it? I'm allergic to sulfa, but I take penicillin like candy!" Don was desperate. Sure he was a flop but if he didn't play, Binkie didn't pay. He *had* to go on.

"Have to go easy on these so-called wonder drugs. They can be habit-forming and . . ."

Don shouted, "Oh you goddamn idiot! I don't give a shit if I live or die!" but it did no good. The doctor departed without leaving a miracle prescription.

Don's understudy went on that night. Virginia and everybody in the cast received a series of large and painful injections which could not have endeared him to the company. The actor who played Bob McKellaway in the Chicago production was flown in, while Don sat in bed stewing in the black bile of melancholy, reading Kierkegaard's *Fear and Loathing* and other inspiring works.

I knew that my father was sick, but I didn't know how sick, in mind as well as body, or how deeply the reviews had wounded him. After a week or so of procrastination, I wrote what I hoped was a cheery letter of commiseration, enclosing a brownie recipe for Virginia to comfort the inner man. I wish I had managed to preserve his reply — it's the only nasty letter I ever received from him. He told me he didn't need my half-hearted sympathy, or my "goddamn" recipe for brownies. It didn't sound like my funny, affectionate father at all.

He was impossible to live with, like a caged beast, literally chasing Virginia into the street at times. Once he threw a Granny Smith apple out the door after her and scored a direct hit on her retreating bottom. Bernard Braden, who had showered him with kindness on this visit to London as in the past, came to his bedside like a Good Samaritan and Don doesn't know what he said to him, but Bernie didn't speak to him again for ten years.

The only visitors who made him feel better were Canadian comedians Dave Broadfoot and Doug Chamberlain, who were performing in the revue *Clap Hands* elsewhere in the West End. They'd seen his reviews, and regaled him with tales of their own past humiliations, whether real or invented. Comedians understand one another.

Don managed to get back to work in six weeks rather than three months, thanks to willpower and having no vices other than weak tea and strong women. By then he was in debt, but flew Mary and me to London for the summer holidays, despite the fact that I was now twelve and no longer qualified for half-fare. At the time, I assumed most fathers made that much effort to see their children.

He felt like a charity case after the panning he had received in the press, although anyone else would have blamed it on hepatitis. I remember the show very clearly, and he was perfect for the part. Bob McKellaway doesn't appreciate the love of a good woman until she gives up the chance to marry a movie star to take him back. I have to admit my sympathies were all with the red-headed wife, and not just because Maggie Smith is a wonderful actress.

On his first Sunday off, during a round of Canasta, Mary and I complained about the drama lessons we were taking from a lady named Lynn Cook, at Dora Mavor Moore's academy. Miss Cook's concept of childhood involved skipping everywhere rather than walking, which didn't suit our sardonic natures at all. I especially hated the way Mary had been given the starring role, while I had a bit part.

Virginia suggested that we try doing some improvisations. As Mary and I were both fascinated by the swans on the Thames in front of the house, we were asked to play swans in an improvised scene. We waddled about for a bit, and then Mary said, "Quick, somebody's coming — into the water and look graceful!" which cracked everybody up. The new game became an instant favourite.

It was a lot more fun than "the truth game," when we had to sit and talk openly about our feelings — sort of like Canasta with your parents holding all the cards. Sometimes Father would come home from the theatre and find the three of us in tears.

Don felt that Virginia was very creative at devising activities and excursions for us, but jealous when he tried to organise something. They had to be sure they both took house keys when we went out, as there was a good chance they would have a tiff and return at different times.

In the middle of our visit, Gloria phoned to say that she wanted to move to London. Mary fired off a letter of protest and I went to bed with the flu, a less efficient way of expressing one's feelings. We were just beginning to make a bit of progress at fitting in with our peer groups in Toronto. Mary had actually been a very popular kid at Rosedale Public School, until they made her a social outcast overnight by skipping her from Grade 4 into Grade 5. She was hoping to make a fresh start at Deer Park Junior High. Without telling us, Donald fired off a letter of his own, telling Gloria she didn't have a hope of getting a job in London, and should stay right where she was.

We heard no more about moving. When we got back to Toronto, we discovered Mother's phone call had been a panic escape attempt because she had fallen in love with the producer who worked across the hall from her at CBC. He had come to Canada as a refugee, one of the student rebels who fought in the Hungarian Revolution of 1956. It's funny, one of my earliest memories is of my mother watching the news on television in Greenwich Village, and sobbing over the fate of those poor Freedom Fighters. Now, she was asking her daughters' permission to marry one.

This seemed to be taking sympathy a bit far. Not only that, he was six years younger than she was, which seemed utterly scandalous in 1963. When she confessed the affair to her producer on *Trans-Canada Matinée*, a witty redheaded Hungarian named Andrew Simon, his reaction was, "You mean the kid in the pullover? An old bag like you?!" She was thirty-six, the kid had just turned thirty.

That fathers should have a sex life seemed unavoidable, but to find one's mother necking with a young foreigner in the kitchen was positively obscene. I phoned my father in London and asked him what to do. However foolish he may be in the conduct of his own affairs, he's still the first person I turn to for advice because it is always wise.

I gave him the facts. I didn't tell him that this interloper had won an Ohio Award for one of his National Film Board documentaries, or founded and edited the magazine *Exchange*, or any of that stuff. I said, "He talks funny and I can't stand him." Children stick to the essentials.

Donald replied, "Okay, so suppose she doesn't marry him because of you. What happens when you're eighteen and ready to leave home? Your mother will be all alone — how will you feel then?" Cripes, I'd never thought of that. The child in me believed that Mummy and Daddy belonged together, and to me, but the budding adult told Gloria to marry anything she wanted, and I really meant it.

So Mother gave up all that alimony as the ex-Mrs. Harron and became Mrs. Stephen Vizinczey. We were given lessons in how to pronounce it: "VIZ-in-say" seemed close enough. We settled for calling him "Viz" and Andy Simon promptly renamed Gloria "G. Viz". Because Mexican divorces aren't recognized in Canada, the wedding took place in Rochester, New York, with Mary and me

as the only witnesses. Viz moved into our apartment at 38A North
Sherbourne St. with his few clothes and many books. One whole
bookcase was devoted to erotica, and we were allowed to read
everything except the kinky stuff like the Marquis de Sade. (Mother
drew the line at that.)

Stephen had already been a successful poet and playwright in
Hungary, and he was determined to be a great writer in his new
language. Soon after moving in, he set about writing his first literary
masterpiece in English, undaunted by the fact that after almost seven
years of unremitting effort, he still couldn't pronounce it.

Meanwhile, back in London, Don was delighted to get two
redheaded wives off his back in the same month. About the time
Gloria gave up her alimony, Maggie Smith left the cast of *Mary,
Mary* for the National Theatre at the Old Vic. She had never been
unpleasant or unkind to him, unlike Gloria, but she was inexplicably
and unpardonably cruel to another actor. One matinée Ron Randell
was replaced by the understudy George C. Cooper, a sweet, mild-
mannered chap who was doing his best to play a Hollywood star
when Miss Smith paused, looked him straight in the eye and said,
"Why don't you get off?"

This was said loudly enough to be overheard in the fourth row.
It was all the poor man could do to complete the scene, and Don,
who happened to be onstage at the time, never spoke to her again.
She was replaced with only a slight drop in box-office by Carole
Shelley, a bubbly personality who was delightful to work with. Don
actually began to enjoy doing the show.

Shortly after Mary and I left London, Don had begun seeing a
psychiatrist again. Virginia and her friend Rita Moreno had been
among the first human guinea pigs to take LSD under clinical
supervision in California, and she felt a good dose of acid might
release all the dybbuks that seemed to inhabit him. After a long
interview the psychiatrist told him that this would be far too
dangerous: there was so much suppressed rage in him, he might
kill someone while under the influence of the hallucinogen.

Virginia didn't argue, although she couldn't see that there was
anything suppressed about his rage. The shrink suggested that Don
write down his dreams, as a safer way of tapping his subconscious.

In one vivid dream, he was standing on a crowded Toronto street-car and saw Marlon Brando sitting at the back. Brando had starred in the film version of *A Streetcar Named Desire* of course, and the psychiatrist interpreted this to mean that Don's desire was to return to Toronto, where we still had streetcars.

Lo and behold, an offer arrived from the CBC to do just what the psychiatrist said — come to Toronto, as host of a daily coast-to-coast radio show. It was a summer replacement series called *Side by Side* in which co-host Pat Patterson would play musical selections of her own choosing, and Don would alternate with excerpts from talking records: comedy, poetry, plays and the like, with the CBC record library at his disposal. The timing was perfect — all the shows would be pre-recorded in late spring, right after *Mary, Mary* was due to end its fourteen-month run. This would enable Pat, who was also the regular season host, to have a summer holiday, and leave Don free for Shakespeare in Central Park. He had heard Joe Papp was planning *Hamlet* as well as *Othello* for his '64 season. If Papp remembered his promise, Harron would have his Hamlet before his fortieth birthday.

In his place, I would have splurged on a transatlantic call, but he waited until *Mary, Mary* closed to fly to New York and get Papp on the phone. Joe remembered about Harron's Hamlet, but offered him something much better, to my way of thinking: Iago to James Earl Jones' Othello. Don was furious. He'd really been counting on this chance to be tortured, neurotic, suicidal *and* a Danish prince. It wasn't fair! He said bitterly, "So who's playing Hamlet for you?"

"Alfred Ryder."

"He's too old," snapped Don, and he was right about that. Ryder was well over fifty and was replaced by his understudy before opening night.

"You were wonderful as Edmund. Iago's the same kind of part," Papp countered, and he was absolutely right about that.

Don seethed, "I'll let you know, Joe. Don't call me, I'll call you," and hung up. The next day an offer arrived from John Houseman to play Edmund in Los Angeles instead. He now had two of the Bard's best villains to choose from, and decided to think it over in Toronto while recording *Side by Side*.

It wasn't until *Side by Side* began taping that he discovered it was a summer replacement for *Trans-Canada Matinée*, edited by Gloria Vizinczey. He was working for his ex-wife.

Anne of Green Gables had traded in her apron and Joan of Arc haircut for business suits, high heels and a hairdo, and was in the ideal position of employing her first husband at the CBC while supporting her second husband to stay home and write. (My mother says in fact she had nothing to do with Don Harron being hired for *Side by Side*. "It was entirely Pat Patterson's idea, and since it was a brilliant idea, of course the rest of us approved.")

She had encouraged Viz to quit his job as a CBC radio producer to concentrate on his first novel. He scribbled away in longhand, listening to Nat King Cole's mellifluous *Ramblin' Rose* until I thought I would go mad. Gloria deciphered his manuscript and typed it up when she got home from work. It was called, appropriately, *In Praise of Older Women*.

During the Harrons' five weeks in Toronto, their relations with the Vizinczeys were remarkably civilised. Gloria and Virginia chatted amicably, and Stephen was almost pathetically grateful to Donald. He later explained to me that it was as if he had been prospecting in the desert and crossed paths with a fellow prospector who said "You can have my claim — there's nothing there!" And what did he find? A little freckled, redheaded goldmine.

Mary and I discovered that having four parents, while overpowering, had definite advantages. I was home alone one afternoon when there was a phone call from the Metropolitan Toronto Police. Mary had been caught stealing an Agathie Christie paperback at Coles' Bookstore, and was in jail.

I didn't know it, but after being skipped a second time at school Mary had taken to skipping a lot more, by forging notes. I guess the signatures were as good as her marks, because she was never caught for it. This time, however, the cops had her red-handed, and wanted one of her parents to come down to the station right away. I promised to get hold of our mother, but I was lying.

Skipping school and stealing — Mother would have had an absolute fit. I phoned Virginia at the Waldorf instead. Her I.D. said Mrs. Harron after all, and she was even more magnificent than I hoped she would be. I picked her up in a cab, which she paid for, and she gave a perfect performance as the distraught parent. It was obvious from the stricken look on Mary's face that being behind real prison bars at age eleven had cured her of a life of crime, so V gave her comfort rather than a lecture as soon as we were back on the street. She never told on her either. (I did, just now.)

Trying to decide between *Othello* and *Lear*, Don was going to let the toss of a coin rule his fate when V pointed out that New York would be packed for the World's Fair, and they would have no trouble subletting their apartment on West 75th St. He could tell she was feeling homesick, and he knew the beach would be much nicer for his daughters than a crowded, sweltering city on $175 a week.

When he told us that we would be spending our summer visit in California, frolicking in the surf while he played the Bastard, we were delighted; but he didn't tell us about Iago in Central Park, or Baby Jane in West Hollywood. When I saw the film version of Olivier's *Othello* the following year, I was transfixed by Frank Finlay's Iago — not just because he was so good, but because I knew it was the perfect part for my father. I little dreamed that he had already turned it down.

He was so worried about making the transition from juvenile lead to leading man, but Edmund was an over-eager kid with a noble streak compared to a full-fledged monster like Iago. In *Final Dress* Houseman recalls that he chose Donald Harron as "an intelligent, attractive and therefore doubly sinister Edmund." He was, but he could have been triply sinister as "the Spartan dog" in *Othello*.

In his memoirs, my father explains his decision this way: "After London, I needed to make a strong impression as an actor again. Iago was a temptation, but New York was bereft of television. Edmund in *Lear* was a sure thing, I felt, and lots of work to follow it if I got the attention from the critics."

"A sure thing"?! A shoe-in for the tiny box?! *What* would Papa Guthrie have said? When I read this I was absolutely livid, and swore it was the one thing he had done I could never forgive. A few years and twenty-one chapters later, as I approach the age my father was then, facing his fortieth birthday with several mouths to feed, I find I understand him better.

It's very difficult to let parents live their own lives, make their own mistakes, grow and change, not always for the better. It's even harder to tag along in silence when they go forth and multiply. Mary and I were now outnumbered two to one, with fireworks on both fronts, and didn't know how lucky we were that all four parents were devoted to us, in their own loony way, and doing their best.

For what it's worth, I would like my father to know that I'm grateful now for all that airfare and dentistry, and the letters and postcards. I forgive him for condemning me to a beach house in Malibu that summer. I forgive everything. But, if he ever turns down another part like Iago without my consent, he's dead meat.

22

TENSION IN TINSELTOWN

DON was right about his Edmund taking Hollywood by storm. Everybody raved about him, and the production in general. They opened on June 8, 1964, and the next day he received an offer to appear as guest star in a three-part *Dr. Kildare*. One guest-star spot a month on the tiny box, and he'd be set for life.

In the meantime, *King Lear* played four weeks at Schoenberg Hall on the U.C.L.A. campus to packed houses and tumultuous applause, those who had fallen asleep after a hard day of sun, fun and cocktails being awakened at appropriate moments by the diehards who were paying attention. During the day and late into the night, Houseman conducted rehearsals to restage the same production at The Pilgrimage Theatre, where they would re-open in mid-July.

Transferring from a small indoor theatre to an outdoor amphitheatre created huge technical problems, and often rehearsals lasted till dawn, only to start again that same afternoon under the blazing sun. This was to be Houseman's final triumph before leaving for Paris, and he had chosen a good friend of Don's from New York, Gordon Davidson, as his assistant director and heir-apparent.

Everyone seems to agree that, as Houseman puts it, "a strange, exciting thing happened" when they moved outdoors: a very good production became a great one, so great the *New York Times* critic had to fly back out to the Coast, poor chap, to give the expanded *Lear* an expanded rave. The Pilgrimage Theatre itself had a lot to do with it. It was carved right into the side of the Hollywood Hills, and the actors were surrounded by real rocks and trees. Sometimes the soldiers were chased onstage by real rattlesnakes.

Max Reinhardt had mounted his *Midsummer Night's Dream* there when he arrived as an exile from Germany in the '30s. Since then it had been in the hands of a religious cult which left behind a huge megawatt crucifix on the top of the hill. The cross continued to blaze nightly, making Shakespeare's three hours of pagan mayhem easy to find. The acoustics were almost as good as the ancients', and the cool night air kept the audience in top form.

Mary and I arrived shortly after the second opening and found ourselves living in a house on a private beach in Malibu, thanks to Virginia's friend Gloria Betz, whose husband Carl was married to Donna Reed on the show of the same name. The Betzes were in Europe and we enjoyed every minute of their absence, mostly on the beach except when we were packing or moving. This usually occurred after Don and Virginia had a fight. Mary and I weren't so dumb as to unpack until we came home again, for torrid-reconciliation-time. Farley seemed quite used to it, and didn't pack at all.

The only time we unpacked in a different place from where we started was during the two weeks another family had been promised the beach house. All four of us moved into Baby Jane's on Lloyd Place. Thank goodness V's sweet, harmless-looking mother had the good sense to clear out, probably taking refuge with a friend, but just being in that house made V more neurotic in a much less charming way than usual. She threw us out one night, and in the morning came to our hotel and said she only meant us to go to the movies. We were already in the movies.

Thank goodness for Monty Hall, who lived nearby and let us use his swimming pool. Don was busy playing in *Dr. Kildare* during the day, *King Lear* at night and *Who's Afraid of Virginia Woolf?* in his spare time. After that I left for two weeks at Camp Tawingo. Mary went back to Malibu Beach with D & V, preferring the game of "pack-or-be-packed" to the torture of outdoor sports and community singing with Jack Pearse.

Don is never more confident than when hiding behind an accent or pretending to be a Bastard, and on the triple *Dr. Kildare* he got to do both as an eccentric Scottish surgeon. They let him keep his long, shaggy Shakespearian locks, which allowed him to sound crusty and look dashing at the same time. But he didn't think long hair was suitable for a "middle-aged" man like himself, and in September had it all cut off in favour of what was known as the "Steve McQueen" look.

It's funny, at no point in his memoirs does he mention that he was preparing at this time for his fortieth birthday on September 19th, 1964, although he describes in loving detail his gallant efforts to escort his second and third wives over this same Great Divide. What's not funny is that the man who gave him the razor cut was hairdresser-to-the-stars Jay Sebring, who later died a horrible death thanks to murderer-to-the-stars Charles Manson.

Television offers were plentiful, thanks to *Lear*, and likely to continue, because invitations to parties were so plentiful — Virginia had a lot of friends. They rented a beautiful house on top of Laurel Canyon, which meant the place was smaller but more funky-chic than our former home on Summitridge Drive. It had huge picture windows and no air conditioning, which made it unlivable on summer afternoons, however pretty to look at and out of, but at least it was above the smog.

Don received an offer to do a comedy show in Toronto, a half-hour with Max Ferguson and his old pal from typing class, Larry Mann. He jumped at the chance, and the Harrons decided to stop off in New York on the way, to give up their apartment on West 75th Street. I was sorry to see that place go, and if I'd known what the next summer in L.A. was going to be like, I'd have been even sorrier.

Mind you, when we had fun it was a riot, although the improvisations sometimes got a little out of hand. In one of them, Mary was assigned the role of Pearl Mesta, the Republican society hostess, and rose to the occasion. I was Democratic First Lady Jacqueline Kennedy, and sank so low as to throw a bowlful of sugar at my Republican rival. D & V didn't get angry, though it was hardly in character. Ah, childhood memories.

A new California game called "Essences" had been added to our repertoire, and we played it again when Father flew us down to New

York for a farewell visit to West 75th. One person would leave the room, and the others would assign you an identity. The only clue you were given on your return was whether you were real or fictional. You had to guess who you were by asking the others questions like "What kind of landscape am I?" or "What kind of hat am I?" The best results came from intuition rather than cleverness or general knowledge, which meant the rest of us could play as equals with Donald the Encyclopedia. I remember once Virginia asked me "What kind of drink am I?" and I replied, "A tall, cool Milk of Magnesia." It was only her second question, but she guessed right away that she was Frank Sinatra. It was almost scary, and we loved it.

After a summer of serious roles on stage and screen, it was a relief as well as a pleasure for Don to work with Max Ferguson and Larry Mann in Toronto, dressing up as airline stewardesses and the like. In a take-off on CBC's *Flashback*, Larry played Krushchev, Max played Hitler and Don was Indhira Ghandi, puckering his lips in front of the mirror and applying lipstick to the centre of his forehead. I mention it because I'm sure this is one sketch you will never see repeated.

It was fun while it lasted, then D & V flew straight back to their new home in Laurel Canyon so Don could do a segment of *Profiles in Courage*, a series based on John F. Kennedy's book. Don had first heard the news of his assassination during *Mary, Mary*, when the stage manager rushed into his dressing room at intermission and said "Kill the line about Jackie Kennedy. Her husband just got shot." Jokes are as fragile as their human subjects.

This episode of *Profiles in Courage* starred Wendy Hiller, the original Eliza Doolittle on film and a "wonderful sport" who served Don a real cup of tea every afternoon at four. It was directed by Cyril Ritchard, who seemed to bear him no grudge for all the nasty comments he'd made during rehearsals of *Everybody Loves Opal*. Sometimes a joke is so fragile it hangs by a thread, like Opal's shawl on Donald's button.

So there he was with the whole Success Kit, house high on a hill and wife to match. One night they gave a dinner party for Don Francks, Robert Goulet, Norman Sedawie and their wives. After her third dry martini Virginia turned to Donald and whispered, "When the hell are they going to serve dinner?"

Don replied gently, "Darling, you're the hostess." When she speaks at Alcoholics Anonymous meetings these days that story gets them rolling in the aisles, and she's got lots more. If Virginia were selling something, she'd make a fortune.

Don was making plenty for all of us in those days, but something was missing. Even though that nag Gloria was thousands of miles away, he decided to try his hand at writing scripts for comedy series in his spare time. He went to see his agent, who seemed bemused by the sight of an actor who thought he could write, but was prepared to humour his golden Canada goose.

Don was told he could submit a script, on spec of course, for a series called *O.K. Crackerby*, starring Burl Ives as an eccentric millionaire with three no doubt spunky children. About two days later he went back to the agent with a completed script. Perhaps inspired by Ernie Kovacs' experiences playing Monopoly for real money with Dean Martin and Jack Lemmon, it was about the kids' desperate Math tutor using the real estate board game as a teaching tool his rich pupils can relate to. They are overheard by the father, who doesn't know it's a game, which sets off a land-grabbing boom in Atlantic City for the real Boardwalk and Park Place.

The production people thought it was great, but a higher-up turned it down flat on the grounds that it would give free advertising to Parker Bros. Don couldn't help being pleased when *O.K. Crackerby* died a quick death. Disappointed but not discouraged, he wrote a script on spec for *The Dick Van Dyke Show* and was told it was unsuitable. They assured him that it was funny enough, but "a little intellectual." This time he was disappointed and completely discouraged.

Nobody at the CBC or BBC had ever accused him of being too intellectual. He should have moved, or splurged on some air mail postage. Instead, he went to parties and appeared as a guest star on all those situation tragedies like *The Fugitive, Burke's Law, Twelve O'Clock High* and *Mr. Novak*. He says *Mr. Novak* was his favourite because working with Burgess Meredith was such a pleasure, and being directed by Ida Lupino positively thrilling.

At parties it was Don, not Virginia, who became notorious for his drinking habits. They went to a Hallowe'en costume party disguised as Nō characters, with black wigs, kimonos and white

Kabuki make-up. The hostess, Eddy Canter's daughter Edna McHugh, told me nobody could identify the mystery couple until the man was offered a drink. They all cried "It's Don Harron!" when he asked for ginger ale.

He was asked to try out for the lead in a situation comedy based on Jean Kerr's *Please Don't Eat the Daisies*, which ought to have proved to him that his performance in *Mary, Mary* was only a disaster in his own mind, apart from the first two nights in London, of course. He had a great time and the laughter from the studio audience was music to his ears, but he lost out in the final selection because he had a "serious face."

All great comedians have serious faces! As Guthrie would say, their job is to make the audience laugh, not do it for them. Buster Keaton would have been thrown out on his ear. Still, Don did land a continuing role in a comedy series: look for him in reruns as the redheaded, redbearded Australian terrorist who keeps leaping off walls on *The Man from U.N.C.L.E.* All that leaping off walls nearly cost him an ankle.

For saddle sores, there was *Willie and the Yank*. Willie was Kurt Russell before he became a sex symbol, playing a little Southern boy who captures a big Northern General. That was Donald the Yank, who had to ride into town at the head of his troops and rein up at a hitching post. He was happy to be captured early — it was one of those marathon three-part Disney specials, and he'd only had three riding lessons.

In back-to-back episodes of *Twelve O'Clock High*, he was *teddibly* brave as a Royal Air Force Wing Commander leading the escape from a German prison camp, and the next week he was awful yeller in the U.S. Army, but, never fear, he ended up being braver than his Commander in the crunch, because he was a slum kid, who wasn't afraid of rats.

In the midst of all this California darkness came light. He was given the lead in Paddy Chayefsky's *Gideon*. He played Gideon, and his old acting teacher Jeff Corey played God. "He always did," says Don, adding wistfully, "It was so wonderful to say real words again."

This was not the Broadway *Gideon*, unfortunately, which had starred Douglas Campbell, but the televised version, which was over all too soon. I'll bet he would have traded his starring role on the tiny box for a smaller part on the stage, just so he and Dangerous Dougie could exchange verbal fastballs again.

At this point another ray of sunshine came from Canada. He was asked to turn his television musical *Anne of Green Gables* into a stage version, to be produced at the Charlottetown Festival the following summer. It was all the Queen Mother's idea. She had heard the title song during the Festival's opening ceremonies in 1964, and said that she would like to see the rest of the show.

Truly a Royal Command Performance. There were a few hitches, though. Father took the big hardbound family copy of the novel away with him, only to discover that thirteen-year-old Martha had carved out the interior with a knife to store her secret hoard of cigarette butts. Mavor Moore, the Festival's director, had bigger problems than this: it took him until April '65 to get the stage rights.

And Mavor's headaches were minor compared with Norman Campbell's. Don recalls, "One of my songs had thirteen lines in the first verse, all rhyming with the same vowel, and eleven lines in the second, all rhyming with a different vowel." That is a completely inaccurate description of *The Apology* from Anne to Mrs. Lynde; the structure was far more bizarre, but by treating it like a Puccini aria Norman made it come out just right.

More songs were needed and Don was off in the desert somewhere chasing David Janssen in *The Fugitive*. Norman's talented wife Elaine, who had helped with the original television version, chipped in a couple of lyrics. And Mavor Moore came up with three of the show's best numbers: the gossip song *Did You Hear, Did You Hear?*; the rousing paean to al fresco education and a healthy curiosity *Open the Windows*; and *The Words*, that eloquent lament of the inarticulate sung by Matthew and later by his sister Marilla.

Arranger John Fenwick wrote a masterful score, and director/ choreographer Alan Lund pulled the whole thing together, adding dance sequences left right and centre. The original Matthew, John Drainie, was at the Festival but tied up in the title role of his Stephen Leacock show. Apart from the orphan herself, a girl from Texas named Jamie Ray, the major *Anne* players all came from the cast of the third Charlottetown production, which happened to be *Spring Thaw '65*.

Don was delighted, especially that Peter Mews would be playing Matthew. His only objection was Alan's casting of Marilla; Barbara Hamilton had been fine as Lucille the general store clerk in the TV production, but he thought she was dead wrong for such a dour spinster — not because she was far too young, or because she couldn't sing, but because she's so funny. He couldn't imagine Barbara without a twinkle in her eye, and Marilla with a twinkle would be unbearable.

While rehearsals for *Anne* were going on in Charlottetown, Mary and I were visiting D & V in California. We remember it vividly because it was the first time we'd ever seen him not working. I think he planned it that way in a misguided attempt to see more of us. Even at Summitridge Drive when he'd been brown on the front, black on the back and white with rage inside, he'd kept busy weeding and writing. This time he was like a caged beast, playing psychodrama with The Brain that Wouldn't Die.

One night Virginia locked herself in the bathroom, ostensibly to cut her wrists. Don rushed out onto the deck, up the stairs and smashed his fist through the bathroom window. She ended up swathing him in bandages, at which point they retired to their nightly routine, and Mary and I to ours.

Our routine consisted of lying stock-still in our bed, each thinking the other was asleep. I composed eloquent speeches of recrimination, never to be delivered, while Mary planned elaborate escape attempts. Once, she actually clawed her way through the tropical underbrush almost to the top of the ridge before turning back.

With Don and Virginia it was always the best of times and the worst of times in rapid succession, but the pace became exhausting now that he had real time on his hands. We drove up the Coast highway to San Francisco, playing word games in the car, sleeping in a cabin in glorious Big Sur on the way up and back. It was nerve-wracking to be having that much fun, knowing that at any moment you might say the wrong thing and change games.

Then, suddenly, Donald got a phone call and disappeared for a few days. I'm sure he told us where he was going, and why, but I didn't notice. Father flying off somewhere was nothing new. If I'd been paying attention, I would have understood the torment he'd been going through, worrying about his musical baby.

The phone call came at four o'clock in the morning from Norman Campbell, who had just siphoned copies of *Anne's* opening night reviews from the local telegraph office. Even Nathan Cohen liked it. Norman says he felt like a doctor in a maternity hospital corridor, announcing "You have a hit, Don, up here in P.E.I., and it's a girl!" The proud father was off to the airport like a flash to see his rusty moppet, leaving his blonde, brown and brunette girls behind.

Mary and I knew that while Virginia might enjoy playing *Hansel and Gretel* now and again, she was perfectly harmless — apart from a 22-caliber tongue of course. One night we went to a drive-in movie, and on the way home she asked, "Why is it that Canadian children are so much more boring than others?" We assumed it was a rhetorical question.

The next day we were submitted to the hideous torture of watching V be nice to her mother. Mary and I spent the afternoon in and beside the swimming pool, trying not to say or do anything to attract attention while they splashed about, laughing gaily. God, she could be cruel. Then she turned to us and said, "You think my mother and I are silly, because we know how to laugh and have fun!" Oh, please.

Joan tucked Baby Jane under her arm and drove away, which would have been bliss except that the pool was in the Valley, while our food and clothing were at the top of Laurel Canyon, miles away. In Toronto, we had bicycles, buses, subways, streetcars and friends. I turned to Mary and said, "I am never, *ever* coming back here." Odd as it may seem, we had never confided in one another before. She had always defended me when I was punished for torturing her, she had always been my best friend, my kindred spirit, my saving grace, and I'd never noticed.

I've never been back to California. Mary goes there frequently — to do television interviews, not to recapture her childhood. The last time she and Virginia had dinner in L.A., I called each of them, both before and after dinner. The next morning, I tracked Father down in Halifax, to compares notes on the summer of '65.

The way I remember it, the four of us sat and watched a drama special on television, starring Don Harron as the famous tragedian Edwin Booth, including a smattering of Hamlet, Brutus, Macbeth etc. as Booth might have played them. After it was over, the phone rang. It was one of the big studios, asking him to come in about a part. He went, and there wasn't any appointment: it had been a crank call, a cruel practical joke.

It's three against one — it never happened. Oh, he played Edwin Booth all right, and the phone rang all right, but it wasn't a crank call, it was an offer to play Edwin's brother, John Wilkes the assassin, on Broadway (to José Ferrer's Edwin, with Lorne Greene as Papa Booth). He turned it down in the end. The "joke" ending I remember was my own re-write of *The Prizewinner*, which I saw on CBC-TV at the age of seven. I can still see my '65 version clear as day: despite all my attempts to lead an uneventful life, I'm as dotty as my father.

I was relieved to hear all three confirm a few unforgettable highlights: Mary's birthday is January 12th, but D & V used to celebrate it in the summer, which seemed unnecessary to me. As usual, all the guests at her twelfth birthday party were adults, all witty and mostly gay, like most witty people in showbiz it seemed. We were all talking and laughing, and everyone except Don and his daughters was drinking.

Virginia was drinking a lot, but I never thought of it as a problem because she was such an adorable drunk, and this night was no exception. She made a quip, everyone laughed and then suddenly, without warning, she announced with the air of one who has received a vision: "I've just realised that life is all pain. It's funny, isn't it? Life is All Pain. . . ." While she sat transfixed by this Truth, our guests beat a hasty retreat. After all, if it was all pain, there was no point in hanging about.

When Don saw Prince Edward Island, he knew for sure that life was not all pain. P.E.I. was so beautiful, so fresh and clean — quite simply the loveliest place he'd ever seen. At the theatre there was excitement in the air, and fresh talent on the stage, as well as some delightfully familiar faces.

After seeing *Anne* that night, the first thing he did was march backstage to see Barbara Hamilton. "I was wrong, Barbara," he confessed.

"Bloody right you were, Harron!" she replied, grinning wickedly. Her dourness had reduced him to tears, and she knew it.

Suddenly California seemed so irrelevant. Whiling away his time in Lotusland, he'd missed the birth of a new festival, another crackpot trip to the moon! Still, it wasn't too late to join in. Mavor suggested turning *Turvey* into a musical for the following season, a project which had been gathering dust since *Separate Tables*. He also invited Don to come up for the whole summer, and perform with the company.

He knew he had to say yes: he had fallen in love with Prince Edward Island. The Charlottetown Festival was going to go on, and it was going to go on doing *Anne of Green Gables*. There was even talk of a national tour to celebrate Canada's 100th birthday in '67. There were big plans afoot, and he wanted to be part of them. The only problem would be breaking the news to his Hollywood wife that he was going home, back to the land of snow and ice and *Spring Thaw*.

He came back to L.A. a changed man, to find two changed children on his hands. He didn't say anything about the change in him, and we resisted his attempts to understand the change in us. One afternoon, after a visit to Baby Jane's, Mary accidentally stepped on my foot as we were getting into the car. When she apologised, Virginia said something like, "Don't say I'm sorry; say, 'I'm a stupid, clumsy little girl who likes to step on people's feet.'"

This in itself was not memorable but for once, finally, our ineffectual tempest-in-a-teapot father really blew his top. He ranted and raved, gesticulating and banging the steering wheel while careering around corners at full speed. There was no way for V to get a word in edgewise, and we were silent as mice in the back seat, not wanting to be responsible for another divorce. The threat of a car crash didn't even enter our minds — he always drives like that.

For a while there, I thought it might be his finest hour, or at least one of his finest performances; then he turned around and yelled at Mary and me for not backing him up. That was the final straw as far as I was concerned. I don't mean that I stopped loving my father, or needing him, or admiring him, I just stopped waiting for him to be my knight in shining armour. It was high time anyway, I was fourteen.

23

LA FORZA DEL DESTINO

WHEN we said goodbye at the airport in L.A., Father was the only one who knew he was planning to come back to Canada to live, and none of us knew that Mary and I would be long gone when he got there. We arrived back in Toronto to find that Stephen Vizinczey's little crackpot trip to the moon, publishing his first novel himself, on borrowed money, had paid off in a big way.

In Praise of Older Women is about many things, unlike the movie version starring Tom Berenger, but the basic premise is simple: that two virgins embarking on a sexual relationship have about as much chance of having fun as two kids without a license, driving down the highway. Evidently Don and Gloria were not alone in experiencing the shock of recognition between its covers: it became a huge international bestseller, and we found ourselves living in a villa near Rome, overlooking the site of Verdi's opera *La Forza del Destino*. Call it fate.

Don comforted himself with the knowledge that his daughters' Roman holiday was just for one year — by which time all of us would be living in Toronto — and kept busy guest-starring in TV series like *The Outer Limits* and *Voyage to the Bottom of the Sea*. On *Time Tunnel* he played Robin Hood, and I would like to tell you that he vaulted palace walls and felled armies with his broadsword, but he insists the credit goes to his double, a stuntman in his sixties who had done the same thing for Errol Flynn.

Sometimes Don had to do his own stuntwork. In a two-part pilot for a series called *Blue Light* starring Bob Goulet, he had to plunge to his death with a brave smile on his face, into a four-foot tank of water. In *One Step Beyond* he had to step off the parapet of his own castle, a young English lord fulfilling the family curse.

The director of *One Step Beyond*, John Newland, asked him what he'd like to play next. He didn't say "Harron's Hamlet"; he said "Camus' *Caligula*," the most twisted psychopath ever to rule the Roman Empire. Instead, Newland offered him the lead in a spy series about identical twins who live on either side of the Berlin Wall. Close, but no *cigare*: it would conflict with his plans for a summer in Charlottetown.

His biggest problem was *Turvey*. Earle Birney had been very receptive to the idea of *The Adventures of Private Turvey* as a play, and had seemed satisfied with the results, so Don assumed he would be pleased about a musical version. As Harron and Birney had (have) the same literary agent, Matie Molinaro, he told her to draw up an agreement satisfactory to both clients. This was not easy.

In fact, it was almost impossible. Earle Birney is an artist, and not a greedy one. As far as he was concerned, a musical was out of the question: war is hell, not a bunch of perky people singing and dancing. Don decided he'd better scare up some jobs in Toronto so that he could work on Earle in person. He was already working on *Turvey*, although Norman Campbell had developed the annoying habit of being hard to find, always flying around producing television specials, which was most inconsiderate.

At this point he received a call from director Paul Almond to do a four-character television play called *Neighbours*, about a black couple and a white couple, with Toby Robins, Ruby Dee and Dick Gregory. Don said yes, yes, YES! He had seen Gregory perform stand-up comedy in several New York nightclubs, and found his sharp philosophy every bit as exciting as the sweet Sahl music of a more innocent time.

It felt like old home week. The producer was Leonard White, his old bunkmate from that other four-character play *A Sleep of Prisoners*. They hadn't worked together since *The Lady's Not For Burning* at the Jupiter Theatre. Paul Almond had last directed Don in the tiny box version of the same play on CBC. Toby Robins and her producer husband Bill Freedman were old friends from Village

Player days. The only twist was that this reunion took place in London. *Neighbours* was a British production, part of ATV's *Armchair Theatre* series masterminded by Canadian Sydney Newman. Toby and Bill were now permanently settled in Mayfair, in Georgian splendour. You Never Can Tell. . . .

Don had no time to socialize or reminisce, however; he was all wrapped up in Dick Gregory. His nights were spent coaching him — not teaching him how to perform, Dick already knew that, although he'd never tried straight acting before — just helping him learn his lines. This was an agonizing business, and for a reason Don found fascinating: as a child, Dick had approached education on the assumption that everything they told him was a tissue of lies, especially in history class. He learned by forgetting, discarding everything except the few things which struck him as true.

This approach had made him the hottest comedian in America. Every day he would receive another bundle of raw material from his prolific writer, Bob Orben. As they rode out to the ATV studios each morning in the limo, Don would read each joke aloud and Dick would accept or reject it. Out of thirty-five jokes he'd forget maybe thirty, and weave the rest into an inspired thirty-minute monologue.

Don says he and Dick Gregory made a lasting impression on each other: Dick's mind and Don's shoes, that is, which were made of Corfam synthetic leather. Gregory, dressed from head to toe in the finest suede, noticed them right away. He was in the process of becoming vegetarian, and had been thinking of giving up the hide as well as the flesh. He was also in the process of giving up his status as a stand-up comedian for that of a sit-down philosopher. On the last day of *Neighbours*, Bertrand Russell's secretary arrived and whisked Dick Gregory off to Wales for a meeting of the minds.

Don would have loved to be a fly on the wall for *that* conversation. Instead, he and Virginia were about to meet us and our minds in Rome, when an urgent telegram arrived asking him to come to Munich. It was from John Newland: the script for the Berlin Wall spy series had gone through many permutations since he and Don worked on *One Step Beyond*, and the identical twins had been reduced to a single double-agent impersonating a dead look-alike (I hope you follow me). It was called *The Man Who Never Was*.

One of the sponsors was a Shakespeare fan, who insisted Harron was The Man for the job. Don wasn't sure, he didn't want anything to interfere with Charlottetown, but he says V convinced him he'd be crazy to turn down the title role in a series, even a Man Who Never Was.

In Munich they had a luxurious suite at the Hotel Continental, to be followed by more of the same in Berlin and Salzburg. This was a big-budget operation, and the shooting was easy: the Germans had cameras equipped to provide instant replays on a miniature screen, so you didn't have to sit around and watch dailies afterwards.

They crossed paths with Robert Goulet and his wife Carol Lawrence. Bob's series *Blue Light* had been picked up, and they were shooting subsequent episodes on location. Don's series, if it came off, would follow the same route in the opposite direction: after an expensive pilot in Europe, they'd go back to Hollywood with their bags full of second unit footage to fluff out the authenticity of subsequent episodes.

The two-part pilot for *The Man Who Never Was* was about the hero's escape from East Berlin and his first confrontation with his dead double's family. They shot a lot of the East Berlin stuff in Munich, where bombed-out buildings were plentiful, and spent Christmas dining on roast goose, wild boar and a four-foot-long hare while the pianist sang, "Zip dee dee doo dah, zip dee dee ay, O mein gutness soch a vonderful day . . ."

When they got to West Berlin it was lit up like Las Vegas. Even the bombed-out church on the Kurfürstendamm was twinkling with coloured lights, and cafés on the Ku'damm were open till three o'clock in the morning. The only problem was Don's stuntman, who suddenly announced that he couldn't do the escape-over-the-Wall bit. This was because he had a bad back, not because someone had just been shot by the East German police for trying the same thing.

Don had to hang by his fingertips on the East side of the Wall, then pull himself up and over to the West. The East German Vopos stood and watched him from twenty-five feet away, Sten guns at the ready and not a smile to be seen anywhere. When it was over, he asked the stuntman (who had come along to watch) if he would be accompanying them to Salzburg. He was just wondering; the script called for him to vault over a barrier and dive into the path of an oncoming train. His double said yes, of course he'd be there.

Don suggested spending New Year's Eve in East Berlin, seeing Brecht's legendary Berliner Ensemble, but Virginia thought that sounded drab, not to mention scary, so they stayed in West Berlin and visited decadent capitalist nightclubs instead.

Chez Nous was the famous drag-queen cabaret which had been forced underground during the Nazi era and boasted Hermann Goering among its best customers. Don says the M.C. was old enough to have performed for Goering in some capacity, but the "girls" were absolutely stunning. He congratulated one French creation on her performance and she said, "Ahhh, Monsieur, but I owe eet all to zee operation!''

He replied gallantly, "My compliments to the chef."

When they got back to the Hotel Bristol-Kempinksi in the wee small hours of January 1, 1966, the laughter and song were still going strong in an apartment across the street. Somebody dropped a couple of champagne bottles out of the window onto the cars parked below and within two minutes the police had arrived, the lights were out and all was silent as the grave. Confronted by such Teutonic efficiency, the Harrons suddenly felt lonely and far from home.

"As often happens when people get thoughtful and nostalgic, Virginia and I ended up having a big argument." Actually, it's not the first impulse of most couples to tear into each other every time they feel the least bit sad, but it seems that it's not all that unusual. Don and Virginia screamed at each other for hours the night after President Kennedy was shot, and Don's shrink told him later that all over America other couples had been doing the same thing.

Early the next morning Don left the hotel alone, walked up to Checkpoint Charlie and handed his passport to a massive, unsmiling woman in East German uniform. She didn't give it back. She told him he could have it when and if he came through the same checkpoint that same day.

He took a bus to the centre of town, where the streets were swarming with people. This happened to be the last day West Berliners were allowed to visit relatives in East Berlin. The ban had been lifted from Christmas to New Year's only, and everyone was anxious to hear what was happening on the other side of the Wall. He was sorry to disappoint all those who greeted him, hoping for news. He had to confess that he was a Canadian, a stranger on both sides of town.

He bought a ticket for the Brecht Theatre, a good seat in the second row. The Berliner Ensemble was being run by Brecht's widow, Helene Weigel, and the play that night would be *The Good Soldier Schweik*, Brecht's World War II sequel to the classic Czech comedy about World War I. This was a choice he would have expected: reminders of the bad old days (before Soviet liberation) were on display in all the immaculate public buildings he visited. However, what he saw that night surprised and uplifted him beyond his wildest dreams.

The Brecht Theatre was not the spartan auditorium he had expected, but a very intimate, handsomely decorated 18th-century playhouse. The prologue was performed by enormous puppets, spitting images of Hitler, Goebbels, Himmler and Goering, who lumbered about the stage in a parody of the Führer's favourite composer, Richard Wagner, with voices provided by singers from the German State Opera.

The play itself took place in a pub, and the backdrop was a beautiful tapestry with a view of Prague. Don had read many books about Brecht's alienation theory ("Don't try to charm the bloody bourgeois, just give them the facts in a dispassionate manner.") but what he saw that night were performers of immense charm and talent who could have convinced him of anything.

As he happened to be working on his own war-is-hell musical at the time, he viewed the proceedings with more than dispassionate interest. When the actors came to a musical number, they simply walked over and put a coin in the jukebox, which provided the instrumental accompaniment to Paul Dessau's songs. It was so clever, so economical — but if you tried it in North America in those days, you'd have the musicians' union rulebook rammed down your throat.

In the Friedrichstrasse station on his way back to the bus, he happened to see one of the last subway trains bound for West Berlin, and couldn't help staring at the little family groups saying goodbye, for who knew how long. He tried to guess who was leaving and who was staying behind: "It was impossible to tell — the good-byes were equally fervent on both sides, just a bunch of relatives taking their last, long look at each other."

The last thing the bus driver did before heading back to West Berlin was to inspect the underside of the vehicle with a big mirror and light on a long handle, looking for escaping East Berliners. As Don passed back through Checkpoint Charlie, a smiling young man handed him his passport and hoped he had a pleasant day.

The next morning they flew the narrow Berlin corridor back to West Germany. Next stop was Salzburg train station, to get run over, but as this was only a couple of hours' drive from Munich they returned to the good life at the Hotel Continentale. As they prepared to depart for the shoot the next day there was no sign of his stunt double. John Newland put his hand sympathetically on Don's shoulder: "Sorry, Donald. He's got chickenpox."

"I'm not so sure about the pox part," Don glowered, and was sent off to buy himself a jockstrap "just in case the train, you know. . . ."

His efforts to purchase a "condominium" (he meant to say "suspensorium") from a bunch of giggling seventeen-year-old girls who were sold out of jockstraps in medium and large sizes proved to be almost as excruciating as being run over by a train. When he came out of the changing room, he was sure their jubilant cry of "Ahhh! Zuh liddle von fits!" could be heard on all seven floors of the Sportschek department store.

Next day they crossed the Austrian border and arrived in Salzburg to find the train already puffing in the station. He was told that the distance between the tip of his nose and the bottom of the train was a close fit, but safe, as long as he lay perfectly flat. They didn't mention anything about the distance between the train and his liddle suspensorium, but he was sure they knew.

He vaulted over a barrier in the crowded station and rolled under the train. He decided the only thing to do was to close his eyes and lie back, to be or not to be, come what may. Soon after the train started rumbling over him, he opened his eyes in spite of himself, then shut them again, fast. Oh, God . . .

I don't know if he prayed this time, but the scene was done in one take and the cast went out to lunch. The last day of shooting took place in an 18th-century castle. Fortunately, the only danger this time was in the script: meeting the family of his dead double. The wife was played by lovely Dana Winter, and her brother by a tall, Gothic-looking young Canadian named Donald Sutherland.

When they parted the next day, Newland asked Harron to cross fingers with him, as they would soon know whether *The Man Who Never Was* would be picked up for the following season. Don crossed his fingers, secretly hoping it wouldn't: "Not for me all these macho heroics. My best performance was making the crew laugh between takes."

D & V took the train to Venice, then on to Rome. They had reservations at the Hotel Inghilterra, where the fun bunch like Tennessee Williams always stayed. When he woke up at ten o'clock the next morning, he tried calling his daughters in Velletri, sixty kilometres away. Then he hung up in confusion and called again, and again. The phone kept being answered by a woman who spoke no English, no Italian, no French and no German, as far as he could tell, but chatted merrily away in something unrecognizable. He gave up in frustration.

Stephen's mother, visiting from Hungary, was the only member of the family who got up before noon. She was probably out in the fields at dawn chatting with the *contadini*, who were surprised to find themselves speaking Hungarian. Mary and I had been expecting to hear from our other parents, so I tried calling the Inghilterra that afternoon. I got through to the hotel, but when I asked for Signore Harron they put me through to some Italian who answered "Prrronto" in a thrilling baritone.

I tried to explain in my best Italian that there had been some mistake, when the suddenly familiar voice said, "Excuse me?" It was my dear father, the Irish tenor. Stephen picked them up in his new Mercedes convertible, we all had dinner in Rome, then they came back with us to the villa (actually a converted monastery), just outside of Velletri.

There, Donald learned that the Vizinczeys had decided not to go back to Canada. Instead, they were moving to England, where the little darlings could get an education worthy of their superior brains. This was a bitter blow. He had "unlimited" visiting rights, but no control over how far he would have to travel to accomplish this feat. "I swallowed hard. My girls would always be half a world away."

There was even talk of sending us to a private school, or so he thought, and Father was afraid they were going to turn us into a pair of insufferable, toffee-nosed little snobs. They may have succeeded in this, but if he'd asked me, I could have told him that a private school was out of the question, because it violated my socialist principles.

Mary and I received an invaluable education in Italy, though not from our Government of Ontario correspondence course — *that* qualified as entertainment. Each in our monastic studies, Mary and I would read instructions involving glass beakers, three-holed stoppers, rubber tubing etc. and laugh heartily. The education came from being surrounded by hard-working tenant-farmers who lived on nothing but pasta all week, with a bit of tomato paste on Sundays. The lady from whom we rented the villa, married to an Italian Communist member of parliament, referred to them as "my peasants."

Our "superior" brains failed to register how much we meant to our father. We assumed that as he had left us of his own free will, he had also chosen to live with the consequences. That Virginia also might crave our companionship seemed beyond the bounds of probability. However, during the three days we spent with them at the Inghilterra in Rome, we couldn't help noticing the extra tension.

Virginia complained even more than usual about Gloria dressing us like orphans to squeeze more money out of Donald, while she and Stephen squandered his child support payments. This was unfair to Gloria: we tried to look spiffy, but I still end up looking like an orphan unless someone else dresses me, and I haven't let Mother do that since Summitridge Drive.

Virginia always made valiant efforts to improve our appearance, despite the fact that by the next visit we would have reverted to our previous state. This time she took us to a hairdresser near the Spanish Steps, and I came out with the best haircut of my life, never to be repeated of course.

Efforts to explore the Eternal City were hampered by the hordes of gypsies eternally accosting us for money. Mary and I were used to it, but V found it intolerable. One of my fondest Roman memories is of my father furtively slipping a handful of coins to a young beggar with a baby in her arms.

When they flew home over the Pole from Copenhagen, Los Angeles seemed more than half a world away. At least their faithful cat Farley was waiting for them. That night, about eleven o'clock, the phone rang. *The Man Who Never Was* had been picked up for the fall. Oh well, what the heck. Don resigned himself to success, and Virginia was delighted.

The next morning, the phone rang again: *The Man Who Never Was* was still going ahead, but with a new sponsor who was not a Shakespeare fan and wanted Robert Lansing in the title role. Harron was out.

That did it. He'd had it with Tinseltown anyway, but this was the final straw. He broke the news to Virginia that after the Charlottetown Festival season ended, they would be moving to Toronto. She knew how badly his pride had been hurt, and didn't argue. Having cleared that hurdle, he began to think about how wonderful it would be to have his daughters living with them there. We could go back to Jarvis Collegiate, back to our old friends, and have a normal family life for a change.

To his relief, Virginia didn't argue about that either. In fact, she seemed quite keen on the idea. Having cleared *that* hurdle, he wrote to Gloria. After all, it seemed only fair that he should have a turn at custody of the children. In the meantime, the Harrons flew to Toronto for another season of *Side by Side* on CBC radio with Pat Patterson.

Side by Side was a lot of fun, again, but he was having trouble with *Turvey*. There were many challenging meetings with Earle Birney, ("I never had this trouble with Lucy Maud Montgomery!") but none with Norman Campbell, who was tied up in other meetings over the possibility of a strike by the Producers' and Directors' Union. Don says they might as well have been on strike, for all the time they spent talking about it. He and Elaine Campbell kept working on the lyrics, and waiting for Norman to emerge and set them to music.

He must have felt bereft, staying at the Waldorf, without his kids
popping in after school, and with Jarvis Collegiate only a few blocks
away. And it must have been devastating when Gloria wrote back
and turned him down flat. I'll bet her trump card was that no school
in Toronto could possibly compete with the academic standards of
Carlyle Grammar School for Girls in Chelsea, which had agreed to
accept us in spite of our being lowly Canadians.

Gloria's faith in the sterling superiority of a British education came
from the Gravenhurst Library, and was unshakeable. She even convinced us that we didn't have a chance of getting into Carlyle
Grammar School. As this seemed to be my only escape from a private
or "public" school I was more nervous than I wanted to admit as
we sat on the hard wooden bench outside the headmistress's office. Suddenly a couple of uniformed schoolgirls burst through the
door to the inner sanctum and one said breathlessly: "Oh, Miss,
we was going to take the bus, but . . ."

"We *was* going"?! Mary and I exchanged knowing looks, as if
to say, "This'll be a piece of cake!" It was, too. Getting in, I mean.

Don fired a letter back to Gloria, announcing that he was cutting off support payments since she refused to let him be with his
children. As for the argument that Toronto wasn't good enough
for them, that really made his blood boil. Between that and waiting
for Norman Campbell, he must have been throwing tantrums at
himself even more than usual. This is a peculiar, harmless habit
picked up from Jimmy Porter which remains with him to this day.
Mary and I remember sitting quiet as mice at Summitridge Drive
while Father fought a pitched battle with a pair of socks, calling
them and himself every filthy name he could think of.

You get used to it. Virginia figured that *The Man Who Never
Was* had been a crushing blow, and tried extra hard to be patient
with him. She even tried to be nice to his parents. He talked to
his old college friend Ross Maclean, who suggested the perfect outlet
to relieve his frustrations: haul the old kit bag out of Pinewood,
and do a political commentary as Charlie Farquharson on CBC-TV's
Sunday newsmagazine, *This Hour Has Seven Days*.

What a great idea. Don put on his old shirt, pants, boots, cap
and glasses, and spoke his mind to the folks at home all across

Canada. His first topic was the rumour that Andrei Gromyko was going to fly from Moscow to Rome for an audience with the Pope: "Now how'd they git an audience fer a thing like that?" Hell, this was *way* more fun than being run over by a train.

The hugely successful and influential series only lasted three more weeks, shot down not by its ratings, which were tops, but as the innocent victim of a custody dispute between the News and Public Affairs departments of the CBC. That's politics for you; but with its dying breath, *This Hour Has Seven Days* breathed new life into the old farmer. Those three short weeks set him on a shining path, and Charlie has remained a political animal ever since.

When Don and Virginia flew back to Los Angeles, he had a paperback book in his pocket, something he'd been meaning to read for years. Now that he was finally reading it, he could see that it had the makings of a great Canadian musical, "about a sensitive spirit, orphaned at an early age, living on an island, who ultimately triumphs although the entire community she lives in seems to be against her." Don't worry, he hadn't flipped. It wasn't *Anne of Green Gables*, but *Klee Wyck*, the real-life story of painter Emily Carr.

While they were packing up at Nash Drive, saying farewell to its patios, huge fireplace, and the dear old tree trunk which ran up the middle of the stairwell, the telephone rang. It was a call from Canada, from Bob Johnston, who was one of the ushers at the very first *Spring Thaw*. Bob was a producer now, and had organized *Thaw's* coast-to-coast tour in 1964. He had just leased the rights from Mavor Moore to produce the twentieth edition, *Spring Thaw '67*, for Canada's centennial year. How about it?

The only thing Don didn't like about it was Bob's idea for the connecting theme: a Brit's-eye view of Canada, the sketches linked by an English narrator, travelling from coast to coast. Don had quite enough of the British point of view from Gloria, thank you very much. He told Bob he wanted to do a Canuck's-eye view, a comic history of Canada from the Age of the Dinosaurs up to Confederation in 1867. Bob said he'd think it over.

Three days later, Johnston phoned back to say he'd thought it over, and the answer was yes, on a tour from sea to shining sea.

Hurray! They packed everything they could into the Volvo, waved goodbye to Lotusland, and headed north-east, going all the way this time, with Farley meowing piteously in the back seat. He kept it up for two hundred miles before deciding, like Virginia, to go with the flow.

They had an absolutely idyllic journey after that, following a winding trail through Las Vegas, the Grand Tetons, Yellowstone Park, with a glimpse of Mount Rushmore and a three-hour wait behind a flock of sheep in Wyoming. They didn't quarrel once in ten whole days, which was unheard of. Don says perhaps he and Virginia should have kept right on moving, because ten-in-one was more like the average after that.

It was bliss all the way to PEI, and their home for the summer. There it was, their picturesque little love nest, a white clapboard cottage with a white picket fence, right on the beach. "Looks darling!" said Virginia. Then she went inside.

It was old inside too, with small rooms and a set of unpainted steps leading up to the loft. Kitchen facilities and plumbing were practically nonexistent. This was more than she had bargained for. "Ugh!" said she, just as Don was drinking in the enchantment of the place.

It reminded him of his grandparents' place in Dunbarton, of the Muskoka cottages of his youth. It felt like everything he'd ever wanted. It felt like *home*. Her "Ugh!" cut him to the quick. He snarled back, "It's a cottage! What the hell did you expect, Doris Day?" That's when the fight started. It was still going on when a letter arrived informing him that, unless he was prepared to support his daughters in the style to which they were entitled, in whatever remote location the Vizinczeys happened to choose, Stephen was going to adopt them.

Even Donald must have been clued in enough to realize that full-time parenting in Toronto would be a mite difficult if he planned to take *Spring Thaw* to every corner of Canada in the coming year, and nothing could stop him from doing that, not even his beloved children. You see, between his former wife's snotty letters about British superiority, and his present wife's constant comments about

Canadian inferiority, the loyal son was rapidly becoming the biggest flag-waver you ever saw.

He was probably prepared to concede the custody issue anyway, and resumed payments to forestall any legal proceedings. The main thing was for *his* girls to spend at least part of the summer in P.E.I. He was sure that *they* would appreciate the cottage. We could play Canasta and Essences, do improvisations that got out of hand, and the rafters would ring with laughter again.

One July day, for no reason other than idle curiosity and the fickle finger of fate, I opened a little desk drawer, certainly not mine, and discovered four or five unopened letters addressed to Mary and me in London, from our father far away. We hadn't heard from him in as many weeks, which was unheard of, but we hadn't thought too much about it. We were full-fledged teenagers, recently transposed from rustic contemplation to a Rolling Stone's throw from the King's Road, Chelsea.

I didn't stop to read the letters, I just stormed off and demanded an explanation. Cowering, Gloria admitted that there was a custody dispute going on, and she had hidden the letters because she didn't want us to be hurt. I told her what to do with *that* limp excuse — as if confiscating our father's letters didn't hurt us! She broke down and confessed that she did it because she was a coward and a cheat. She was sure that if we knew, we would insist on moving back to Toronto with our favourite parents.

It's true that I'd always been Daddy's girl, worshipped Virginia, hated Stephen and pitied my feeble-minded little mother, but still there was no doubt in my mind. I said, "What on *earth* makes you think we'd rather live with Father and Virginia?"

Her mouth dropped open. "Well, wouldn't you?"

I snapped, "Oh come on, Mother, two weeks of Strindberg is enough for anybody." We had just seen Olivier in *The Dance of Death* at the Old Vic. I might have added that living on Woodfall Street, a few doors down from the author of *Look Back in Anger*, was more like D'Annunzio. Ah, the Osbornes and the Vizinczeys, psychodrama in stereo. . . .

This was Gloria's first hint that all was not sweetness and light on the other side. Emboldened, she broke the news that Stephen, her sweet angel, was willing to adopt us. Mary and Martha Vizinczey? Of all the nerve! Apparently he thought he deserved some credit for being willing to foot our bills as well as our thinly-veiled contempt. I heaped such scorn on this proposal it was never mentioned again.

However, because of my clever little crack about Strindberg, Gloria decided not to communicate this fact to her ex-husband until after the summer holidays, when her little darlings would be safely back in school. Don and Virginia were left with the impression that Gloria was the heartless bitch depriving them of the sticky little hands and faces that keep couples together during trying times. That wasn't Gloria, that was me.

When Mary and I calmed down enough to read F.B.'s letters, we discovered that our mother had misjudged him: there was not one word about paternal rights, or a father's feelings, just affectionate greetings and vivid descriptions, if fewer jokes than usual. The closest he came to luring us over was by raving about the beauty of his new love, Prince Edward Island, and he couldn't help that.

Imagine writing week after week without a word of reply, not knowing if his daughters had disowned him or not. The poor Bastard must have felt like King Lear. Imagine Virginia giving up Lotusland for the prospect of full-time parenting in the Frozen North. They could have spared themselves months of anxiety and frustration if they hadn't been so anxious to spare our feelings in the dispute. And we couldn't even spare them a few weeks' friendly psychoplay on the beach in P.E.I.

Looking back on it, my heart bleeds for all of my parents. At the time, I was an unforgiving fifteen-year-old who viewed their ridiculous antics with a jaundiced eye. I'd seen a lot of Shakespeare, but until I found myself playing psychodrama in front of my own stepdaughter, I didn't know that grown-ups have about as much control over their own destiny as a bunch of kids without a license, driving down the highway.

24

HOME IS THE HERO

JUST before the Harrons left L.A., Virginia consulted an astrologer who told her that her husband was about to enter a new phase in his career and she would be divorced. Don was outraged at this latter suggestion, although there was no denying the former. From the moment he moved back to Canada in 1966 he reverted to his true state as a workaholic. He was blissfully happy rehearsing all day, performing at night and writing all the time.

Virginia was not pleased. Far from home, stepdaughters and friends, she responded by having a brief, indiscreet fling with a handsome young member of the company. She succeeded in getting her husband's attention, but it was the only thing she could have done to break the bond between them.

The Charlottetown season opened with *The Ottawa Man*, Mavor Moore's version of Gogol's *The Government Inspector*, with Don in the title role, Eric House playing the mayor and Kate Reid his wife. Kate agreed to take part in *Turvey* as a drunken derelict, so Don and Norman Campbell wrote a song just for her. *Buy a Drink for Old Mother* was composed backstage during a single performance of *The Ottawa Man*, with Don tossing snatches of lyric to Norman between frantic exits and entrances.

The third production was a revival of *Anne of Green Gables*. The day of the opening, Don heard a Voice. It was The Voice of an Angel, as her first album was so aptly titled, rehearsing in the cabaret next door. He told the Festival's producer, Jack McAndrew, he needed that Voice for his *Thaw*. McAndrew replied, "Catherine McKinnon? She's a big star. She doesn't need *Spring Thaw*!"

281

Don recalls, "A meeting was arranged." The next morning,
Catherine was having breakfast in the Confederation Centre dining room with her sister Patricia, when a handsome older man walked
up to the table and asked if he could join them. He was wearing
a tank top, shorts, loafers without socks and a faded jeans jacket
he thinks he stole from John Houseman.

He offered her a six-month bus ride through fog and blizzard
in a show yet to be written, with a cast yet to be determined, all
for a Finn's pee, and she thought that sounded like fun. She said
she would try to rearrange her schedule (in other words, get out
of a lucrative concert tour), and he left without mentioning his name
or where he could be reached. Patricia turned to Catherine and said,
"Who is that man?"

Catherine replied, "I don't know!" She knew he had written the
musical *Anne*, but that was all. Ask her the same question today,
and she'll probably give you the same answer.

When *Variety's* chief critic Hobe Morrison came up to review all
three shows, he touted *Turvey* as the most likely prospect for Broad-
way. Don thought that the whole cast was magnificent and Jack
Duffy was a perfect *Turvey*, but the script needed a lot of work.
He had cast himself as the chaplain, giving his first sermon since
"Greasepaint and the Pulpit" in *Tenth Times*.

Danny Kaye's production company phoned from Hollywood
about acquiring the film rights to *Anne*. They hadn't seen or heard
the show, but already planned to have André Previn rewrite the
score. Norman told them politely no thanks, but Don was tempted
to tell them a lot more than that. He was fed up with people assum-
ing Yanks and Brits could do everything better.

D & V moved to Toronto in September, to Virginia's relief, and
he set to work in earnest on his *Thaw*. Already it was lumbered with
the tag "controversial," although he couldn't see anything controversial about a comic song-and-dance review of Canadian history
from the Pleistocene to Confederation. As far as he was concerned,
the only departure from tradition was the one-man writing team,
instead of the usual handful.

For his cast he naturally chose Peter Mews, who had appeared
in every one of the previous nineteen *Thaws*. Barbara Hamilton was

an equally obvious choice. Most of the others were *Thaw* veterans like Doug Chamberlain, Diane Nyland and Dean Regan. To this core he added Quebecker Ron Tanguay, Robert Christie's statuesque daughter Dinah and the little songbird from Nova Scotia, Catherine McKinnon.

Shortly after rehearsals began, the Harrons invited Catherine to dinner at their townhouse off Avenue Road. Afterwards Don offered her a ride home, as is his gallant custom. While she and Virginia stood chatting in the front hall, he went upstairs to look for his car keys. Suddenly a huge rumpus broke out on the floor above. There were sounds of a violent struggle, and she could hear Don screaming obscenities at his opponent. To her amazement, Virginia went right on talking as if nothing was happening.

She remembers thinking, "This woman's a monster! Can't she see that poor man needs help?" After a few minutes the battle ended as abruptly as it began, and Don returned to the foyer seemingly none the worse for wear. No explanation was given. Perhaps there was an insane relative in the attic?

Catherine and Patricia popped in one night on the way home from a gig — perhaps to make sure Don was all right. Mary and I happened to be there for the Christmas holidays, and Virginia had played Catherine's album for us. I was impressed by the two sisters — The Voice of an Angel and The Face of an Angel, twenty-one and seventeen respectively. Catherine seemed to be very pretty too, underneath all the makeup, fake hair and false eyelashes. I wondered what a young woman in her position could possibly have to feel insecure about.

As the McKinnon sisters were leaving, Virginia smiled at Patricia and said quietly, "You're a very pretty little girl, and don't you *ever* come here again." Obviously V's acute radar had picked up a danger signal; only she had the wrong target, and the effect was not what she intended. Catherine's protective instincts were now doubly aroused, and she made up her mind she was going to rescue that man from the witch who had insulted her sister.

The first performance of *Spring Thaw '67* was a matinée in Edmunston, New Brunswick. The audience was composed of high school students, mostly French-speaking but fluently bilingual. These kids knew their Canadian history, and laughed at every "histerical" reference, as Charlie would say. This never happened again. Slowly and painfully, as they wended their way ditto across the country, the show had to be made just as funny to grown-ups who didn't know or care about Canadian history, namely the vast majority.

Campbellton went well, but when they got to home-sweet-home Charlottetown everything went wrong. The business manager, who had been sent on ahead, tried to commit suicide just before they arrived. The truck carrying the sets and costumes broke down and had to wait for a service station to open, and the manager of the Forty Winks Motel was on the phone complaining about a stolen pillow. The dress rehearsal went on until almost 3 a.m., not helped by Virginia giving everyone her personal notes.

The opening night audience in Charlottetown sat as though carved in stone, and Don knew that he had failed, miserably. The Toronto press duly recorded the event: the *Evening Telegram* headline read, "*Thaw '67*: Saved by the Performers". The *Star* sent a young know-it-all named Peter Gzowski, who penned the blame directly on Harron: "He has looked at Canada, and he has not been able to make it sound funny."

Don realised that his work was just beginning. He was a man with a mission; there was no question of turning back. He had just begun to write, and re-write, the story of this country, and was determined to get laughs doing it. It is a process which continues to this day, but the tour of *Spring Thaw* hadn't even made it to Fredericton before Bob Johnston quietly informed him that the entire cast was threatening to walk out if he didn't get his wife off the bus.

After six years as Mrs. Harron, Virginia's idea of roughing it was an insufficiently dry martini. While the cast and crew slaved away, she sat around in her lynx parka telling everybody how to do their job, and complaining about everything Canadian. Don says the final straw was when she tried to tell the director, Alan Lund, how to fix the show. I heard it was when she stole Barbara Hamilton's seat, and told her where to get off when Barbara asked for it back. Whichever straw was last, they were patient people, but not gluttons for punishment like their author and leading man. Whether or not V was trying to get thrown off the bus (as I suspect), she immediately agreed to tough it out with Baby Jane in California until the *Thaw* tour was over.

As the tour went on, Don couldn't help wondering if all those years away, despite the frequent trips home, had left him out of touch with what made Canadians tick, or at least what tickled them. He certainly didn't blame them. In Sackville, while the bus ploughed through a blizzard, the audience had waited patiently for six hours. He felt he'd let the whole country down, never mind the cast and crew who struggled to keep pace with his rewrites.

He thanked heaven for his box-office insurance: little Catherine McKinnon was so shy, so stoic, so delightfully repressed. She never complained about anything. During restructuring, they would find themselves rehearsing a scene one way and performing it another. One night in Winnipeg, she came out for the Ice Age sketch pretending to be a mosquito, and realised she was supposed to be a horse. Diane Nyland was also buzzing, instead of whinnying, beside her. The Voice of an Angel was so scared, she says she sang flat for five months.

Some of the reviews were good, but Frank Morriss gave Don a panning in the *Winnipeg Tribune* that really struck home: "I'm not asking Mr. Harron to be rude, but he has the skill and the gift to sting our sense once in a while, instead of tickling our sensibilities with timid little titters at our history and our customs. His contribution to the show is the weakest because he is afraid to give offense."

He was afraid, all right, but it was much more than that. When he set out to deliver a birthday gift in person to his vast homeland, he was already a changed man. He had always had the common touch, admired the hard-working poor more than the idle rich, but now he was a fervent populist, and his whole style of comedy had changed with him.

Gone were the multilingual puns, the literary references, the dazzling wordplay, the operatic spoofs which so delighted the cultivated urban audience of early *Thaws*. To Don it was not a question of talking down to the average small-town Canadian, but of giving up fancy props (all my favourite bits) and getting down to basics.

He suspected the more sophisticated critics would continue to make mincemeat out of him, and he hated to think what would happen when the show played Toronto, but he couldn't help it.

As on the *Sleep of Prisoners* tour across America, the more remote the location, the more inspiring he found the audience reaction. In Timmins it was 40° below (Fahrenheit *and* Celsius), and the movie house stage wasn't even big enough to hold the nine-foot screen for their magic lantern show. Don decided the narrator would have to ad lib his way through. The narrator happened to be Charlie Farquharson, one comic crutch from *Thaw '52* he need not do without. The farmer from Parry Sound's descriptions of what the audience was supposed to be seeing got more laughs than the real slides had, and loosened up the rest of the show.

The reaction seemed to get warmer as they went West, and by the time they reached the Coast he was beginning to think he might have a hit on his hands. In Victoria, Audrey Johnson's review hailed it "the best *Thaw* we've theen for years." On the way back, however, the critical reception cooled rapidly. In Trail, B.C. the local paper called the show "a chilly mush of cold slush." Saskatoon and Regina weren't much better, but none of these rejections discouraged him, even if they hurt.

By the time they got to Moose Jaw, he thought the tightly knit company of adventurers had braved every obstacle Mother Nature or human nature could throw in their path, but he was wrong. That night, as the crew was desperately trying to turn yet another high school gymnasium into a theatre, there was a horrifying thud. A member of the crew named Lyle Ayton had fallen while rigging up some lights.

It was just like the opening of *Measure for Measure*, but this was Canada, not Connecticut, and there was no happy ending. Lyle Ayton was dead, really and truly dead. Don felt that he had sacrificed a human life on his fool's errand, and he didn't want to go on.

The show did go on, against his will. At the beginning of Holy Week, the cast arrived back in Toronto for a well-deserved rest before opening at the Royal Alex. After all the pre-publicity hailing the hero's return, Don dreaded the Toronto opening so much he decided to get away from it all. He spent the time in Montreal, preparing material for a television special about the World's Fair, Expo '67.

Virginia flew back from California, and went with him to Mont-real. He couldn't bear to tell her he was admitting defeat, that his crackpot trip to the moon had been a ghastly mistake with tragic consequences. "I thought the best thing to do was quietly sneak back to the U.S. and return to the round of television shows, and weekends playing volleyball at the beach." She would be so pleased.

He had a special permit to roam around the Expo site. It turned out to be a sea of mud, with only a few weeks to go before opening day. He didn't know how they were going to get it done, but as he sloshed around he could see what they were trying to do, and the vast scope of it moved him. He decided that, "come hell or high water," he would find a place in his own country.

He doesn't remember the opening night performance in Toronto, just all the cameras flashing at him during the lavish party thrown by "Honest Ed" Mirvish in his Warehouse restaurant after the show. All he could think about was what those "hired assassins" were writing about his *Thaw*. He found out at four o'clock in the morn-ing from cast member Dean Regan, reading the reviews hot off the press from a pay phone.

Herbert Whittaker's headline in *The Globe* read "Harron's Humor Gives *Spring Thaw* its Lilt". *Telegram* critic Ron Evans called it "Hysterical History" and suggested they put on *Thaw '67* in the Canadian Pavilion at Expo "to show the world we're not the poor, pompous, humourless, opinionless clods they take us to be." This was followed by six record-breaking weeks at the Royal Alex, and two sold-out months touring Southern Ontario.

Don couldn't figure it out. He says the best part was that Nathan Cohen's review didn't make it into *The Star* until the following day. His reliable enemy wrote that "*Spring Thaw '67* has been conceiv-ed for an unsophisticated and undemanding public. Even on that basis it does not do. By any other test, it is a grisly experience."

Spring Thaw '67 turned out to be the longest-running, most pro-fitable edition of the show in that institution's glorious history, which ended with the ignominious "nude" *Thaw* in the late '70s. While *Thaw* was still going strong, *Anne of Green Gables* was making its first triumphal procession across the country, including three weeks at Expo '67. Nathan Cohen attacked the show, of course, but the other critics were as happy as the audience.

Mary joined D & V in Montreal that summer, and saw *Anne* at Expo. I wasn't interested; I had a boyfriend. I didn't see my other parents until Christmas, when they came and stayed with us at Coleherne Court, the block of flats in London the Vizinczeys still call home (when they're there). One morning I walked into the kitchen to find Mother and Father having tea, just like old times. Drawing herself up to her full diminutive height, she announced tragically, "It's all right, your father has told me everything. There will be no more lies between us!" With that, Gloria Swanson swept out of the kitchen, her nightie billowing behind her.

"What's eating her?" I asked.

My father, who was sitting at the table reading the *Guardian*, looked up and replied casually, "Oh, she asked me if I thought you were a virgin, and I said 'I doubt it, she's sixteen.'" Then he went back to reading the paper.

He and Virginia were very subdued that Christmas. They didn't tell us what they already knew, that this was the last time we would all be together. He had fallen in love with Catherine McKinnon, and to this day believes that he pursued her relentlessly. He did pursue her, but if you know the relentless determination of the sweet songbird of Nova Scotia, it was a foregone conclusion.

Right after *Spring Thaw* closed in Montreal, Catherine had disappeared from his life, off on a frantic round of one-nighters to make up for the financial loss of all those months in *Thaw*. He tracked her down in Surinam, off the South American coast. The only commitment he could get out of her was "We shall see." She was not interested in being his mistress, playing second-fiddle to his second wife.

After Christmas in London, Don and Virginia had gone their separate ways, he to Toronto and she to California, or so he thought. Farley stayed in Toronto but went to live with Tommy Tweed's daughter, actress Terry Tweed. Farley had walked into D & V's life on the night of their very first torrid reconciliation, and it wouldn't have been right for him to take sides. I wish I could do his memory justice, for he was a prince among cats, grey with white gloves, spats, shirtfront and half a moustache. He lived to be as old as he was wise, that is to say ancient.

Don began 1968 alone, and the first thing he wanted to do was revive Jane Mallett Associates with Jane and Robert Christie. Jane was too frail now for a full-blown revue, and her voice not strong enough for a full-sized theatre, but it still had its thrilling hoarse, breathy quality, and the famous timing and delivery were intact. He wanted to create something just for her.

He chose Paul Hiebert's *Here Lies Sarah Binks*, a gentle Canadian spoof on all those ladies who write nature poetry. Tommy Tweed, a former student of Hiebert's at the University of Manitoba, had already written a one-hour radio version, in which all three Jane Mallett Associates had appeared with great delight. Tommy was a radio man, and said he was too tired to write the stage version. He told Don he'd come opening night, when it would be too late to nag him about anything.

The show was booked to run for six weeks in the cosy little auditorium of the Central Library, which also housed the Canadian drama archives. Using Lucio Agostini's original radio score, Don wrote a ''mini-musical'' for a cast of six, including the pianist Horace Lapp, who had a traffic accident during rehearsals; his subsequent lapses of memory at the keyboard kept the rest of them on their toes.

To recreate the atmosphere of rural Saskatchewan in the early '30s, Don chose a village hall for his setting; and for his occasion, the dedication of a monumental stone to the departed poetess. At intermission, the cast did not retire backstage, but marched down the aisle and, still in character, joined the patrons for lemonade and cookies, the only refreshments served.

During one of the preview performances, Don heard a familiar existential cackle in the audience and Virginia, whose laugh it was, says he turned chalk white. She had come back hoping for another torrid reconciliation, even if she didn't understand what he was doing to his career. (Frankly, neither did I.) Instead, he took her to a well-known folk club, The Riverboat on Yorkville.

Catherine McKinnon walked onstage with her sidemen and assessed the situation. She picked up the microphone, looked straight into Donald's eyes and sang *This Masquerade*. Virginia looked at her husband and knew it was all over. He was transfixed, mesmerized, enthralled. ''He bought it!'' she says with wonderment, after all these years.

Virginia admitted defeat and gave him his second Mexican divorce.

He gave her the boot, $10,000 and a Volvo station wagon. For once, a psychiatrist had been right about something, even if for the wrong reason: as predicted at their wedding, the marriage lasted seven years.

Don needed Catherine's Voice: he had begun work on his Emily Carr musical, and wanted her to star in it. But it was more than that. He says, "I have never met a human being with more raw courage than this little Maritimer." One of the things that captivated him most was her eagerness to make disastrous career moves, not content to rest on her laurels as a "straight" singer. "For some reason, some stubborn streak, Catherine has never been satisfied just to excel at a specialty she has developed. She wants to try it all." Sound familiar?

Meanwhile, someone else's *Spring Thaw '68* had just opened in St. John's, Newfoundland, to the usual round of "It's not as good as last year!" from the critics. In the *Star* Patrick Scott out-Cohened Cohen by declaring it to have "all the grace and charm of a giant squid". Don was glad he had done *Thaw '67*, but said never again: he might be a glutton for punishment, but there are limits.

Here Lies Sarah Binks opened to rave reviews and, as Don had intended, it was a personal triumph for Jane Mallett. The critic from *The Varsity*, his old college paper, had never seen Jane before, and his review was a paeon of wonder to her comic genius. Alan Gordon later attempted to revive *Spring Thaw,* brave chap.

Sorry to be predictable, but the only dissenting critical voice against *Sarah Binks* was good old Nathan Cohen, who didn't like Hiebert in the first place, and called adaptor Harron and director Christie "the real malefactors of the mess. Like the coelecanth and the cockroach, a few vestigial forms of theatrical diversion turn up eons after they have outlived their purpose. . . . It is not to laugh, it is to weep."

"Otherwise everything okay, Nat?" replies my father, the Wandering Coelecanth. There must have been a cockroach and coelecanth convention in Toronto that Spring, because they flocked to *Sarah Binks* for the whole six weeks. Don declares, "I never had such a good time in all my years in the theatre."

He says the greatest official accolade he received in Canada's centennial year was an offer by the Ministry of Revenue in Ottawa to write and perform a series of comic films about income tax. There were to be four of them, five minutes each, featuring no fewer than twelve characters, all played by Harron. He had no agent at the time, except the ones in London, New York and L.A. he never called, and accepted the paltry fee they offered him, $1500 for the lot.

The civil servant who hired him asked him out to lunch, then left him at the cash register to pay for himself. It was a hint of what was to come. As well as writing the scripts Don played a video jockey on a Tax-a-phone show, fielding questions from himself as an Arab sheik asking about oil depletion allowances, a Scots curler, a John Lennon hippie with long hair and grannie glasses, a patient swathed in bandages, a female civil servant with an English accent, some senior citizens and, of course, the farmer from Parry Sound.

Considering he could never make head or tail of his own taxes, he was pretty proud of his efforts to make the whole worrisome business less intimidating and easier for the average taxpayer to understand. He figured it was a nice way to round off the country's birthday, even if the government was getting him practically Scot-free.

Finally, after months of waiting, the $1500 cheque arrived from the federal government. The very next day he received a reassessment notice increasing his taxable contribution to the national pot by $1500. When Charlie talks about yer Department of the Infernal Revenyoo, he knows whereof he speaks.

25

MEASURE FOR MEASURE

WHEN I was fourteen, during our last summer high-on-a-hill in L.A. overlooking the smog, my father said to me out of the blue, "Look, if you find when you're grown up that we don't have anything in common, I don't want you to feel you have to visit me or anything. Please, don't bother!" I took him at his word, while he was still paying my bills, and he didn't flinch. How could any child, no matter how selfish, not want to spend time with a parent like that?

Neither my father nor my mother ever asked me for gratitude or respect, and until I became a parent never received any. From birth, they treated Mary and me like people who were at least as intelligent as they were, just new in town. They took us by our sticky little hands, showered us with devotion and led us out into the world, asking nothing in return.

Looking back, Mary and I agree that having one parent like that is an incredible stroke of luck, but two is a little rich for anyone's blood. We even had four adorable, adoring grandparents. The addition of a few step-parents, of operatic proportions, was probably necessary to redress the balance.

To this day, Don and Gloria never burden the little darlings with their problems if they can possibly help it. Until I read his memoirs, I didn't know how hard it was for my father to come home to Canada. This does not prevent him from viewing it as entirely A Good Thing, but for the benefit of the next generation of Canadian performers who tire of Tinseltown and decide to come home, allow me to remove my father's rose-coloured glasses for a moment. That is, after all, what children do best.

Throughout his acting career, Don Harron had received a steady stream of offers from Canada, principally from the CBC. Every time he came back for a visit, he was flooded with work. This time, however, once word circulated that he had given up his L.A. success kit and was actually *living* in Toronto, he found that producers preferred long distance to local calls more than ever.

With the new-found national pride he had helped to foster, their attitude seemed to be, "So, you've come crawling back, eh? Well, if you're not good enough for them, you're *certainly* not good enough for us!" The British and the Americans had been good to him, but he was no longer in a land of "We're the Greatest!" He was back in the land of "We May Not Be Much, But You're Worse!" — the Canadian way of saying the same thing.

There were calls for Charlie Farquharson, but Don the actor seemed to have been completely forgotten. They still remembered him in England, mind you. One of our first dinner guests at Coleherne Court was Dennis Norden. He and Stephen met on *The David Frost Show*, while Vizinczey was being attacked as a filth-monger by that caricature of the Queen Mother, Barbara Cartland. Dennis was so delightful in his defence of *In Praise of Older Women* that Viz invited him over for dinner.

Norden's first question, even before folding his tall lanky frame into a chair, was "You folks are Canadian aren't you? You wouldn't happen to know a friend of mine, an actor named Donald Harron?"

To which Gloria replied: "Actually, he's my ex-husband and these are his daughters." (I remember thinking "Dennis must think Canada is an awfully small country.")

Don flew these same daughters to Toronto the following Easter, 1968. It was one of the few times we ever saw him not working, and the first time we could remember seeing him without a wife. It sounded ideal, but was hard to get used to. *Here Lies Sarah Binks* closed shortly before we arrived, but they put on a special performance in Jane Mallett's house for the benefit of ourselves and a few friends. It was a precious gift to be appreciated later, like parents.

At the time, I repaid his kindness by flying home a week early, which must have cost him a bundle, because I missed my boyfriend. As soon as I got back to London I split up with him. At sixteen I had lost the clear vision of childhood and joined the traffic on the highway, leaving my sister holding the bag. Looking back, I realise that what upset me was not just my father courting a child bride, but the discovery that my old Jarvis Collegiate friends' normal, stable fathers were fleeing the comforts of Rosedale like lemmings in pursuit of inner truths and younger women. I didn't believe in love any more, and marriage was just a dirty lie designed to give children a false sense of security.

I didn't explain any of this to my father because I didn't understand it myself. Did he sulk, storm, berate me for my thanklessness? No, he just drove me to the airport, kissed me goodbye and put it out of his mind. A few months later, he phoned up and offered me a holiday in the South of France. What a saint.

In the meantime, Hollywood had not forgotten him, even if he wasn't good enough for the CBC, so he flew down to star in another episode of *The F.B.I.* He asked the director what happened to the real F.B.I. agent, the one who used to breathe down their necks to make sure the episodes were "authentic." The reply was, "Oh, he'll be by, don't you worry. Always pops in for a few minutes every morning."

Sure enough, he breezed by just after ten. It was the same agent, but what a change! His game was tennis now, and he had traded in his gun, green suit and fedora for a racquet, white shirt and shorts. Don remarked on this transformation to his co-star, Barry Morse. They were rooming together, when they weren't busy running around the set as a couple of gay Communist subversives.

Barry told Don about his brother, who had spent his entire working life as a London Bobby. Asked if he never tired of this occupation, pounding the same old beat, his brother replied that he couldn't possibly, not "watching Life's Rich Pageant flowing by!" Watching Life's Rich Pageant, or "L.R.P.", became an instant byword in the Harron family, and remains our favourite game.

Barry armed Don with that bit of Morse family philosophy just in time for yet another event he describes as "the biggest disaster" of his career, two rain-soaked weeks at the C.N.E. The 1968 Grandstand Show was a historical pageant called *Sea to Sea*, with the National Ballet and a few vocal performers like Charlie Farquharson, Catherine McKinnon and Robert Christie as Sir John A. Macdonald of course.

Scripting a huge outdoor spectacle was a new field for Don, and he had a football field to do it in. He was so worried, he did something he's never done before or since: he went to a tea-cup reader. She told him he was about to have one of the biggest successes of his career. "As it turns out, I worry about the kind of tea that woman was using."

For his theme, he chose the creation of the Canadian National Railway because, as Charlie says, "It's hard to say whether yer coast-to-coast Canada come about 'cause of yer sea-by-sea railroad or the vicey of yer versey. It's a sorta chick-in-yer-aig argument to guess who got laid first." *Sea to Sea* would begin where *Thaw 1967* left off, in 1867, and end with the last spike in the C.N.R. rail fifteen years later.

The morning after they opened, the *Toronto Star* blasted him in stereo. On one page was Ralph Hicklin. Don's old college chum with no axe to grind "except possibly into the back of my neck" who wrote: "Give me anything but *Sea to Sea*, the new-type, dreary-type, indescribable-type spectacle that made its curtsey last night." On the opposite page, Sid Adilman echoed his sentiments with the proviso that "Miss McKinnon, one of Canada's best popular singers, creates the depth and mood of the moment with unmannered elegance. Harron who wrote the show also appears as Charlie Farquharson. His script is to blame."

This was followed by two weeks of the worst weather the Ex has ever known. The heavens opened, the rain came down and didn't stop. Don felt that he had sinned in more than the eyes of Man. One night during an electrical storm several actors refused to handle the microphones, so Charlie strode out, mic in hand. This was one way of dying in front of an audience he hadn't tried yet.

Kamikaze Kate went out there too, not a horse or a mosquito this time but a Métis maiden. As Charlie explains it, sometimes the Scottish immigrants got along with the Cree already in residence, and sometimes not. When they did, the result was "what they call bein' 'Matey.' "* Don Had given Gordon Lightfoot a book about Louis Riel hoping it would inspire a song for Catherine and it did.

*Did I say "gone were the multi-lingual puns"? I was wrong!

She sang *The Land with No Name* every night come hell or high water, which pretty well describes it.

As soon as it was over, Catherine flew off to repair the damage to her career and Donald decided to get out of the country for a while, "before they cancelled my citizenship." He had been so successful in putting my un-Holy Week behaviour out of his mind, he recalls: "My daughters hadn't seen me for a year, so I phoned them in London." I was the only one there. Mary was with the Vizzes in St. Tropez. He said, "The Riviera? Let's go!" And we did.

There was one hitch, however. Just as he was about to leave for the airport, the phone rang. It was Bob Allen from the CBC, who had directed him in Galsworthy's *Justice*, the second play ever performed on Canadian television. He urged Don to drop by his office and pick up a screenplay.

A call from the CBC, for any dramatic role, was too rare to be resisted, so he picked up the script on his way to the airport, and left his phone number in St. Tropez with Allen's secretary. She glanced at it and said, "This show starts taping next week."

"Really," said Don. "Who turned it down?" She rattled off a long list of American stars which included his old pal from *Man from U.N.C.L.E.* David McCallum, Keir Dullea, Robert Reid and Aldo Ray. Don said, "Aldo Ray? What kind of part is this?!"

"A United Church minister."

"Oh, I see," he replied. "Typecasting."

Truer words were never spoken. From then on, whenever my father received a local call for a straight dramatic part, they were looking for Don-in-a-dog-collar. It suited him, frankly, and he enjoyed it. Anyway, he read enough in the cab to see that it was the title role, and a terrific part. He had to say yes to *Reddick*, which he did from a pay phone at the airport.

"Good. See you Monday."

It was Wednesday, and by the time he landed at Heathrow it was Thursday morning. It was wonderful to see him. I had been working as a volunteer visiting the poor, old, lonely, sick and tired. It had come as a terrible shock to discover that people lived in wretchedness and isolation all around me, behind closed doors. I'd almost stopped feeling sorry for myself, and was grateful to be whisked off to the South of France.

Before we knew it, he had acquired a deep tan and was gone, script in hand, but this was nothing new. It was nice to know we were still a family, F.B., the Vizzes, Mary and I, all talking at the same time and finishing one another's sentences.

Back in Toronto, Don found himself in a rehearsal hall with a bunch of eager young actors. Several of them wanted to do improvisations based on situations in the play and the director told them it was all right to improvise, as long as they used the exact words in the text. "Now that a generation gap had been clearly established," says Don, they began shooting.

The location was Bathurst Street United, the church of his youth. He had been baptized in its font, and now he was preaching a sermon from the pulpit where his father had stood forty-two years earlier, trying to be heard over his son's cries of "Big Bum, Big Bum!" The turbulent '60s had finally caught up with TV drama, and being heckled was not enough — he would have to get stabbed by a member of his hippy congregation to make a point.

Reddick was such a success that Fletcher Markle, back from the coast and in charge of TV drama at CBC, decided in retrospect that it was the pilot for a series. In fact there was only one sequel, *Reddick II* a year later, and Don hated the script. He says it was all talk and no action, i.e. no knives, just lots of nagging and doubts. For the series, they opted for a young "mod" minister in a black leather jacket, who hopped on his Harley-Davidson and vroom-vroomed off the air with God's speed.

Between *Reddicks*, Don took off his collar and put on his Charlie cap. By December 1968 he was on top of the world, visiting the 200 men who live closer to the Pole than anyone else because they're stuck on Alert, the Canadian Armed Forces base. When the entertainers stepped off the plane, it was -60°F. Don recalls the sensation vividly: "My fingers started to fold inward like a bunch of rotten bananas." This is known as a "CBC concert party".

You have to go out of your way to find an audience as warm as that. They did two shows, one for each shift, and in between the camp personnel pooled their rations to put on a magnificent feast. Miss Canada 1968, Marie-France Beaulieu, was moved to tears and asked if there was anything she could do in return. There was: the dignified base commander asked for an autographed pair of her underpants for the trophy room wall. If you're ever in Alert, check it out. You'll find a pair of Catherine McKinnon's there, too.

Don proposed to Catherine soon after he got back to Toronto. He popped the question in an elevator, without warning, on their way down from a rooftop restaurant. Catherine says it was the result of a particularly lousy meal, but she accepted anyway.

They joined Mary and me at Coleherne Court for Christmas. Needless to say, we did not refer to them as "D & C". This was more than a get-acquainted session for the Harron family Mark III. Catherine had some TV shows to do, and Don was getting ready for the West End production of *Anne of Green Gables*. The producers, Donald Albery and Toronto boy Bill Freedman, had chosen an English girl for the title role. Don chased all the way to the southwest coast, where she was playing in a Christmas pageant, to make sure this Polly James looked like she could have been left on somebody's doorstep. She did.

My father describes the evening of December 31 this way: "New Year's Eve was spent with my Martha and Mary, and Martha's boyfriend, an Algerian Frenchman who turned up wearing my ex-wife's beaver coat. He cooked us an excellent ratatouille and sang us a lot of French love songs while we played an Italian version of Monopoly with Venetian street names." There's nothing you can teach a seventeen-year-old about one-upmanship: my boyfriend was five years older than my father's fiancée.

Just before midnight, Don took Catherine, a split of champagne and two glasses, in a cab to Trafalgar Square. As they toasted the New Year, 1969, he suggested they get married as soon as possible. Their relationship had just survived a typical Harron family gathering, and he was probably anxious to clinch the deal before she backed out.

Catherine said they'd have to check their datebooks, and Don said that because of his Mexican divorces, they'd have to get married in the States. Fortunately they hadn't forgotten Don the actor down there. He would be flying straight from London to Chicago, to star in another production of ever-fateful *Measure for Measure*.

He would not play Claudio this time, the spineless, handsome young hero. All that kid's stuff was behind him now. He was going to play Angelo, the Bastard who condemns Claudio to death. Sweet maturity, at last.

On his last night at the Goodman Theatre, he interrupted the final curtain call to make an important announcement: "Ladies and gentlemen, I got married this afternoon. They insisted I come here tonight and attempt to rape this nun, when I could have been much happier in my hotel suite with *this*!" He ran to the wings and returned pulling Catherine after him. She had remained backstage to be less conspicuous in her long white dress.

The audience cheered like a bunch of kids at a rock concert and gave them a standing ovation. He didn't think of it as a parting gesture to All That, his career as a classical actor, standing with one foot in front of the other, spouting soaring verse with appropriate gestures; but so it proved to be. During rehearsals for *Measure for Measure*, he had received another phone call from those two crackpot Canadians, Frank Peppiatt and John Aylesworth.

Frank had produced the Expo '67 special with Don in Montreal, but now he was back in L.A. with his drinking partner and they had another sure-fire idea for a hit series: a country version of *Laugh-In*. Don replied, "Sure, sure. Last time it was a country version of *The Perry Como Show*."

They told him it was different this time, not a pilot but a definite series. CBS had thrown *The Smothers Brothers* off the air for having content, and picked *Hee Haw* as a no-risk replacement. The original working title was *Country Corn*, which pretty well describes it, and they wanted Charlie Farquharson to be their anchorman.

Don told them he wouldn't be free until the first of June. He had to fly straight back to London after *Measure for Measure*, and Catherine to the Imperial Room in Toronto. He didn't even have time for a honeymoon until *Anne of Green Gables* opened in the West End. They said, "Fine. While you're over there, write us ten two-minute newscasts, and bring them with you to Nashville the first week in June."

"Bring them down to where?"

"Nashville. It's in Tennessee."

Don joined us at Coleherne Court the third week in March, and set to work on *Anne* re-writes with Norman Campbell, who "as ьsual,'' says Don reprovingly, was doing double-duty. While in London (with Elaine and all six children) he had also contracted to produce a television series for Liberace.

Bill Freedman was very anxious that their show not seem derivative. Already the opening was sandwiched between two other musicals: *Ann Veronica* the night before, and *Belle Starr* starring Betty Grable the night after. *Mame* was coming too, hot from Broadway, and had musical numbers called *Open a New Window* and *Bosom Buddies*. Even though *Anne of Green Gables* had premièred two years before *Mame*, Anne's *Open the Window* and *Bosom Friends* would have to be changed.

Open the Window was simply retitled *Learn Everything*. *Bosom Friends* presented more of a problem because the word ''bosom'', which occurs throughout the song, provoked titters in the English. It would have to be completely rewritten. Norman mentioned his difficulty to Liberace, and to his surprise found a piano delivered to his flat the next day.

Don began poring back through the original novel (obviously not my copy) for a suitable phrase to replace ''bosom friends.'' Norman pointed out that the expression ''kindred spirit,'' which occurs several times in the book, had been coined by Lucy Maud Montgomery herself. *Kindred Spirits* has been Anne and Diana's duet ever since.

To his chagrin, only three members of the Canadian touring company had been selected for the London production: Diana (Susan Anderson), Gilbert Blythe (Robert Ainslie) and, to his relief, untwinkly Barbara Hamilton as Marilla. He particularly missed *Thaw* pal Peter Mews, Charlottetown's best Matthew, but his replacement was the adorable, cuddly American Hiram Sherman, a dear friend from two summers of Shakespeare-on-the-Houseman-tonic.

Chubby was already a West End favourite, ever since playing Art Buchwald (perfect casting) in a revue based on his newspaper columns full of brilliant observations on Life's Rich Pageant. The producers wanted a big, up-tempo solo for Chubby to replace *The Words*, which didn't suit him. Don and Norman resisted because Mavor Moore's simple lament is so powerful in its quiet way, so quintessentially Canadian; but they had Liberace's piano, so they set to work and came up with a real Yankee showstopper, *When I Say My Say*.

They kept Marilla's version of *The Words*, sung to Anne after Matthew's death, and Barbara Hamilton had the weeping masses in the palm of her hand. Matthew's *The Words* has since been restored to its rightful position in productions from Osaka to Kuala Lumpur, and everybody gets the message even if Matthew can't find the words.

Catherine arrived in time for the London opening. The morning after, the Connaught Hotel delivered a copy of *The Times* with breakfast to the honeymoon suite. Don was so haunted by the memory of *Mary, Mary* (and, as Dave Broadfoot says, "Maggie Maggie Smith Smith") that he refused to read the review, so Catherine read it aloud to him. It was a rave.

Bill Freedman phoned soon after to tell him that the rest were raves too, not one exception. *Anne of Green Gables* turned out to be one of those classic showbiz sleepers. She snuck into town unnoticed and captured the critics' hearts, as well as the '69-'70 Plays and Players Awards for Polly James, Chubby Sherman and Barbara Hamilton, as well as best musical.

Mind you, Urjo Kareda flew over to give it a good panning in the *Toronto Star*. Nathan Cohen showed up about 200 performances later to give it another blast of Canadian hoar-frost, but it kept on running. Strangely, both critics went all gooshy inside over subsequent productions in Charlottetown. Must be something in the air out there.

With *Anne* the toast of London, Freedman turned his attention to a film deal he was negotiating with Columbia Pictures. It was based on a book by Montgomery Hyde, the true story of a World War Two Mata Hari spying on the Vichy French in Washington, D.C. He wanted Jane Fonda to play the lead, and he wanted Don Harron to write the screenplay. The studio executive said, "You mean the cat who wrote *Anne of Green Gables*? What's so sexy about that? Forget it! Get somebody else."

When United Artists acquired the movie rights to Stephen Vizinczey's *An Innocent Millionaire*, he told them he wanted Don Harron to write the screenplay, and received the same kind of reply. Always, my father's greatest challenge has been to remain a Renaissance Man in typecast world. United Artists has since spent millions finding out what Vizinczey already knew: that writers like Don Harron are a rare breed, adaptors whose first impulse is not to prove themselves smarter that the original author.

An Innocent Millionaire is about many things, and we'll see how the movie starring Tom Cruise turns out, if he doesn't get too old waiting for a decent script. The hero's father is partly *my* father, but Viz is quick to point out that Don Harron, unlike Dana Niven, was never an unsuccessful actor.

While Columbia Pictures was rejecting Don the writer for an "adult" film because he had written a hit family musical, the CBS television network was trying to reject him for *Hee Haw* on the grounds that he was a successful "straight" actor. The argument had been going on since his rave reviews in *Measure for Measure* appeared, damning proof that he was unfit to be the King of K.O.R.N.

Unfortunately, Peppiatt and Aylesworth stood their ground. "Admittedly, Charlie had never appeared in the U.S.," says Peppiatt, "but we knew he had been making Canadians laugh for years. We also knew that making Canadians laugh for years was not easy unless you were a politician."

When *Hee Haw* went on the air, Patrick Scott declared in the *Toronto Star*, "If you watch this show you do not deserve to own a television set." Evidently this applied to over 45 million viewers. It shot to #1 in the ratings, and last I heard is still around. The president of CBS said he particularly liked "that funny farmer fella whose wife was a Drain on her father's side."

The first time Virginia saw Charlie Farquharson, she told Don he could make a million dollars with that character — but she hoped he wouldn't.

26

MOURNING AND *MORNINGSIDE*

WHEN I confiscated my father's memoirs to write my own version, he set only one condition: that I squeeze his whole life into one volume. I achieved this only by cutting more than I can bear, and skipping the last twenty years of his career, the ones he considers by far the most important. I had hoped to do something to please him, for once, but the poor man was absolutely horrified.

He read everything I said about him without complaint (although there was the occasional gasp of "Is that *all* you say about Katharine Cornell?!"), but now he was begging for mercy: "Please, Martha, don't do it to me. Some people even called Pierre Berton conceited for thinking *his* life worth more than one volume, and his literary reputation is far greater than mine!" Of course, what living Canadian could possibly be worth more than one volume?

My defense was that *Harronside* ended with the birth of *Hee Haw* in 1969, leaving nothing more for me to contradict. He was puzzled, and said he thought there was more. I went back through the boxes of clippings and, sure enough, found a black folder containing pages 555 to 580, written on the back of an old script as usual.

The manuscript ends with his mother's funeral in February 1976. Lionel, who had cancer and didn't know it, followed his darling Dutzie five weeks later, just like her parents before them. Those final weeks were so agonizing, rather than put them on paper Donald left the other 580 pages to gather dust.

From the time he came back to Canada in 1966 until the end of their days, he did everything in his power to make his parents

303

happy, including doing their grocery shopping, chauffeuring, and finally providing round-the-clock nursing care so they could stay in their own home. Any neglect they might have suffered during his years away had been more than made up for. Still, he is tortured by regret.

Back in 1969, when I announced that I was giving up the privilege of a free British university education to attend my parents' Alma Mater, at my father's expense, he was delighted. At the time I thought my motive was to be with my crazy French boyfriend, whose British visa had expired and who came to Canada with me, also at my father's expense. (There were no abused children in my family — only abused parents.)

Looking back, I think I was more concerned with making sure Catherine didn't usurp my position as Number One Daughter in my father's heart. Either way, when I moved into their little love nest without so much as a by-your-leave, Catherine got this sick feeling in the pit of her stomach; but she repressed it for the moment. Being under the impression that clothes and dishes washed themselves, I treated a twenty-four-year-old star like my personal maid.

For his forty-fifth birthday on September 19, 1969, Catherine decided to surprise her husband by replacing their small portable television with a six-foot-long stereo/TV console. I will never forget the look on her face, staring at my father staring at his new present. It took up half the living room, and he didn't notice. She decided to wait and see how long it would take him to notice she was pregnant.

I certainly noticed it, but when I asked him about it he laughed and said, ''No, we're just happy and in love, and both putting on a little weight!'' All of her weight gain was in one place, but I could see it was pointless to argue. She finally gave up waiting and broke the news to him a few weeks before the baby was born.

The stork found them in Trinidad, where Catherine was filling in for another singer too advanced in her pregnancy to perform. Although not due until March, Kelley weighed in at five pounds, five ounces on January 9, 1970, brought on by the turbulent flight down. I confess to feeling relieved that Catherine's Ouija board was wrong, and Jason turned out to be a girl. My father also records that "Secretly, I was glad." King Lear had his Cordelia, at last.

When they came back to Toronto the other twin bed in my room was replaced by a crib with something tiny and perfect in it. Every time the baby uttered a peep I would pick her up, rock her in my arms and croon to her. Catherine was so determined to be the perfect wife she was prepared to put up with anything — except the torture of listening to a Harron sing. I was asked to move out, and a nanny moved in. Germine Leys was and remains the only stable member of the Harron family.

Being paid an allowance to move in with your boyfriend sounds like every teenager's dream come true, but I was miffed at being deprived of my big moment, the one where you leave your parents sobbing on the doorstep. In any case, going to Victoria College had been a big mistake. I discovered this the first time I walked into the Registrar's office and the woman behind the counter asked if I was related to Don Harron. When I confessed to being his eldest, the rest of the staff turned and stared at me and the woman said "We all remember your father. He was *perfect* — academically . . . and romantically!"

Some children may enjoy basking in their parents' reflected glory, but for me it was agony. Everywhere I went the professors had either taught him or gone to school with him. I didn't dare go near Dr. Frye, spoken of with such reverence by both my parents, which was a terrible waste of a golden opportunity. Instead, I would wait in the Wymilwood coffee shop to hear about "Norrie's" lectures from friends.

My entire academic career became a search for fields not yet cultivated by my father's furrowed brow. I even tried linguistics, and he gave me a free lecture on Chomsky's theories. He was only trying to be helpful, but it drove me crazy. When U of T offered me a chance to go to the University of Nice as one of three students on a pilot exchange programme, I jumped at the chance. My boyfriend reacted by getting drunk, dragging me around by the hair, threatening me with a knife and breaking my nose. I knew then I had made the right decision.

As you know if you read the preface, I wrote my father a hate letter on my twenty-first birthday. I realise now that I forgot to include the things I *really* hated about him, namely: "I hate you for being so smart, I hate you for being so talented, and I hate you for being so famous!" The trouble with famous parents — and I have several — is that you feel like a hopeless failure before you get started. And even if you do make it, you know everyone will say, "Oh well, it was easy for *her*!"

When I learned that the computer in Nice had eaten my exam results it was a matter of complete indifference to me, but my father had spent a lot of money on my university education, and for some reason wanted a piece of paper to show for it. As it was the only thing he ever asked me for, I decided to humour him. Mary and I came to Canada for Christmas, 1973, after which she would go back to Oxford University and I would remain in Toronto just long enough to complete my B.A. (I'm still living in Toronto.)

Donald had never given a thought to buying rather than renting a house in his life, but during our absence he and Catherine had acquired two of them. Catherine wisely did not leave the selection up to him. The first purchase occurred when he took Catherine to see his mother's birthplace, the old post office in Painswick, near Barrie. Catherine dubbed their new country house "Barrie Sound", in honour of Charlie Farquharson's home town. Their city house is two blocks away from where Don and Virginia used to live.

When Mary and I arrived at the house in Toronto, Catherine had a banquet prepared and Kelley, who was almost three, came down to greet us in her best party dress. She had been so excited at the prospect of meeting her sisters at last, and was bitterly disappointed by the two sour-faced grown-ups standing at the bottom of the stairs. She introduced us to guests by explaining "First my daddy married their mummy, then he left her and married my mummy."

Mary and I exchanged a look that said "Ah, the abridged version." In private, Goneril and Regan referred to her as "Scarlett O'Hara", although it was hardly her fault (and she wouldn't be caught dead in anything frilly today).

We learned that during our absence Catherine had mastered the intricacies of "the truth game" and "pack-or-be-packed". She had obviously realised that waiting for Donald to notice her feelings — or anything else for that matter — was a waste of time. When she told me about the time she went to dinner at D & V's, she added: "Now, when people come over for dinner, Donald offers them a ride home, goes to look for his car keys, all hell breaks loose upstairs, and you know what? I go right on talking as if nothing was happening!"

One night they went to a party at Farley Mowat's in Port Hope and had a huge fight. Catherine locked him out of the car and drove the sixty miles back to Toronto alone. Donald, with no money in his pockets because he was wearing his McKinnon tartan kilt, was forced to take a taxi. When he reached home for torrid-reconciliation-time, Catherine greeted him at the door and paid for the cab.

All this was to be expected, I suppose. However, something truly bizarre had developed while we'd been away. Don took his daughters to a restaurant for lunch, and all these people kept barging up to the table, greeting our father like he was an old friend — except they called him "Charlie". I said to my sister, "What the hell is going on here?!"

It was Farquharson fever, of course, brought on not just by *Hee Haw* but by something much more important: the publication of his first book, Charlie Farquharson's *Histry of Canada*. Although he'd been a scriptwriter since college days, with many successful comedy sketches, plays and musicals to his credit, he never thought of himself as a *real* writer (still doesn't). He would never have had the audacity to produce something between hard covers if he hadn't found himself in a desperate situation.

Right after he signed the mortgage on the house in Toronto, *Hee Haw* was cancelled. The CBS network had acquired a new program director whose first move was to get rid of all the country corn shows, namely *The Beverly Hillbillies, Petticoat Junction, Green Acres,* all of which can still be seen in reruns, and of course *Hee Haw.* By then Don Harron was hopelessly typecast as that rube with his sweater buttoned wrong, not only in Canada but also in the States. Don reacted in typical Canadian style: he sat and waited for the phone to ring.

It rang. The call was from Paddy Chayefsky, who hadn't forgotten his Tenth Man and wanted him to play the harried hospital administrator in his new movie, *The Hospital*, starring Diana Rigg and George C. Scott. The director was Don's old schoolmate from the University of Toronto, Arthur Hiller. Needless to say, he went to New York, where they were shooting the film in a new unfinished wing of the Metropolitan Hospital on the edge of Spanish Harlem.

One of the plot lines involved the hospital's attempt to expand by expropriating several adjacent tenament buildings. In the script there was a protest demonstration which fizzled out due to lack of support. When they began shooting the scene, with actors playing policemen, hospital workers, militant students and residents bearing placards that said "SAVE OUR HOMES", real residents poured out of the tenements to join in the protest. They thought their homes were threatened; a riot ensued and one of the actor-policemen was injured. Chayefsky bowed to reality, changing the ending and won the Academy Award for best script.

The movie was over all too soon and Don returned to Toronto wondering what to do next. One of Catherine's old school friends is married to Al Majeika, who was at that time working for McGraw-Hill Ryerson publishers. Over brunch one Sunday, Al said "Why don't you write a book, Herring?" Don said he didn't write books, but Al said "Try a couple of chapters and I'll take it over to McGraw-Hill. But make it funny. Humour sells."

His first impulse was to write about politics, but Al told him to try something new. Don settled for something old: history, Canadian history, the subject he had tackled in *Spring Thaw '67*. On his next visit to his parents' house on Pinewood Avenue, he found his old second form (Grade 10) textbook. The little blue book by Stewart Wallace was already pretty funny, and he decided to use it as his model.

Wallace's book didn't go back far enough, he felt, so he began at the beginning, with the creation of the Universe, or as Charlie puts it, with "yer cremation of yer Universal". Don wrote three chapters, about two pages each, handed them over to Majeika and turned his attention to less lofty matters — *much* less lofty. Saying to himself "Baby needs new shoes," he became a daytime TV game show host.

Called *Anything You Can Do*, it pitted teams of men against women, racing against the clock to make complete fools of themselves. Their host felt like the biggest fool: right after he signed the contract, he learned that *Hee Haw* was going back on the air.

Don calls it "*Sesame Street* for grown-ups", which is an insult to
Oscar the Grouch, Grover and Big Bird, but being the K.O.R.N.
anchorman was positively dignified compared to refereeing battle-
of-the-sexes egg-and-spoon races.

CBS had not changed its mind about *Hee Haw*. It was revived
on syndication, picked up by over two hundred individual TV sta-
tions — twenty more than the entire CBS network. Right after that,
Norman Campbell phoned to say that the head of CBC drama,
Fletcher Markle, had commissioned a ninety-minute musical for
television, based on Don's film treatment of the life of Emily Carr.
It was called *The Wonder of it All*, which pretty well sums up both
Emily's and Don's feelings about Life's Rich Pageant.

The best thing about being on *Hee Haw*, as opposed to almost
every other series on television, was that it was not a full-time job.
As the newscaster, Don was involved in very few group scenes. He
could fly down a couple of times a year, tape all his segments and
be back in Toronto in two or three days. Instead of *The Man Who
Never Was*, getting run over by trains, he could be The Man Who
Was Hardly Ever There and still pay his bills. (The second best part
was that he got to write his own material.)

However, there was still the little matter of hosting *Anything You
Can Do*. He would fly up to Ottawa and tape twenty shows at a
time, five a day for four days, and he did everything he could to
get fired. He made fun of the contests, he made fun of the prizes,
he even made fun of the director. The only thing he couldn't do
was make fun of the contestants, because he doesn't have a mean
bone in his body. The more he made fun of the show, the harder
the audience laughed. He was stuck with it, for two long years.

In the meantime he had a *Histry of Canada* to write, a project
to which he could devote himself heart and soul. For *Spring Thaw
'67* he had obtained permission from the family of C.W. Jeffreys
to parody his famous illustrations. The artist had done seven, and
done a good job, but more were needed for the book. He provided
McGraw-Hill's illustrator with a list of captions, and kept asking
to see the new drawings, but they stalled him with excuses and
"metaphorical pats on the head" until the *Histry* was printed. The
new ones were so bad he was convinced his book was ruined.

The cover was a different matter, fortunately. Don insisted that there be no printing on it, only his crabbed handwriting, and that it should look like it had been covered with wrapping paper at home. The publisher assigned a twenty-year-old named Frank Hammond to design it, and the result far surpassed Don's expectations. He calls it the most brilliant book cover he ever saw, and I agree. Hammond used plain brown wrapping paper, an Instamatic snapshot of Charlie stuck on with gaffer's tape and, for a crowning touch, the tell-tale ring of a teacup stain on one corner of the photograph. If you know my father the tea granny, it was also singularly appropriate.

Don still says the cover was what made Charlie's *Histry of Canada* such a phenomenal bestseller. It did create some problems, however. The owner of a bookstore in Sudbury sent his whole order back, complaining that some careless drinker in the shipping department had stained all two hundred copies.

When it was released in the fall of 1972, McGraw-Hill's computer predicted that *The Histry of Canada* would sell 18,000 copies at a time when the national average for a Canadian book was 5,000. It sold over 200,000 copies, at last printing. Being the author's daughter I can't claim to be objective, but it seems to me that the text might have had something to do with it.

Apart from Kildare Dobbs, few critics sang its praises — perhaps because Charlie doesn't write "proper" English. Don's agent Matie Molinaro gave a copy to another of her famous clients, Marshall McLuhan, for Christmas that year. She says that McLuhan was very involved in the James Joyce revival taking place at the time, and she had to confess to him that she found *Finnegan's Wake* rather tough going. McLuhan admonished her: "Should be no trouble at all, if you read it out loud. Good heavens, Matie, you read Charlie Farquharson, *of course* you can handle Joyce!"

Perhaps because he had just made publishing histry, Charlie was invited to speak at the Prime Minister's dinner in 1973. Pierre Trudeau's Liberals had narrowly defeated the Conservatives under Robert Stanfield, and Charlie parodied Pierre's comment on the victory by declaring that "yer universe is folding up, as it should." He went on to say that Valeda, the wife and former sweetheart, became a "Trudyo-maniac" in 1968 — "But she sure never voted fer yiz in '72 after you tole us that the guvmint couldn't do its business in the middle of our bedroom, and then you went and let all them homeo-sectionals have the free abortions.'' Trudeau almost fell out of his chair laughing.

The next time Charlie was supposed to perform in front of the Prime Minister, Trudeau refused to attend. The occasion was a Canada Day '74 celebration at the National Arts Centre in Ottawa, televised on CBC, and the reason was that Don had chosen as his partner Dorris Lussier, best known as the Plouffe family's beloved Uncle Gedeon. Lussier also happened to be secretary of the separatist Parti Québecois, and had announced his intention of running as a P.Q. candidate in the Gaspé.

It's a pity he wasn't there, because Trudeau would have enjoyed the sketch. They played two farmers who had come to Ottawa for the day, with their tractors, to participate in a milk strike demonstration. There really had been such a demonstration a couple of months earlier. In the Don n' Dorris version, when the farmers sent a message via the Sergeant-at-Arms demanding to know what the Prime Minister was going to do about the milk situation, Trudeau's reply was "Leave one quart and a pint of cream.''

In addition to *Hee Haw*, Charlie had a Canadian TV show called *And That's the News, Goodnight!* on the fledgling Global Television Network, and Don went to great lengths to assemble a talented team of eager young comedy writers. The budget was lousy, but it was great fun working with a cast which included *Thaw* stalwarts like Catherine McKinnon, Jack Duffy and Barbara Hamilton, as well as Patricia McKinnon and Helen Burns, between marriages to Michael Langham.

My favourite regular features were Don as Charlie with Barbara as a delightfully dour Valeda, sitting watching TV and commenting on L.R.P. Billy Van played the boy Orville. The same three played a rich urban family, with Don playing Charlie's city cousin Valerie Rosedale, Barbara as her husband Charles and Billy as their daughter Stephanie. He ended a hockey sketch by collapsing sideways with his stick onto the floor, and lost seventy percent of the hearing in one ear — permanently.

Charlie followed up his *Histry of Canada* with *The Jogfree of Canda*, the only writer I know whose spelling gets worse with every book. Again his effort was virtually ignored by the literary press and

sold in vast amounts. He has published five times since then, without
appearing on bestseller lists, and the pattern remains the same. He
says he doesn't care, as long as people read them.

Don Harron is the most learned man I ever met, a true scholar
because it comes from curiosity rather than a desire to impress.
Disguising himself as Charlie Farquharson gave him the freedom
to speak his mind to the folks at home all across the country, and
being snubbed by the cultural establishment was a small price to pay.

One day he happened to read an article about a French-Canadian
comedian he greatly admired. Like Harron, Yvon Deschamps was
a 'legitimate' stage actor who became a comedy star through his
inspired monologues. In the interview, Deschamps said that he
wanted to work with Charlie Farquharson so they could exchange
political views in a comic setting.

Don was eager to take him up on it, but doubtful that any television network would go for the idea because Deschamps was an
unabashed separatist. Considering the amount of political pressure
that had been exerted on CBC a couple of years earlier to prevent
his milk sketch with Lussier from going on the air, he was surprised
when Jack McAndrew, the head of TV Variety, said he liked the
idea too.

Don went to Trois-Rivières, where Deschamps was captivating
audiences in a two-character play with Jean-Louis Roux. When they
met backstage, Deschamps came straight to the point: he wanted
to do a show about national unity, culminating in a real debate
with Charlie taking the federalist side, of course, and he the
separatist. It didn't take long to find a title they both liked, even
if it meant something different to each of them: *The Let's Save
Canada Hour*.

The only hitch was that much of the show would have to be
prepared in California, where Yvon would be spending the winter
along with a whole colony of French-Canadian stars like Diane
Dufresne and Ginette Reno. CBC agreed to that too because Don
was working on another project for them, and could conduct interviews for it while he was down there. This was back in the good
old days before drastic budget cuts and staff reductions by the Prime
Minister Charlie refers to as "Briney Bullroney".

The second project was something Don had been badgering them to do for six years: honour the memory of Tyrone Guthrie, who had died in 1970. The CBC had finally given in, thanks to the persistence of its producer, Norman Campbell. He had worked with Guthrie on *The Mikado*, the first Gilbert and Sullivan production at Stratford, Ontario. Don's tribute would mark the twenty-fifth anniversary of the Festival in 1978, a labour of love entitled *The Unselfish Giant of Stratford*.

Don flew down to Los Angeles with Catherine and six-year-old Kelley. Even in the good old days the CBC had to run a pretty tight ship: the expert skeleton crew was covering three assignments at the same time, juggling interlocking schedules. Two of them were Don's, but this was nothing new. Norman vividly recalls their previous trip to L.A., trying to work on *The Wonder of It All* while his partner was guest-starring on *Mission: Impossible* —

"I would just work up an approach to the elusive Don and in mid-thought he would say 'Excuse me, Norman', pick up a Luger pistol and dash onto the set to play a Nazi. He'd yell and scream Third Reich double-talk until the take was over, then come back and in his typical soft voice say, 'Now Norman, about Emily . . . where were we?'"

To Don, *The Let's Save Canada Hour* was a satiric version of the kind of show Americans do so often, and take so seriously — what he calls the "What a Great Country We Have Here" syndrome. He loved working with Deschamps, and they both seemed to find Hollywood a great source of inspiration. They did an un-Hollywood version of *The Exorcist*, where a little girl awoke from a nightmare speaking nothing but French, and a Canadian *All in the Family* (the most popular American sitcom of the day, itself based on the British series *Till Death Us Do Part*). The Bunkum family had a Québecois son-in-law, played by Deschamps, and an uncle who was a priest: mimic Jean-Guy Moreau doing a devastating impression of P.Q. leader René Lévèsque. Al Waxman was Archie and Don was Edith, singing off-key to his heart's content.

As *The Let's Save Canada Hour* was supposed to be a comedy special, Don insisted the great debate at the end had to have a satirical framework, no matter how serious the topic. They did a take-off on *This Hour Has Seven Days*, the show that first made Charlie a political animal. It was aptly titled *This Country Has Seven Days*, and Jean-Guy Moreau was brilliant as pipe-smoking, tear-stained moderator Laurier Lapierre.

In comic terms Charlie won the debate hands down. Separatism was not a subject on which Deschamps was inclined to be funny and his impassioned, highly personal approach provided the perfect foil for Charlie's argument that all of Canada is separate already, united only by a common hatred of Toronto. He takes a similar approach today in the great Free Trade debate, arguing that if we commit to it with the United States, and it works, we should try it between the provinces of this country.

As far as Don is concerned, Deschamps won the separatism debate hands down. Yvon's main argument was that if Canada stayed together the French Canadian language, which for him was his identity, would be gone within the next quarter-century. The phrase he kept repeating was "I don't want to disappear." This struck a deep chord in his opponent, even if it didn't make him stop wanting to save Canada.

He had just finished interviewing Lorne Greene, Lloyd Bochner and William Shatner about the first three years of Stratford-on-Tario under Guthrie. All of his Canadian actor friends who were still living in Hollywood seemed to be blending comfortably into the landscape. Lorne Greene had a house as big as the Ponderosa, with saddles for bar stools. Don realised that he had the same problem with California that Deschamps had with English-speaking Canada: the reason he left the States eleven years earlier was not because he didn't like it, but because he didn't want to disappear.

To me it seemed that he *had* disappeared, consumed by a dybbuk more powerful than Jimmy Porter or Arthur Landau could ever be, a clown with his sweater buttoned wrong. It was Mary who crawled under a chair and cried the first time we saw Charlie Farquharson, and I wrote that "even now she can't watch the Doctor of Personal Experience without a twinge of pain." But that wasn't Mary, that was me.

Don't get me wrong, I really love Charlie, it's just that I love my father the Renaissance Man a lot more. I resented Charlie for robbing my brilliant Bastard of his Iago, his Macbeth, his Richard III, all the parts I wanted to see him play. It made me furious to see him snubbed by the theatrical establishment because he was a funny-looking farmer.

In private, he would just shrug and say he wasn't smart enough or hard-working enough to be a farmer. In public, he reacted by dressing up in drag and making the establishment laugh at themselves as Valerie Rosedale, the society matron who believes a woman's place is in the country club. This public gesture was also a private tribute to Jane Mallett. Valerie is not Jane's clubwoman character — she is irreplaceable — but a member of the same set.

One person remembered Don the actor, and it was another unforgettable character named Paul Thompson, the driving force behind Toronto's innovative Theatre Passe Muraille. He had seen the *Reddick* specials on CBC, and wanted to know if Don would like to play the real Reddick, whose life was far more dramatic. He hesitated because looking after his ailing parents had become a full-time job, but after driving to Chatham, Ontario and talking to former members of Rev. Russell Horsburgh's congregation, he had to say yes.

On February 1, the day before rehearsals started, Don picked his father up from the nursing home he had just moved into temporarily, and drove him to the hospital where Delsia was undergoing tests. "As they breathed through each other's lungs, my father could not stay in the house without her."

Delsia suffered from arteriosclerosis and could not speak, but when the ambulance attendants had come to Pinewood to take her away from her home, she had resisted with every ounce of strength that was in her, which was quite a lot. Don has never forgiven himself for not fighting for her. He had been to visit her the night before with a bunch of flowers and some home-made butter tarts, but she was sound asleep. When he and Lionel walked in the next morning, she had been dead for almost an hour. His father clung to her like a baby and cried and cried.

Don told Paul Thompson to get someone else to play Horseburgh. Instead, Thompson postponed rehearsals for a week. Lionel spent the next five weeks tortured by modern medicine's attempts to keep him alive. He died on March 9, just before *Horsburgh* opened. Thompson postponed the opening for a week, after which Don-in-a-dog-collar carried on, grateful for catharsis onstage nightly.

In 1954, Don had to choose between playing the cowardly Dauphin in Shaw's *St. Joan* all the way to James Bay, or starring in *Home is the Hero* on Broadway. He says he made the wrong decision. In 1976, soon after *The Horsburgh Scandal* closed, he received a phone call from the woman he refers to as his St. Joan.

It was early morning, he was half asleep and whoever it was wanted to know if he was interested in hosting a coast-to-coast radio show five mornings a week. He said, "You mean like Peter Gzowski's *Discomfort in the Morning*? I couldn't do that!"

"Why not?" the woman replied. "I've heard you being interviewed and I think you have a very interesting mind."

"I'm an actor, not a host," he protested. "Let me come on as Charlie Farquharson and . . ."

"I'm not interested in Charlie Farquharson," she said firmly. "I'm interested in Don Harron." There was a stunned silence, on his end. She said, "Think about it," and left her extension number at CBC. He didn't even catch her name, just that she was executive producer of *Morningside*.

The offer frightened him far more than it intrigued him. Having just lost both parents, he was in no condition to start ripping off masks. He turned it down, and the next day signed a contract to tour the United States as Charlie from Labour Day to Christmas, flogging his *K.O.R.N. Allmynack* for Books Canada.

He had intended to write Charlie's version of American history for the Bicentennial, but stopped after reading *Bury My Heart at Wounded Knee*: "There was no way I could tell Americans that their tragic litany of genocide was food for satire." Some had managed it, but coming from an outsider it would sound unbearably smug. He settled for a take-off on the *Farmers' Almanac*, with "Advice fer the Future and the Pasture."

In 1966 Stephen Vizinczey set off on his first American book tour full of high hopes. He had faced starvation, interrogation, censorship, Nazi guns and Russian tanks. He had even tackled the Harron girls, and nothing had daunted his spirit, but he says he came through the publicity treadmill a broken man, after months of answering the same questions nine times a day, "and none of the interviewers had read the book!"

Don Harron is often asked if he never tires of being Charlie Farquharson. His answer is always that he did get sick of him once, in the fall of 1976. Imagine three solid months of pursing your lips in imitation of the north end of a chicken heading south, fielding nine rounds a day of, "Is Roy Clark growing his own hair? Is it a transplant from some other part of his body?" and "Are the breasts on those girls for real? Are they transplants from some other part of their body?"

Only one interviewer surprised him, and that was singer-turned-talk-show-host Dinah Shore. Right in the middle of discussing his "racy almanac" she stopped, put down the book and looked searchingly at his stubbled face. "Donald, you've done Shakespeare." He admitted it was true, over three decades in three countries. She said, "Do me some right now."

It must have looked carefully rehearsed, because he dutifully removed his cap and glasses, and launched into Edmund's first soliloquy from *King Lear*, which begins "Thou, Nature, art my goddess;" and it all came flowing back to him, right up to "stand up for bastards!"

Back in Toronto, Don appeared on *Morningside* — as Charlie Farquharson, of course. He had twelve minutes with two hosts, Maxine Crook and the delightfully witty Harry Brown, which made the conversation seem pretty crowded. He was dying to hang around afterwards and talk shop with them, but was whisked out the studio door as another guest was whisked in. *Morningside* was a busy show.

Almost a year to the day after St. Joan's first attempt, Don's phone rang at an ungodly hour. She said, "Mr. Harron."

"Yes."

"Don Harron."

"Of course."

"I heard you on *Morningside*."

"Who is this?!" He had recognized the voice immediately, he just didn't know her name.

"This is *Morningside*." He insisted she must have some other identity, so she spelled her Estonian name for him: Krista Maeots, as in "MY-oughts". "We still want you for our show," she said. "Have lunch. We'll talk about it."

She spent $1.50 on wining and dining him and convinced him it was his patriotic duty to take the job. "It's not the railroad that threads its way across this country every day, it's radio."

"What about television?" he countered.

"Television can't do it any more, it's been cable-ized. Radio is our national dream now, the one medium that can link up this whole country, every day."

"And you think radio is going to keep this country together?"

She looked at him with a serious face and blue eyes that wanted desperately to be amused. "We can try. You too."

But first he had to audition, by doing a sample hour of *Morningside*. He says he hasn't known such fear since his training flight as a navigator, which he failed miserably, and Krista looked more nervous than he was. He was placed in a tiny room with reams of research material, mostly Xeroxed newspaper clippings, and given an hour to prepare. They warned him anything that could go wrong might go wrong on the air, and he would be expected to react gracefully.

Trying desperately to speed-read his way through the pile of information, wondering what on earth he was going to do, he pulled an old trick that had seen him through many auditions in his youth: even though it usually wasn't true, he would say to himself, "I don't need this job." It still worked.

He skipped the rest of the material on the guest: "Hell, I know who Dalton Camp is. He's the one who stuck the first knife into John Diefenbaker." He introduced Camp by commenting on the provincial election the day before, in which the Ontario Tories had been reduced to a minority government. "And from over in London, where he is visiting Buckingham Palace, the voice of John Diefenbaker could be heard crying, "It's all the fault of Dalton Camp!"

Camp laughed heartily, everyone relaxed a bit and the rest of the hour sped by in a blur. One minute he would be talking to a delightful couple of senior citizens with their own TV show in Ottawa. ("Senior citizens get so little chance to have anybody listen to them, they did all my work for me.") The next second he'd be playing disc jockey, and after a couple of minutes to collect his thoughts there'd be a young reporter on the line, tracking down the dumping of fissionable material in the Northern bush.

They saved the curve ball for the very end. A listener requested Bing Crosby singing *When the Blue of the Night Meets the Gold of the Day*, but the control room flashed him a card saying they didn't have the record. Presumably he was meant to coax an alternate request out of the listener, but instead he burst into song. He bub-bub-bub-a-booed his way through a tune he hadn't heard in twenty years, and the voice on the other end was laughing uncontrollably.

He asked how *anyone* could keep that up for fifteen hours a week. Krista Maeots, drenched with sweat at the end of his trial hour, told him "Nobody gets that much chance to talk to the rest of the nation, not even the Prime Minister."

When it was announced that Don Harron would be celebrating the twenty-fifth anniversary of the birth of Canadian television by going back into radio, the headline in the *Toronto Star* read "Don Harron drops the mask: Can he still make it?" Well, he was sure going to try. The ratings climbed to 1.3 million people from coast to coast, and he kept it up for five years.

I was very lucky that my father's unmasking followed closely on the heels of my firstborn learning to walk. A show like *Morningside* on the radio lets you at least try to keep up with the kids, dishes and laundry and still feel like part of the human race. In my case, I had the unique privilege of listening to my dear father the Renaissance Man.

When he announced on the air that he was stepping down as host of *Morningside* I cried like a baby, although I knew it was coming. A friend in Toronto phoned her sister in Charlottetown and, both in tears, they said simultaneously "He's tired!". He was tired, and handed the microphone back to Peter Gzowski, who was waiting anxiously in the wings. Before he left, Don gave the CBC top brass a list of suggestions for weekly shows he'd like to do, and hasn't heard from them since.

POSTSCRIPT

IN CONCLUSIVE

WHEN I confiscated *Harronside*, I had no idea that the manuscript was virtually complete. It begins with the first phone call from Krista Maeots, in June 1976, and ends with Don's mother's funeral on February 4th that same year. After 580 pages, he came within four months of coming full circle before leaving it to gather dust.

I had to write my own version to come full circle myself, and realise that I was completely wrong about my father's career. He's right, and I was wrong: the last twenty years of his career *are* the most important, and not just because of *Morningside*. There are other brilliant Shakespearean actors in this world — and Don Harron was certainly one of the best — but there is only one Charlie Farquharson, a man outstanding in his field, because it's too far to go back to the house.

Before I became a parent, my father warned me that in the dark days ahead, maybe not in his lifetime but probably in mine, the only things that will mean anything will be fresh air to breathe, fresh water to drink and fresh food to eat, because there won't be any left. His prediction is coming true: the future belongs to our children, and we've spent it already. Charlie's latest piece of ''litry fluff'' is entitled *Cum Buy the Farm*.

When I left home there were only two things I knew for sure: I was never going to get married, and I was never going to be a crazy writer like my father and stepfather. I still refuse to get married, for what it's worth. I call Gary Cormier my husband because "boyfriend" sounds silly after all these years, with three kids and mortgages to match.

When I met my knight in shining armour, he kept reminding me of someone. I tracked Virginia down in California (it was easy — I called her mother's house) and there she was, with the same thrilling, dangerous voice — not the phony one Natasha gave her in the movies, but the one with the existential cackle. I said, "Virginia, remember how you used to tell me that I'd never be happy with a man because I'd always be looking for my father? Well, you were wrong. I was looking for my stepmother — and God help me, I've found him." She laughed — I knew she would.

I love her from a distance, and Gary has the phone bills to prove it. He looked at me the other day and said, "You're starting to change your mind about leaving me when the kids have grown, aren't you?"

My mouth dropped open. I hadn't told him about the first thoughts, never mind the second ones. I said, "How did you know?"

He laughed. "Martha, I can read you like a book!"

Nobody has *ever* said that about my father. When he told me he was going to write his autobiography, I was thrilled. He paid me to file his research material in chronological order, and I couldn't help reading as I did so. When I read what he had done with it, I was appalled. Quoting all his bad reviews at length, referring to the raves merely in passing, he described himself as a "failed cartoonist" and a "fake farmer."

At the time, I told him to stop being so bloody Canadian, but a couple of years later I said, "On second thought, let *me* handle this." What got me started was meeting someone from the Board at Stratford in the Spring of 1986. I had just heard they were planning to do *Othello*, and couldn't resist telling him that Joe Papp and I thought Don Harron would make a fantastic Iago. From the look on that Board person's face, you would have thought I'd said, "Dolly Parton would make a fantastic Desdemona!"

This got me so upset I phoned Herbert Whittaker and recounted the conversation, adding: "Be honest. Was that such a stupid thing for me to say?"

He laughed and replied, "Martha, they don't know! They don't know the history of their own culture, let alone your father's great part in it."

I said, "Oh they don't, eh? Well, I'm going to tell them!" My subject cooperated by returning the boxes of research material, except the one I was looking for — the one with all the newspaper clippings from birth to 1969. It had vanished, completely. I was going to give up, but it's amazing what having to pay back a publisher's advance can do for your sense of determination.

On April 3, 1987 I was listening to *Gzowskiside* when it was announced on the CBC news that Don Harron had collapsed while hosting the opening ceremonies of the new Arts Centre in North Bay, Ontario, and had been rushed to the hospital. When I called the hospital and told them I was his daughter, the voice on the other end said, "I'll put you through to Intensive Care."

I sat on hold for what seemed like an hour but was probably ten minutes. My father had dragged his I.V. unit down the hall to the nurses' station to tell me it was a dirty, filthy lie: "I did *not* collapse on-stage — I finished the show first!"

Gee, and there we all were thinking, "That lazy bum, anything to get out of an honest night's work!" I've known Don Harron all my life, but I didn't know how hard he worked until I started doing the research for his speeches. I once heard him patiently explaining to someone that he could not travel thousands of miles to speak to their group for free because a snowmobilers' association is not a registered charity. There are plenty of those, however, and like sharks in a feeding frenzy, they almost ate him alive.

Just as I was putting the finishing touches to *A PARENT CON-TRADICTION*, my father showed up at the door with the missing box of clippings. It had been in a basement flood in Barrie Sound. The pages are all stuck together and stink to high heaven. Gary won't even let me put the box in the garage, and I can hardly blame him. As I write, it's sitting in a plastic garbage bag on the back deck.

I realise now that this was a blessing in disguise. I would have bored everyone to death with all those "dazzlings" and "brilliants," and there was no room for them anyway. I had to include every flop, every mistake, every foolish, thoughtless deed Don Harron has ever committed (fortunately not too many) because I knew that if I left *one* out, he'd say "Oh sure, they like me now, but if they knew!. . ."

I would gladly chart the rest of my father's exploits as an unsung Canadian hero — the only kind we have unless we hang 'em first, or Harron and Campbell write the musical — but that could easily fill another volume, and his career is far from over.

Don and Catherine spend their "holidays" in a white clapboard cottage in P.E.I., performing in a tent on the north shore. Their first show was called *Loitering Within Tent*, and their latest is a musical version of *Olde Charlie Farquharson's Testament*, produced by Frank Peppiatt. It was so hot in the tent opening night that when Catherine appeared as the angel Gabriel her moustache fell off. Just like in *A Sleep of Prisoners*, Shadrach, Meschach and Abednego brave the fiery furnace nightly, but this time it's a musical number called *Heat, Hot Heat* with The Hick from Vic and his spiritual son Bill Carr dressed in spangled red longjohns.

My father says that *Olde Charlie Farquharson's Testament* is the *Spring Thaw* version of the Bible. Needless to say, they plan to take it across the country.

P.P.S.–I take back what I said, F.B. Don't ever stop being so bloody Canadian.

ACKNOWLEDGEMENTS

To my family, especially Gary Cormier, who gave me his office and a computer, and tried to sleep while I wrote the whole thing in bed. To Amy, Ben and Zoe Cormier, for their patience and understanding, and eating all that take-out food. To Gloria and Stephen Vizinczey, for their unflagging and indispensable encouragement, and for providing an editing job that money can't buy — so I won't try. (Gloria says Stephen did the editing, but as my sister Mary so wisely observed, "When one eats, the other digests.") To Virginia Leith, for letting me read whole chapters to her over the phone and laughing at all my jokes, even the ones at her expense. And to assorted Harrons and Haddens, especially Mary Harron Stan, for family history.

To my father's friends and colleagues, too numerous to mention, for the invaluable feedback. The following performed thankless tasks too heroic to be ignored: Bill Bremner, Dave Broadfoot, Susan Brower, Sharron Budd, Norman Campbell, Dr. Northrop Frye, Lou Jacobi, Norman Jewison, Matie Molinaro, Mavor Moore, Don Murphy, Frank Peppiatt, Paul Simmons, Lister Sinclair and Herbert Whittaker, who deserves the last word:

> "Don Harron is a genuine Canadian star, one of that slow-blossoming breed. To become one he has demonstrated a truly dazzling array of talents, each of which would have made him a star in a more generous country."